MARTIN BUBER
AND HIS CRITICS

GARLAND REFERENCE LIBRARY
OF THE HUMANITIES
(VOL. 161)

MARTIN BUBER AND HIS CRITICS

An Annotated Bibliography of Writings in English Through 1978

Willard Moonan

GARLAND PUBLISHING, INC. • NEW YORK & LONDON
1981

Library of Congress Cataloging in Publication Data

Moonan, Willard.
　Martin Buber and his critics.

　(Garland reference library of the humanities; v. 161)
　Includes indexes.
　1. Buber, Martin, 1878–1965—Bibliography.　2. Philosophy—
Bibliography.　3. Hasidism—Bibliography.
4. Judaism—20th century—Bibliography.　I. Title.
II. Series.
Z8127.4.M66　[B3213.B8]　　　016.2963　　　78-68278
ISBN 0-8240-9779-3　　　　　　　　　　　　AACR2

Printed on acid-free, 250-year-life paper
Manufactured in the United States of America

To Sara and Alex

*Love is an existence which lives
in a kingdom larger than the
kingdom of individuals. It is
in truth the Bond of Creation,
that is, it is in God.*

M.B.

CONTENTS

ACKNOWLEDGMENTS

Many people have contributed to this book. I would like to express my thanks to the staffs of the following libraries: the University of Illinois Library at Urbana-Champaign; the Norman and Helen Asher Library at Spertus College of Judaica; the Klau Library of the Hebrew Union College; the Joseph Regenstein Library at the University of Chicago; the Indiana University Library at Bloomington; the Purdue University Library; the University of Minnesota Library at Minneapolis; and the Library of Congress. My thanks also to David Doman and his fellow toilers throughout the interlibrary loan system for their efforts on my behalf. I especially appreciate the patience and understanding shown to me over the last two and a half years by my family and by my colleagues at Milner Library, Illinois State University. Finally, my thanks to Janette Buckman and Marion Sandell who, with typewriters, exercised that God-like quality of bringing order out of chaos. Needless to say, any errors in the book are my own responsibility.

INTRODUCTION

Martin Buber has been acclaimed as one of the major philosophical and religious thinkers of the twentieth century. The centenary of his birth in 1978 was celebrated in speech and article. His distinction between the I-Thou and the I-It relationships has been called a "Copernican revolution" in modern thought.* The terminology of his major work, *I and Thou* (item A17), has become part of our modern religious language. A list of Buber's major achievements would include his contributions to the German Jewish community prior to World War II, his Zionist activities, the development of his philosophy of dialogue and philosophical anthropology, his efforts to bring the world view of the Hasidic movement into modern consciousness, the Buber-Rosenzweig translation of the Bible, and his attempt to reinterpret the essence of Judaism for modern man.

Yet in each of these areas Buber's work has been severely criticized and his influence called into question. One critic devoted a recent article to what he called Buber's failures as a scholar, teacher, translator, philosopher, and Zionist (item B651). A close associate of Buber stated that "it is universally conceded ... that praise of Buber far exceeds his influence" (item B662).

The purpose of the present work is to bring together in a systematic arrangement all significant material by and about Buber published in English through 1978. The two primary goals were completeness and usefulness. Indexes and abstracts were checked, library collections perused, and references traced. All items discovered were searched for clues to additional items. To make the bibliography as useful as possible, the critical material was annotated and various indexes were constructed, includ-

*A remark attributed to both Karl Heim and Emil Brunner.

ing an extensive subject index to both Buber's works and the criticism. It was hoped that the indexing would extend the usefulness of the work beyond the limitations of a bibliographic list.

Abstracts, Indexes, and Bibliographies Consulted

This is a list of the abstracts, indexes, and bibliographies used for the present work with inclusive dates when appropriate. This will enable the researcher to continue the bibliographic search begun in this book.

Writings by Buber

This section contains a checklist of 378 items by Buber arranged chronologically by year of publication in English. Within each year, items are arranged alphabetically by title. Complete bibliographic information is given including the translator when available and, for books, the presence or absence of a subject index. Separate items collected in books under Buber's authorship are listed under the book citations in the order they appear in the books. When there was a question of whether to list the parts of a book or only the book as a whole, the determining factor was the manner of original publication. If the parts of a book were originally published separately, they are so listed here. Exceptions to this are collections of short excerpts from material previously published in English, and collections of Hasidic stories. These are listed only as books.

The earliest publication of each work is listed and indexed. Reprints and later editions are listed only if (1) they represent new translations, (2) the original work is included in a later collection published under Buber's authorship, (3) there is a variant title which might suggest a different work, or (4) significant new material has been added. Item numbers for Buber's works are preceded by an "A." Eight items included were not available to the compiler; this is indicated in the notes following the citations.

A list of Buber's works published in other languages can be found in a bibliography compiled by Moshe Catanne* and in the bibliography appended to *The Philosophy of Martin Buber* (item 377).

---

*A Bibliography of Martin Buber's Works: 1859–1957 (Jerusalem: The Bialik Institute, 1958).

Writings about Buber

This section contains an annotated bibliography of 668 items about Buber arranged chronologically by year of publication in English. Within each year, items are listed alphabetically by author or, if the author is unknown, by title. Complete bibliographic information is given for each item including, for books, the presence or absence of a subject index.

While the goal was to list all significant commentary on Buber, in practical terms this goal was unreachable, particularly when dealing with parts of books. Material discovered was included if it presented information on Buber's life, his thought, the influence of his thought, or critical opinion, either positive or negative. Explicit concern with Buber was the primary criterion for inclusion.

Three types of materials were excluded from this bibliography: (1) dissertations, because they are already controlled bibliographically through *Dissertations Abstracts International*; (2) brief descriptive book reviews, because it was felt that they did not contain useful information; and (3) general encyclopedia articles on Buber, because of the superficial nature of the information given.

The earliest publication of each work is listed, annotated, and indexed. Reprints and later editions are listed only if (1) they are included in a collection dealing with Buber, (2) there is a variant title which might suggest a different work, or (3) significant new material has been added. To distinguish these item numbers from those referring to Buber's works, item numbers for writings about Buber are preceded by a "B."

Twenty-three works listed were not available to the compiler; this is indicated in the notes following the citations. They are included because there is evidence to suggest that they contain important information.

Title Index: Writings by Buber

This is an index to the translated titles of Buber's works. To find other translations with variant titles, the reader must go to the item numbers given.

Translator Index: Writings by Buber

The presence of this index reflects the importance of the translators. Many of the translations included in this bibliography
have engendered considerable criticism.

Author Index: Writings about Buber

All authors cited are included in this index.

Subject Index: Writings by and about Buber

When Buber's works and critical works are both listed under a
subject heading, the item numbers for Buber's works are listed
first, each preceded by an "A," followed by the item numbers for
critical works, each preceded by a "B." Cross-references are included when appropriate.

The subject heading "Overview" is used for works that describe Buber's thought with little or no commentary on that
thought. Five subject headings, "Dialogue, philosophy of,"
"God-man relation," "Hasidism," "I-It relationship," and "I-
Thou relation," have subdivisions labeled "Overview," again des-
ignating descriptive works containing little or no critical commentary.

ABSTRACTS, INDEXES,
AND BIBLIOGRAPHIES CONSULTED

Abstracts of English Studies. 1958–1978, No. 4.

American Humanities Index. 1975–Spring 1979.

American Jewish Year Book. 1900–1979.

Annual Bibliography of English Language and Literature. 1920–1975.

Art Index. 1929–1979.

Bibliographic Index. 1937–August 1979.

Biography Index. 1946–November 1979.

Book Review Digest. 1905–November 1979.

Book Review Index. 1965–September/October 1979.

Book Review Index to Social Science Periodicals. 1964–1971.

British Humanities Index. 1962–September 1979.

British Museum General Catalogue of Printed Books. Through 1970.

British National Bibliography. 1950–August 1979.

Canadian Periodical Index. 1970–November 1979.

Catholic Periodical and Literature Index. 1967–October 1979.

Catholic Periodical Index. 1930–1966.

Central Conference of American Rabbis Yearbook. 1890–1940.

Christian Periodical Index. 1956–June 1979.

Cumulated Magazine Subject Index. 1907–1949.

Cumulative Book Index. 1928–1979.

Education Index. 1929–December 1979.

Educational Resources Information Center: Current Index to Journals in Education. 1969–November 1979.

Educational Resources Information Center: Resources in Education. 1966–November 1979.

Essay and General Literature Index. 1900–1978.

Existentialism and Phenomenology: A Guide to Research. Compiled by
Leonard Orr. Troy: Whitstan Publishing Company, 1978.

German Jewry. Wierner Library. Westport, Conn: Greenwood Press,
1975.

Guide to Catholic Literature. 1888–1967.

Guide to Social Science and Religion in Periodical Literature. 1965–1979,
No. 2.

Historical Abstracts. 1965–1970.

Historical Abstracts: Part A. 1971–Summer 1979.

Historical Abstracts: Part B. 1971–Summer 1979.

Humanities Index. 1974–December 1979.

Index of Articles on Jewish Studies. 1969–1978.

Index to Book Reviews in Historical Periodicals. 1972–1976.

Index to Book Reviews in the Humanities. 1960–1976.

Index to Festschriften in Jewish Studies. Compiled by Charles Berlin.
Cambridge: Harvard College Library, 1971.

Index to Jewish Festschriften. Compiled by Jacob R. Marcus and Albert
Bilgray. Cincinnati: Hebrew Union College, 1937.

Index to Jewish Periodicals. 1963–1978.

Index to Little Magazines. 1890–1970.

Index to Periodicals by and about Blacks. 1950–1977.

Index to Religious Periodical Literature. 1949–June 1979.

International Index to Periodicals. 1907–1965.

Language and Language Behavior Abstracts. 1973–1978, No. 6.

Leo Baeck Institute Year Book. 1956–1978.

Library Literature. 1921–October 1979.

Library of Congress Subject Catalog. 1950–June 1979.

London Bibliography of the Social Sciences. 1931–1977.

MLA Bibliography. 1922–1978.

Magazine Index. 1977–April 1979.

New York Times Index. 1975–1978.

Nineteenth Century Readers Guide. 1890–1899.

Personal Name Index to the New York Times Index. 1851–1974.

Philosopher's Index. 1967–1979, No. 3.

*Philosopher's Index: A Retrospective Index to Non-U.S. English Language
Publications from 1940*.

Philosopher's Index: A Retrospective Index to U.S. Publications from 1940.

Poole's Index to Periodical Literature. 1802–1906.

Popular Periodical Index. 1973–1978.

Psychological Abstracts. 1927–October 1979.

Readers' Guide to Periodical Literature. 1900–December 25, 1979.

Religious and Theological Abstracts. 1958–1978.

Science Citation Index. 1961, 1964–August 1979.

Social Science and Humanities Index. 1965–March 1974.

Social Science Citation Index. 1976–August 1979.

Social Science Index. 1974–December 1979.

Sociological Abstracts. 1953–1979, No. 1.

Subject Guide to Books in Print. 1977/1978–1979/1980.

Subject Index to Periodicals. 1915–1922, 1926–1961.

Times (London) Index. 1906–1978.

Writings by Buber

A1   "Rabbi Wisdom." *Living Age*, 14 October 1922, pp. 87-90.
      [No translator given.]

1929

A2   "Sayings of the Baal-Shem-Tov: Collected by Martin Buber."
      Translated by Clifton Fadiman. *Menorah Journal*, 17
      (October 1929), 52-8.

A3   "Theodor Herzl and History." *Theodor Herzl and We*. By
      Martin Buber and Robert Weltsch. Translated by Chaim
      Arlosoroff. New York: Zionist Labor Party "Hitachduth"
      of America, 1929, pp. 5-16.

1931

A4   *Jewish Mysticism and the Legends of Baalshem*. Translated
      by Lucy Cohen. London: J.M. Dent and Sons Ltd., 1931,
      230 pp. [No subject index. Includes items A5 though
      A7 below.]

    A5   "The Life of the Chassids." Pp. 1-38. [In item A4
          above. Another translation as items A134 and A181.]

    A6   [Twenty-one Chassidic Stories.] Pp. 39-211. [In
          item A4 above. All stories except "The New Year's
          Sermon" translated again as item A135.]

    A7   "A Fragment from Baalshem's Life, and Some of His
          Sayings." Pp. 212-24. [In item A4 above.]

1934

A8   "The Third Leg." *The Best Fruits*. Translated by Leo W.
      Schwarz. New York: New School for Social Research,
      1934, n.p. [Another translation as item A284.]

1935

A9   "The Central Myth." *Rebirth: A Book of Modern Jewish Thought*. Edited by Ludwig Lewisohn. New York: Harper and Brothers, 1935, pp. 103-4. [Probably translated by the editor.]

A10 "The Meaning." *Rebirth: A Book of Modern Jewish Thought*. Edited by Ludwig Lewisohn. New York: Harper and Brothers, 1935, pp. 90-5. [Probably translated by the editor.]

A11 "Of Oneness." *Rebirth: A Book of Modern Jewish Thought*. Edited by Ludwig Lewisohn. New York: Harper and Brothers, 1935, pp. 95-8. [Probably translated by the editor.]

A12 "The Only Way." *Rebirth: A Book of Modern Jewish Thought*. Edited by Ludwig Lewisohn. New York: Harper and Brothers, 1935, pp. 104-7. [Probably translated by the editor.]

A13 "The Primal Powers." *Rebirth: A Book of Modern Jewish Thought*. Edited by Ludwig Lewisohn. New York: Harper and Brothers, 1935, pp. 107-8. [Probably translated by the editor.]

A14 "The True Foundation." *Rebirth: A Book of Modern Jewish Thought*. Edited by Ludwig Lewisohn. New York: Harper and Brothers, 1935, pp. 100-2. [Probably translated by the editor.]

A15 "Ultimate Aims." *Rebirth: A Book of Modern Jewish Thought*. Edited by Ludwig Lewisohn. New York: Harper and Brothers, 1935, pp. 98-100. [Probably translated by the editor.]

1936

A16 "The Prayer-Book, a Tale of the Baal Shem." Translated by Simon Chasen. *Menorah Journal*, 24 (October 1936), 272-5.

1937

A17 *I and Thou*. Translated by Ronald Gregor Smith. Edin-
      burth: T. and T. Clark, 1937, 119 pp. [No subject
      index. Another translation as item A370.]

1938

A18 "Keep Faith." *Palestine Post*, 8 July 1938. [Not avail-
      able for indexing.]

1939

A19 *Two Letters to Gandhi from Martin Buber and J.L. Magnes*.
      Jerusalem: Rubas Mass, 1939, pp. 1-22. [No trans-
      lator given. Abridged versions as items A89 and
      A169.]

1943

A20 "My Road to Hasidism." *Memoirs of My People*. Edited by
      Leo W. Schwarz. New York: Farrar and Rinehart, 1943,
      pp. 514-22. [Probably translated by the editor.
      Another translation as item A180.]

1944

A21 "Advice to Frequenters of Libraries." *Branch Library
      Book News* (New York Public Library), 21 (May 1944).
      [Indexed from reprint in *Library Journal*, 69 (July
      1944), 589. No translator given.]

A22 "Social Experiments in Jewish Palestine." *New Palestine*,
      13 October 1944, pp. 14-5. [No translator given.]

1945

A23 "The Crisis and the Truth." *Australian Jewish Review*,
      September 1945, p. 3. [No translator given.]

A24 "Eternal Truths." *Zionist Record New Year Annual*, 9
      (November 1945). [Not available for indexing.]

A25 *For the Sake of Heaven.* Translated by Ludwig Lewisohn.
     Philadelphia: Jewish Publication Society, 1945, 316 pp.
     [No subject index.]

A26 "God's Word and Man's Interpretation." *Palestine Post,*
     April 1945, p. 8. [Not available for indexing.]

A27 "Judah Halevi's 'Kitab al Kusari.'" *Contemporary Jewish
     Record,* 8 (June 1945), 358-68. [No translator given.]

A28 "Moses Hess." *Jewish Social Studies,* 7 (1945), 137-48.
     [No translator given.]

A29 "The Passover." *Palestine Tribune,* 27 March 1945, pp.
     5+. [No translator given. Reprinted in item A45.]

A30 "The Philosophical Anthropology of Max Scheler." Trans-
     lated by Ronald Gregor Smith. *Philosophy and
     Phenomenological Research,* 6 (December 1945), 307-21.

                              1946

A31 "The Beginnings of the National Ideal." *Review of
     Religion,* 10 (March 1946), 254-65. [No translator
     given.]

A32 "The Education of Character." Translated by Ronald
     Gregor Smith. *The Mint.* Edited by Geoffrey Grigson.
     London: Routledge and Sons Ltd., 1946, pp. 1-14.
     [Reprinted as item A52.]

A33 Introduction to *Chinese Ghost and Love Stories,* by
     P'u Sung-ling. New York: Pantheon Books Inc., 1946,
     pp. 9-13. [No translator given.]

A34 *Mamre: Essays in Religion.* Translated by Greta Hort.
     Melbourne: Melbourne University Press, 1946, 190 pp.
     [No subject index. Includes items A35 through A44
     below.]

     A35 "The Faith of Judaism." Pp. 1-17. [In item A34
          above. Reprinted as item A70.]

     A36 "The Two Centers of the Jewish Soul." Pp. 18-31.
          [In item A34 above. Reprinted as item A71.]

     A37 "Imitatio Dei." Pp. 32-43. [In item A34 above.
          Reprinted as item A74.]

A38 "Biblical Leadership." Pp. 44-61. [In item A34 above. Reprinted as items A80 and A354.]

A39 "Trust." Pp. 62-3. [In item A34 above.]

A40 "Interpretation of Chassidism." Pp. 65-148. [In item A34 above. Just a subtitle for items A41 through A43.]

A41 "Spirit and Body of the Chassidic Movement." Pp. 67-99. [In item A34 above. Reprinted as item A63. Another translation as item A197.]

A42 "Spinoza, Sabbatai Zwi, and Baalshem." Pp. 99-121. [In item A34 above. Reprinted as item A64. Another translation as item A196.]

A43 "Symbolism and Sacramental Existence in Judaism." Pp. 121-48. [In item A34 above. Reprinted as item A65. Other translations as items A198 and A203.]

A44 "The Beginnings of Chassidism." Pp. 149-80. [In item A34 above. Reprinted as item A61. Another translation as item A194.]

A45 *Moses.* Oxford: East and West Library, 1946, 226 pp. [No translator given. Subject index.]

A46 "Oral Testimony before Anglo-American Committee of Inquiry." With Judah L. Magnes and Moses Smilansky. *Palestine: A Bi-National State.* New York: Ihud (Union) Association of Palestine, 1946, pp. 30-74. [Originally in English? Reprinted as item A47.]

1947

A47 *Arab-Jewish Unity: Testimony before the Anglo-American Inquiry Commission for the Ihud (Union) Association.* With Judah Magnes. London: Victor Gollancz Ltd., 1947, pp. 43-96. [Originally in English? Reprint of item A46.]

A48 *Between Man and Man.* Translated by Ronald Gregor Smith. London: Routledge and Kegan Paul, 1947, 210 pp. [Subject index. Includes items A49 through A53.]

A49   "Dialogue." Pp. 1-39. [In item A48 above.]

A50   "The Question to the Single One." Pp. 40-82. [In
      item A48 above.] Reprinted as item A102.]

A51   "Education." Pp. 83-103. [In item A48 above.]

A52   "The Education of Character." Pp. 104-17. [In
      item A48 above. Reprint of item A32.]

A53   "What Is Man?" Pp. 118-205. [In item A48 above.]

A54   "Palestine: Can the Deadlock be Broken?" *Picture Post*,
      12 July 1947, pp. 22-5. [No translator given.]

A55   *Tales of the Hasidim: The Early Masters*. Translated by
      Olga Marx. New York: Schocken Books, 1947, 355 pp.
      [No subject index.]

A56   *Ten Rungs: Hasidic Sayings*. Translated by Olga Marx.
      New York: Schocken Books, 1947, 127 pp. [No subject
      index.]

A57   *Towards Union in Palestine*. Edited by Martin Buber,
      J. L. Magnes, and E. Simon. Jerusalem: Ihud (Union)
      Association, 1947, 124 pp. [Includes items A58 and
      A59 below.]

A58   "The Bi-National Approach to Zionism." Pp. 7-13.
      [No translator given. In item A57 above.]

A59   "Our Reply." Pp. 33-6. [No translator given. In
      item A57 above.]

                            1948

A60   *Hasidism*. New York: Philosophical Library, 1948, 207 pp.
      [Subject index. Includes items A61 through A68 below.]

A61   "The Beginnings of Hasidism." Translated by
      Greta Hort. Pp. 1-33. [In item A60 above.
      Reprint of item A44. Another translation as
      item A194.]

A62   "Foundation Stone." Translated by Carlyle Witton-
      Davies and Mary Witton-Davies. Pp. 34-59. [In
      item A60 above. Another translation as item A195.]

A63 "Spirit and Body of the Hasidic Movement." Translated by Greta Hort. Pp. 60-94. [In item A60
 above. Reprint of item A41. Another translation
 as item A197.]

A64 "Spinoza, Sabbatai Zevi, and the Baalshem." Translated by Greta Hort. Pp. 95-116. [In item A60
 above. Reprint of item A42. Another translation
 as item A196.]

A65 "Symbolical and Sacramental Existence in Judaism."
 Translated by Greta Hort. Pp. 117-44. [In item
 A60 above. Reprint of item A43. Other transla-
 tions as items A198 and A203.]

A66 "God and the Soul." Translated by Carlyle Witton-
 Davies and Mary Witton-Davies. Pp. 145-58. [In
 item A60 above. Another translation as item
 A199.]

A67 "Love of God and Love of One's Neighbor." Translated by Immanuel Olsvanger. Pp. 159-83. [In
 item A60 above. Another translation as item
 A184.]

A68 "The Place of Hasidism in the History of Religion."
 Translated by Carlyle Witton-Davies and Mary
 Witton-Davies. Pp. 184-201. [In item A60 above.
 Another translation as item A201.]

A69 *Israel and the World: Essays in a Time of Crisis.* New
 York: Schocken Books, 1948, 255 pp. [No index. Includes items A70 through A91 below.]

A70 "The Faith of Judaism." Translated by Greta Hort.
 Pp. 15-27. [In item A69 above. Reprint of
 item A35.]

A71 "The Two Foci of the Jewish Soul." Translated by
 Greta Hort. Pp. 28-40. [In item A69 above.
 Reprint of item A36.]

A72 "The Prejudices of Youth." Translated by Olga
 Marx. Pp. 41-52. [In item A69 above.]

A73 "The Love of God and the Idea of Deity." Translated by I.M. Lask. Pp. 53-65. [In item A69
 above. Reprinted as item A117.]

A74   "Imitatio Dei." Translated by Greta Hort. Pp. 66-
      77. [In item A69 above. Reprint of item A37.]

A75   "In the Midst of History." Translated by Olga Marx.
      Pp. 78-82. [In item A69 above.]

A76   "What Are We to Do About the Ten Commandments?"
      Translated by Olga Marx. Pp. 85-8. [In item
      A69 above. Reprinted as item A351.]

A77   "The Man of Today and the Jewish Bible." Translated
      by Olga Marx. Pp. 89-102. [In item A69 above.
      Reprinted as item A344.]

A78   "Plato and Isaiah." Translated by Olga Marx. Pp.
      103-12. [In item A69 above. Reprinted as items
      A172 and A355.]

A79   "False Prophets." Translated by Olga Marx. Pp.
      113-8. [In item A69 above. Reprinted as item
      A357.]

A80   "Biblical Leadership." Translated by Greta Hort.
      Pp. 119-33. [In item A69 above. Reprint of item
      A38. Reprinted as item A354.]

A81   "Teaching and Deed." Translated by Olga Marx. Pp.
      137-45. [In item A69 above.]

A82   "Why We Should Study Jewish Sources." Translated
      by Olga Marx. Pp. 146-8. [In item A69 above.
      Another translation in item A220.]

A83   "On National Education." Pp. 149-63. [In item A69
      above. No translator given.]

A84   "The Jew in the World." Translated by Olga Marx.
      Pp. 167-72. [In item A69 above.]

A85   "The Power of the Spirit." Translated by Olga Marx.
      Pp. 173-82. [In item A69 above.]

A86   "The Spirit of Israel and the World of Today."
      Translated by I.M. Lask. Pp. 183-94. [In item
      A69 above. Reprinted as item A337.]

A87   "The Gods of the Nations and God." Translated by
      Olga Marx. Pp. 197-213. [In item A69 above.]

A88 "Nationalism." Translated by Olga Marx. Pp. 214-
26. [In item A69 above.]

A89 "The Land and Its Possessors." Pp. 227-33. [In
item A69 above. No translator given. Abridged
from item A19.]

A90 "'And If Not Now, When?'" Translated by Olga Marx.
Pp. 234-9. [In item A69 above.]

A91 "Hebrew Humanism." Translated by Olga Marx. Pp.
240-52. [In item A69 above. Another translation
as item A361.]

A92 *Tales of the Hasidim: The Later Masters*. Translated by
Olga Marx. New York: Schocken Books, 1948, 352 pp.
[No subject index.]

1949

A93 "Let Us Make an End to Falsities." *Freeland* (New York),
5 (January/February 1949). [Not available for indexing.]

A94 *Paths in Utopia*. Translated by R.F.C. Hull. London:
Routledge and Kegan Paul, 1949, 152 pp. [Subject
index.]

A95 *The Prophetic Faith*. Translated by Carlyle Witton-
Davies. New York: Macmillan Company, 1949, 247 pp.
[No subject index.]

1950

A96 "Myth in Judaism." Translated by Ralph Manheim.
Commentary, June 1950, pp. 562-6. [Another translation as item A334.]

A97 "A New Venture in Adult Education." *The Hebrew Univer-
sity in Jerusalem, 1925-1950*. Jerusalem: The Hebrew
University, 1950, pp. 115-9. [No translator given.
Reprinted in item A372.]

A98 "Remarks on Goethe's Concept of Humanity." Translated
by Maurice Friedman. *Goethe and the Modern Age*. Edited
by A. Bergstraesser. Henry Regnery Company, 1950,
pp. 227-33. [Reprinted as item A159.]

A99   "A Talk with Tagore." *India and Israel*, 15 October
       1950, p. 18. [No translator given. Another transla-
       tion as item A305.]

A100   *The Way of Man, According to the Teachings of Hasidism*.
       London: Routledge and Paul, 1950, 46 pp. [No index.
       No translator given. Reprinted as item A182.]

                              1951

A101   "Distance and Relation." Translated by R.G. Smith.
       Hibbert Journal, 49 (January 1951), 105-13. [Reprinted
       as item A230.]

A102   "Individual and Society." Translated by Ronald Gregor
       Smith. *Marriage and the Jewish Tradition*. Edited by
       Stanley R. Brav. New York: Philosophical Library,
       1951, pp. 130-8. [Reprinted from item A50.]

A103   "Israel's Land: Habitation of God: The Zionism of Rabbi
       Nahman." Translated by Francis C. Golffing.
       Commentary, October 1951, pp. 345-54.

A104   "Judaism and Civilization." *The Present Contribution
       of Judaism to Civilization*. London: World Union for
       Progressive Judaism 25th Anniversary Conference, 1951,
       pp. 70-7. [No translator given. Reprinted as items
       A110 and A338.]

A105   "Religion and Reality." Translated by Norbert Guterman.
       Religious Faith and World Culture. Edited by A.
       William Loos. New York: Prentice-Hall, Inc., 1951,
       pp. 49-58. [Reprinted as item A115.]

A106   "Society and the State." Translated by Maurice Fried-
       man. *World Review*, N.S. 27 (May 1951), 5-12. [Re-
       printed as item A171.]

A107   *Two Types of Faith*. Translated by Norman P. Goldhawk.
       London: Routledge and Paul, 1951, 177 pp. [Subject
       index.]

1952

A108   "Adult Education in Israel." *Torah: The Magazine of
       the National Federation of Jewish Men's Clubs of the
       United Synagogue of America*, 11 (June 1952). [Not
       available for indexing. May be reprint of item A97
       or item A372.]

A109   *At the Turning: Three Addresses on Judaism.* New York:
       Farrar, Straus and Young, 1952, 62 pp. [No subject
       index. Includes items A110 through A112 below.]

       A110   "Judaism and Civilization." Pp. 11-26. [In
              item A109 above. No translator given. Reprint
              of item A104. Reprinted as item A338.]

       A111   "The Silent Question." Pp. 29-44. [In item
              A109 above. No translator given. Reprinted
              as item A339.]

       A112   "The Dialogue between Heaven and Earth." Pp. 47-
              62. [In item A109 above. No translator given.
              Reprinted as item A340.]

A113   *Eclipse of God.* New York: Harper and Brothers
       Publishers, 1952, 192 pp. [Subject index. Includes
       items A114 through A122 below.]

       A114   "Prelude: Report on Two Talks." Translated by
              Maurice S. Friedman. Pp. 3-9. [In item A113
              above.]

       A115   "Religion and Reality." Translated by Norbert
              Guterman. Pp. 13-24. [In item A113 above.
              Reprint of item A105.]

       A116   "Religion and Philosophy." Translated by
              Maurice S. Friedman. Pp. 27-46. [In item A113
              above.]

       A117   "The Love of God and the Idea of Deity." Trans-
              lated by I.M. Lask. Pp. 49-62. [In item A113
              above. Reprint of item A73.]

       A118   "Religion and Modern Thinking." Translated by
              Maurice S. Friedman. Pp. 65-92. [In item A113
              above.]

A119   "Religion and Ethics." Translated by Eugene
       Kamenka and Maurice S. Friedman. Pp. 95-111.
       [In item A113 above.]

A120   "On the Suspension of the Ethical." Translated
       by Maurice S. Friedman. Pp. 115-20. [In item
       A113 above. Also printed as item A127.]

A121   "God and the Spirit of Man." Translated by
       Maurice S. Friedman. Pp. 123-9. [In item A113
       above.]

A122   "Supplement: Reply to C.G. Jung." Translated by
       Maurice S. Friedman. Pp. 133-7. [In item A113
       above.]

A123 "Hope for This Hour." Translated by Maurice Friedman.
      World Review, N.S. 46 (December 1952), 20-4. [Re-
      printed as item A175.]

A124 *Images of Good and Evil*. Translated by Michael Bullock.
      London: Routledge and Kegan Paul, 1952, 83 pp. [No
      subject index. Reprinted in item A130.]

A125 *Israel and Palestine: The History of an Idea*. Translated
      by Stanley Godman. London: East and West Library,
      1952, 165 pp. [No subject index. Reprinted as item
      A375.]

A126 *Right and Wrong: An Interpretation of Some Psalms*.
      Translated by Ronald Gregor Smith. London: SCM Press,
      1952, 62 pp. [No subject index. Reprinted in item
      A130.]

A127 "The Suspension of Ethics." Translated by Maurice S.
      Friedman. *Moral Principles of Action*. Edited by
      Ruth N. Anshen. New York: Harper and Brothers, 1952,
      pp. 223-7. [Also printed as item A120.]

                              1953

A128 "The Cultural Role of the Hebrew University." Translated
      by David Sidorsky. *Reconstructionist*, 26 June 1953,
      pp. 29-32.

A129 Foreword to *Community and Environment*, by E.A. Gutkind.
      London: Watts, 1953, pp. vii-ix. [No translator given.
      Another translation as item A283.]

A130   *Good and Evil: Two Interpretations*. Translated by
        Ronald Gregor Smith and Michael Bullock. New York:
        Scribner, 1953, 143 pp. [No subject index. Reprint
        of items A126 and A124.]

                            1954

A131   [Message.] Translated by Maurice Friedman. *Pulpit
        Digest*, June 1954, p. 36. [Reprinted as item A311.]

                            1955

A132   "Genuine Conversation and the Possibilities of Peace."
        Translated by Maurice Friedman. *Cross Currents*, 5
        (Fall 1955), 292-6. [Reprinted as items A177 and
        A310.]

A133   *The Legend of the Baal-Shem*. Translated by Maurice
        Friedman. New York: Harper and Row, 1955, 222 pp.
        [No subject index. Includes items A134 and A135
        below.]

        A134   "The Life of the Hasidim." Pp. 17-50. [In item
                A133 above. Another translation of item A5.
                Reprinted as item A181.]

        A135   [Twenty Hasidic Stories.] Pp. 51-208. [In item
                A133 above. Another translation of item A6.]

A136   "A Realist of the Spirit." Translated by Maurice
        Friedman. *To Dr. Albert Schweitzer: A Festschrift
        Commemorating His 80th Birthday from a Few of His
        Friends*. Edited by Homer A. Jack. Evanston: Friends
        of Albert Schweitzer, 1955, pp. 11-3. [Reprinted as
        item A275.]

A137   "Revelation and Law." *On Jewish Learning*. By Franz
        Rosenzweig. Edited by N.N. Glatzer. New York:
        Schocken Books, 1955, pp. 109-18. [No translator
        given.]

A138   "We Need Arabs, They Need Us!" *Frontpage* (Israel),
        20 January 1955. [Not available for indexing.]

1956

A139   "Abraham the Seer." Translated by Sophie Meyer.
       Judaism, 5 (Fall 1956), 291-305. [Reprinted as
       item A346.]

A140   "Between Man and Man: Education." Translated by Ronald
       Gregor Smith. *Pastoral Psychology*, 7 (December 1956),
       41-5. [Reprinted from item A51.]

A141   "Character Change and Social Experiment in Israel."
       Translated by Maurice Friedman. *Israel: Its Role in
       Civilization*. Edited by Moshe Davis. New York:
       Seminary Israel Institute of the Jewish Theological
       Seminary of America, 1956, pp. 204-13.

A142   "Greetings to Dr. Mordecai M. Kaplan." *Recon-
       structionist*, 4 May 1956, p. 17. [No translator
       given.]

A143   *The Tales of Rabbi Nachman*. Translated by Maurice
       Friedman. New York: Horizon Press, 1956, 214 pp.
       [No subject index.]

A144   *Writings of Martin Buber*. Selected, edited, and intro-
       duced by Will Herberg. Cleveland: World Publishing
       Co., 1956, 351 pp. [No subject index. Selection of
       materials previously published in English.]

1957

A145   "Elements of the Interhuman." Translated by Ronald
       Gregor Smith. *Psychiatry*, 20 (May 1957), 105-13.
       [Reprinted as item A231.]

A146   "Guilt and Guilt Feelings." Translated by Maurice
       Friedman. *Psychiatry*, 20 (May 1957), 114-29. [Re-
       printed as item A234.]

A147   "Israel's Mission and Zion." Translated by Maurice
       Friedman. *Forum*, 4 (Spring 1957), 145-7. [Reprinted
       as item A217.]

A148   *Pointing the Way: Collected Essays*. Edited and trans-
       lated by Maurice S. Friedman. New York: Harper and
       Brothers, 1957, 239 pp. [No subject index. Includes
       items A149 through A177 below.]

A149 "Books and Men." Pp. 3-4. [In items A148 above.
      Another translation as item A204. Reprinted as
      item A260.]

A150 "Productivity and Existence." Pp. 5-10. [In
      item A148 above.]

A151 "The Demon in the Dream." Pp. 11-5. [In item
      A148 above.]

A152 "The Altar." Pp. 16-9. [In item A148 above.]

A153 "Brother Body." Pp. 20-4. [In item A148 above.]

A154 "With a Monist." Pp. 25-30. [In item A148
      above.]

A155 "The Teaching of the Tao." Pp. 31-58. [In item
      A148 above.]

A156 "To the Contemporary." Pp. 59-60. [In item
      A148 above.]

A157 "Drama and Theatre." Pp. 63-6. [In item A148
      above.]

A158 "The Space Problem of the Stage." Pp. 67-73.
      [In item A148 above.]

A159 "Goethe's Concept of Humanity." Pp. 74-80. [In
      item A148 above. Reprint of item A98.]

A160 "Bergson's Concept of Intuition." Pp. 81-6.
      [In item A148 above.]

A161 "Franz Rosenzweig." Pp. 87-92. [In item A148
      above.]

A162 "Healing through Meeting." Pp. 93-7. [In item
      A148 above. Reprinted as item A299.]

A163 "Education and World-View." Pp. 98-105. [In
      item A148 above.]

A164 "What Is to Be Done?" Pp. 109-11. [In item
      A148 above.]

A165 "Three Theses of a Religious Socialism." Pp.
      112-4. [In item A148 above.]

A166 "Recollection of a Death." Pp. 115-20. [In item
 A148 above.]

A167 "China and Us." Pp. 121-5. [In item A148 above.
 Reprinted as item A306.]

A168 "Gandhi, Politics, and Us." Pp. 126-38. [In
 item A148 above.]

A169 "A Letter to Gandhi." Pp. 139-47. [In item
 A148 above. Abridged from item A19.]

A170 "People and Leader." Pp. 148-60. [In item
 A148 above.]

A171 "Society and the State." Pp. 161-76. [In item
 A148 above. Reprint of item A106.]

A172 "The Demand of the Spirit and Historical Reality."
 Translated with Olga Marx. Pp. 177-91. [In
 item A148 above. A reprint, in part, of item
 A78.]

A173 "Prophecy, Apocalyptic, and the Historical Hour."
 Pp. 192-207. [In item A148 above. Reprinted
 as item A358.]

A174 "The Validity and Limitation of the Political
 Principle." Pp. 208-19. [In item A148 above.]

A175 "Hope for this Hour." Pp. 220-9. [In item A148
 above. Reprint of item A123.]

A176 "Abstract and Concrete." Pp. 230-1. [In item
 A148 above.]

A177 "Genuine Dialogue and the Possibilities of Peace."
 Pp. 232-9. [In item A148 above. Reprint of
 item A132. Reprinted as item A310.]

1958

A178 *Hasidism and Modern Man.* Edited and translated by
 Maurice Friedman. New York: Horizon Press, 1958,
 256 pp. [No subject index. Includes items A179
 through A184 below.]

A179 "Hasidism and Modern Man." Pp. 21-43. [In item A178 above.]

A180 "My Way to Hasidism." Pp. 47-69. [In item A178 above. Another translation of item A20.]

A181 "The Life of the Hasidim." Pp. 74-122. [In item A178 above. Another translation of item A5. Reprint of item A134.]

A182 "The Way of Man According to the Teachings of Hasidism." Pp. 126-76. [In item A178 above. No translator given. Reprint of item A100.]

A183 "The Baal-Shem-Tov's Instruction in Intercourse with God." Pp. 179-222. [In item A178 above.]

A184 "Love of God and Love of Neighbor." Pp. 225-56. [In item A178 above. Another translation of A67.]

A185 *Hasidism and the Way of Man*. Title for two-volume work which includes *Hasidism and Modern Man* (item A178) and *Origin and Meaning of Hasidism* (item A193).

A186 *I and Thou*. Translated by Ronald Gregor Smith. 2nd edition. New York: Charles Scribner's Sons, 137 pp. [No subject index. Reprint of item A17 plus item A186 below.]

A186a "Postscript." Translated by Ronald Gregor Smith. Pp. 123-37. [In item A186 above.]

A187 "Israel and the Command of the Spirit." Translated by Maurice Friedman. *Congress Weekly*, 8 September 1958, pp. 10-2. [Reprinted as item A216.]

A188 "It Is Now High Time." *London Letter*, 1958. [Not available for indexing. May be reprint of items A131 and A311.]

A189 *Tales of Angels, Spirits and Demons*. Translated by David Antin and Jerome Rothenberg. New York: Hawk's Well Press, 1958, 61 pp. [No subject index.]

A190 *To Hallow this Life: An Anthology*. Edited by Jacob Trapp. New York: Harper and Brothers Publishers, 1958, 174 pp. [Subject index. Excerpts from many works.]

A191 "What Is Common to All." Translated by Maurice Fried-
      man. *Review of Metaphysics*, 11 (March 1958), 359-79.
      [Reprinted as item A232.]

                              1960

A192 "Dialogue between Martin Buber and Carl Rogers."
      *Psychologia: An International Journal of Psychology
      in the Orient*, 3 (December 1960), 208-21. [Origin-
      ally in English? Reprinted as item A236.]

A193 *The Origin and Meaning of Hasidism*. Translated by
      Maurice Friedman. New York: Horizon Press, 1960,
      254 pp. [No subject index. Includes items A194
      through A202.]

      A194 "The Beginnings." Pp. 24-57. [In item A193
            above. Another translation of items A44 and
            A61.]

      A195 "Foundation Stone." Pp. 59-88. [In item A193
            above. Another translation of item A62.]

      A196 "Spinoza, Sabbatai Zvi, and the Baal-Shem."
            Pp. 89-112. [In item A193 above. Another
            translation of items A42 and A64.]

      A197 "Spirit and Body of the Hasidic Movement." Pp.
            113-49. [In item A193 above. Another transla-
            tion of items A41 and A63.]

      A198 "Symbolic and Sacramental Existence." Pp. 151-81.
            [In item A193 above. Other translations as
            items A43, A65, and A203.]

      A199 "God and the Soul." Pp. 183-99. [In item A193
            above. Another translation of item A66.]

      A200 "Redemption." Translated with Elisha Nattiv.
            Pp. 201-18. [In item A193 above.]

      A201 "The Place of Hasidism in the History of Religion."
            Pp. 219-39. [In item A193 above. Another
            translation of item A68.]

      A202 "Christ, Hasidism, Gnosis." Pp. 241-54. [In
            item A193 above.]

A203 "Symbolic and Sacramental Existence in Judaism." Trans-
        lated by Ralph Manheim. *Spiritual Disciplines*.
        Papers from the Eranos Yearbook, vol. 4. New York:
        Pantheon Books, 1960, pp. 168-85. [Other translations
        as items A43, A65, and A198.]

1961

A204 "Books and People." Translated by Harry Zohn. *Jewish
        Affairs*, January 1961, pp. 7-8. [Other translations
        as items A149 and A260.]

A205 "The Word That Is Spoken." Translated by Maurice
        Friedman. *Modern Age*, 5 (Fall 1961), 353-60.
        [Reprinted as item A233.]

1962

A206 Fellows, Lawrence. "Reform Jews Get Israel Synagogue."
        New York Times, 15 April 1962, p. 3. [Excerpts of a
        message sent by Buber. Originally in English?]

A207 [Interview.] *Life International*, 10 September 1962.
        [Not available for indexing.]

A208 "Man's Duty as Man." *Massachusetts Review*, 4 (Autumn
        1962), 55. [No translator given. Another transla-
        tion as item A307.]

A209 "Martin Buber on Good and Evil." *Listener*, 18 January
        1962, p. 127. [Originally in English?]

A210 "Samuel and Agag." Translated by Maurice Friedman.
        Commentary, January 1962, pp. 63-4. [Reprinted as
        item A257.]

1963

A211 "Believing Humanism." *Leo Baeck Institute Year Book*,
        8 (1963), 260-1. [No translator given. Another
        translation as item A292.]

A212 [Civil Disobedience.] *A Matter of Life*. Edited by
        Clara Urquhart. Boston: Little, Brown and Company,
        1963, pp. 51-2. [No translator given. Another
        translation as item A308.]

A213 "The End of the German-Jewish Symbiosis." *Jewish
       Existence Today*. Edited and translated by Herbert
       Strauss. New York: American Federation of Jews from
       Central Europe, [1963?], n.p. [Two pages. Another
       translation as item A364.]

A214 "Interpreting Hasidism." *Commentary*, September 1963,
       pp. 218-25. [No translator given.]

A215 *Israel and the World*. 2nd ed. New York: Schocken
       Books, 1963, 266 pp. [No subject index. Reprint of
       item A69 plus items A216 and A217 below.]

       A216 "Israel and the Command of the Spirit." Trans-
              lated by Maurice Friedman. Pp. 253-7. [In
              item A215 above. Reprint of item A187.]

       A217 "Israel's Mission and Zion." Translated by
              Maurice Friedman. Pp. 258-63. [In item
              A215 above. Reprint of item A147.]

A218 "Man and His Image-Work." Translated by Maurice
       Friedman. *Portfolio*, No. 7 (Winter 1963), 88-99.
       [Reprinted as item A235.]

A219 "Reflections on Theology, Mysticism, and Metaphysics."
       *Horizons of a Philosopher: Essays in Honor of David
       Baumgardt*. Edited by Joseph Frank, Helmut Minkowski,
       and Ernest J. Sternglass. Leiden: E.J. Brill, 1963,
       pp. 52-5. [No translator given. Slightly revised
       from German version of item A341.]

A220 "Why Learning." *Jewish Existence Today*. Edited and
       translated by Herbert Strauss. New York: American
       Federation of Jews from Central Europe, Inc., [1963?],
       n.p. [Two pages. Another translation, in part, of
       item A82.]

                              1964

A221 "Church, State, Nation, Jewry." Translated by William
       Hallo. *Christianity: Some Non-Christian Appraisals*.
       Edited by David W. McKain. New York: McGraw-Hill
       Book Co., 1964, pp. 176-88.

A222 *Daniel: Dialogues on Realization*. Translated by Maurice
       Friedman. New York: Holt, Rinehart, and Winston,
       1964, 144 pp. [No subject index.]

A223 "Interrogation of Martin Buber." *Philosophical Inter-*
       rogations. Edited by Sydney Rome and Beatrice Rome.
       New York: Holt, Rinehart, and Winston, 1964, pp. 13-
       117. [Originally in English? For annotation see
       item B242.]

                          1965

A224 "Buber's Farewell: The Fiddler." *Jerusalem Post*,
       18 June 1965, p. 7. [No translator given. Reprinted
       in item A226. Another translation as item A322.]

A225 "Elijah: A Mystery Play." Translated by Maurice Fried-
       man. *Judaism*, 14 (Summer 1965), pp. 260-6. [Selec-
       tions only. Complete play as item A363.]

A226 "The Fiddler." *Jewish Heritage*, 8 (Summer 1965), 54.
       [No translator given. Reprint of item 224. Another
       translation as item A322.]

A227 *Between Man and Man*. Translated by Maurice Friedman.
       New York: Macmillan Company, 1965, 229 pp. [Subject
       index. Reprint of item A48 plus item A228 below.]

       A228 "The History of the Dialogical Principle."
              Translated by Maurice Friedman. Pp. 209-24.
              [In item A227 above.]

A229 *The Knowledge of Man: Selected Essays*. New York:
       Harper and Row Publishers, 1965, 186 pp. [Subject
       index. Includes items A230 through A236 below.]

       A230 "Distance and Relation." Translated by Ronald
              Gregor Smith. Pp. 59-71. [In item A229 above.
              Reprint of item A101.]

       A231 "Elements of the Interhuman." Translated by
              Ronald Gregor Smith. Pp. 72-88. [In item A229
              above. Reprint of item A145.]

       A232 "What Is Common to All." Translated by Maurice
              Friedman. Pp. 89-109. [In item A229 above.
              Reprint of item A191.]

       A233 "The Word that Is Spoken." Translated by Maurice
              Friedman. Pp. 110-20. [In item A229 above.
              Reprint of item A205.]

A234 "Guilt and Guilt Feelings." Translated by Maurice
      Friedman. Pp. 121-48. [In item A229 above.
      Reprint of item A146.]

A235 "Man and His Image-Work." Translated by Maurice
      Friedman. Pp. 149-65. [In item A229 above.
      Reprint of item A218.]

A236 "Dialogue between Martin Buber and Carl Rogers."
      Pp. 166-84. [In item A229 above. Originally
      in English? Reprint of item A192.]

                          1966

A237 *Addresses on Judaism*. Translated by Eva Jospe. New
      York: Schocken Books, 1966. [Although Maurice Friedman
      includes this title in his bibliography in *The Philo-
      sophy of Martin Buber* (item B377), to the best of my
      knowledge no such title has been published. Friedman
      states that it includes a translation of *Reden uber
      das Judentum* and *At the Turning* (item A109). The
      eight addresses included in *Reden uber das Judentum*,
      translated by Eva Jospe, are included in *On Judaism*
      (item A327).]

A238 Smith, Robert C. "Correspondence with Martin Buber."
      Review of Existential Psychology and Psychiatry, 6
      (Fall 1966), 246-9. [Originally in English?]

A239 *The Way of Response: Martin Buber, Selections from His
      Writings*. Edited by N.N. Glatzer. New York: Schocken
      Books, 1966, 223 pp. [No subject index. Selections
      from previously published materials.]

                          1967

A240 "Autobiographical Fragments." *The Philosophy of Martin
      Buber*. Edited by Paul Arthur Schilpp and Maurice
      Friedman. LaSalle, Ill.: Open Court, 1967, pp. 3-39.
      [Includes items A241 through A260 below. Reprinted
      as items A325 and A374.]

  A241 "My Mother." Translated by Maurice Friedman.
        Pp. 3-4. [In item A240 above.]

  A242 "My Grandmother." Translated by Maurice Friedman.
        Pp. 4-5. [In item A240 above.]

A243 "Languages." Translated by Maurice Friedman.
Pp. 5-6. [In item A240 above.]

A244 "My Father." Translated by Maurice Friedman.
Pp. 6-7. [In item A240 above.]

A245 "The School." Translated by Maurice Friedman.
P. 8. [In item A240 above.]

A246 "The Two Boys." Translated by Maurice Friedman.
Pp. 8-10. [In item A240 above.]

A247 "The Horse." Translated by Ronald Gregor Smith.
P. 10. [In item A240 above. Reprint of
material from item A49.]

A248 "Philosophers." Translated by Maurice Friedman.
Pp. 11-3. [In item A240 above.]

A249 "Vienna." Translated by Maurice Friedman.
Pp. 13-4. [In item A240 above.]

A250 "A Lecture." Translated by Maurice Friedman.
Pp. 14-5. [In item A240 above.]

A251 "The Cause and the Person." Translated by Maurice
Friedman. Pp. 16-9. [In item A240 above.
Another translation of material from item A69.]

A252 "The Zaddik." Translated by Maurice Friedman.
Pp. 19-22. [In item A240 above. Reprint of
material from item A181.]

A253 "The Walking Stick and the Tree." Translated by
Maurice Friedman. Pp. 22-3. [In item A240
above. Reprint of material from item A222.]

A254 "Question and Answer." Translated by Maurice
Friedman. Pp. 23-5. [In item A240 above.]

A255 "A Conversion." Translated by Ronald Gregor
Smith. Pp. 25-6. [In item A240 above. Reprint
of material from item A49.]

A256 "Report on Two Talks." Translated by Norbert
Guterman. Pp. 26-31. [In item A240 above.
Reprint of material from item A105.]

A257 "Samuel and Agag." Translated by Maurice Fried-
      man. Pp. 31-3. [In item A240 above. Reprint
      of item A210.]

A258 "Beginnings." Translated by Maurice Friedman.
      Pp. 33-5. [In item A240 above. Reprint of
      material from item A228.]

A259 "A Tentative Answer." Translated by Maurice
      Friedman. Pp. 35-7. [In item A240 above.]

A260 "Books and Men." Translated by Maurice Friedman.
      Pp. 37-9. [In item A240 above. Reprint of
      item A149. Another translation of item A204.]

A261 *A Believing Humanism: My Testament, 1902-1965.* Trans-
      lated by Maurice Friedman. New York: Simon and
      Schuster, 1967, 252 pp. [No subject index. Includes
      items A262 through A324 below.]

A262 "Reminiscence." Pp. 29-30. [In item A261 above.]

A263 "To Create New Words." P. 31. [In item A261
      above.]

A264 "Confessions of the Author." P. 33. [In item
      A261 above.]

A265 "In Heidelberg." Pp. 34-5. [In item A261 above.]

A266 "Elijah." P. 37. [In item A261 above.]

A267 "The Word to Elijah." P. 39. [In item A261
      above.]

A268 "The Disciple." P. 41. [In item A261 above.]

A269 "The Magicians." P. 43. [In item A261 above.]

A270 "Power and Love." P. 45. [In item A261 above.]

A271 "The Demonic Book." Pp. 46-7. [In item A261
      above.]

A272 "On the Day of Looking Back." P. 49. [In item
      A261 above.]

A273 "Do You Still Know It...?" P. 51. [In item A261 above.]

A274 "Spirits and Men." Pp. 52-4. [In item A261 above.]

A275 "A Realist of the Spirit." Pp. 55-6. [In item A261 above. Reprint of item A136.]

A276 "Memories of Hammarskjold." Pp. 57-9. [In item A261 above.]

A277 "On Leo Shestov." P. 60. [In item A261 above.]

A278 "On Richard Beer-Hofmann." Pp. 61-9. [In item A261 above.]

A279 "Hermann Hesse's Service to the Spirit." Pp. 70-9. [In item A261 above.]

A280 "Authentic Bilingualism." Pp. 80-4. [In item A261 above.]

A281 "Since We Have Been a Dialogue." Pp. 85-6. [In item A261 above.]

A282 "Comments on the Idea of Community." Pp. 87-92. [In item A261 above.]

A283 "Community and Environment." Pp. 93-5. [In item A261 above. Another translation of item A129.]

A284 "The Third Leg of the Table." Pp. 96-7. [In item A261 above. Another translation of item A8.]

A285 "Educating." P. 98. [In item A261 above.]

A286 "The Task." Pp. 99-101. [In item A261 above.]

A287 "On Contact." P. 102. [In item A261 above.]

A288 "Style and Instruction." Pp. 103-5. [In item A261 above.]

A289 "An Example: On the Landscapes of Leopold Krakauer." Pp. 106-8. [In item A261 above.]

A290   "Religion and God's Rule." Pp. 109-12. [In
       item A261 above.]

A291   "Fragments on Revelation." Pp. 113-6. [In item
       A261 above.]

A292   "Believing Humanism." Pp. 117-22. [In item
       A261 above. Another translation of item A211.]

A293   "House of God." P. 123. [In item A261 above.]

A294   "Hasidut." P. 125. [In item A261 above.]

A295   "Religious Education." P. 126. [In item A261
       above.]

A296   "On the Science of Religion." Pp. 127-9. [In
       item A261 above.]

A297   "Philosophical and Religious World View." Pp.
       130-5. [In item A261 above.]

A298   "On the Situation of Philosophy." Pp. 136-7.
       [In item A261 above.]

A299   "Healing through Meeting." Pp. 138-43. [In
       item A261 above. Reprint of item A162.]

A300   "On the Psychologizing of the World." Pp. 144-52.
       [In item A261 above.]

A301   "The Unconscious." Pp. 153-73. [In item A261
       above.]

A302   "Politics Born of Faith." Pp. 174-9. [In item
       A261 above.]

A303   "In Twenty Years." P. 180. [In item A261 above.]

A304   "On Two Burckhardt Sayings." Pp. 181-2. [In
       item A261 above.]

A305   "A Conversation with Tagore." Pp. 183-5. [In
       item A261 above. Another translation of item
       A99.]

A306   "China and Us." Pp. 186-90. [In item A261 above.
       Reprint of item A167.]

A307 "On 'Civil Disobedience.'" P. 191. [In item
      A261 above. Another translation of item A208.]

A308 "More on Civil Disobedience." Pp. 192-3. [In
      item A261 above. Another translation of item
      A212.]

A309 "On Capital Punishment." P. 194. [In item
      A261 above.]

A310 "Genuine Dialogue and the Possibilities of Peace."
      Pp. 195-202. [In item A261 above. Reprint of
      items A132 and A177.]

A311 "Stop." Pp. 203-4. [In item A261 above. Reprint
      of item A131.]

A312 "On the Ethics of Political Decision." Pp. 205-
      10. [In item A261 above.]

A313 "On the Problem of the Community of Opinion."
      P. 211. [In item A261 above.]

A314 "To the Clarification of Pacifism." Pp. 212-4.
      [In item A261 above.]

A315 "Greeting and Welcome." Pp. 215-7. [In item
      A261 above.]

A316 "The Three." P. 219. [In item A261 above.]

A317 "November." P. 221. [In item A261 above.]

A318 "Rachman, a Distant Spirit, Speaks." P. 223.
      [In item A261 above.]

A319 "World Space Voyage." P. 224. [In item A261
      above.]

A320 "Expression of Thanks, 1958." P. 225. [In item
      A261 above.]

A321 "Beside Me." P. 227. [In item A261 above.]

A322 "The Fiddler." P. 229. [In item A261 above.
      Another translation of items A224 and A226.]

A323 "Expression of Thanks, 1963." P. 230. [In item
      A261 above.]

A324 "After Death." P. 231. [In item A261 above.]

A325 *Encounter: Autobiographical Fragments.* Translated by
      Maurice Friedman. LaSalle, Ill.: Open Court, 1967,
      136 pp. [No subject index. Reprint of item A240.
      Reprinted as item A374.]

A326 *Kingship of God.* Translated by Richard Scheimann. New
      York: Harper and Row Publishers, 1967, 228 pp.
      [Subject index.]

A327 *On Judaism.* Edited by Nahum N. Glatzer. New York:
      Schocken Books, 1967, 242 pp. [No subject index.
      Includes items A328 through A340 below.]

      A328 "Preface to the 1923 Edition." Translated by Eva
            Jospe. Pp. 3-10. [In item A327 above.]

      A329 "Judaism and the Jews." Translated by Eva Jospe.
            Pp. 11-21. [In item A327 above.]

      A330 "Judaism and Mankind." Translated by Eva Jospe.
            Pp. 22-33. [In item A327 above.]

      A331 "Renewal of Judaism." Translated by Eva Jospe.
            Pp. 34-55. [In item A327 above.]

      A332 "The Spirit of the Orient and Judaism." Trans-
            lated by Eva Jospe. Pp. 56-78. [In item A327
            above.]

      A333 "Jewish Religiosity." Translated by Eva Jospe.
            Pp. 79-94. [In item A327 above.]

      A334 "Myth in Judaism." Translated by Eva Jospe.
            Pp. 95-107. [In item A327 above. Another
            translation of item A96.]

      A335 "The Holy Way: A Word to the Jews and to the
            Nations." Translated by Eva Jospe. Pp. 108-
            48. [In item A327 above.]

      A336 "Herut: On Youth and Religion." Translated by
            Eva Jospe. Pp. 149-74. [In item A327 above.]

A337 "The Spirit of Israel and the World of Today."
Translated by I.M. Lask. Pp. 179-90. [In item
A327 above. Reprint of item A86.]

A338 "Judaism and Civilization." Pp. 191-201. [In
item A327 above. No translator given. Reprint
of items A104 and A110.]

A339 "The Silent Question." Pp. 202-13. [In item
A327 above. No translator given. Reprint of
item A111.]

A340 "The Dialogue between Heaven and Earth." Pp.
214-15. [In item A327 above. No translator
given. Reprint of item A112.]

A341 "Replies to My Critics." Translated by Maurice Fried-
man. *The Philosophy of Martin Buber*. Edited by Paul
Arthur Schilpp and Maurice Friedman. LaSalle, Ill.:
Open Court, 1967, pp. 689-744.

1968

A342 *Biblical Humanism: Eighteen Studies*. Edited by Nahum N.
Glatzer. London: Macdonald and Co., 1968, 247 pp.
[Subject index. British publication of item A343.]

A343 *On the Bible: Eighteen Studies*. Edited by Nahum N.
Glatzer. New York: Schocken Books, 1968, 247 pp.
[Subject index. Reprinted as item A342. Includes
items A344 through A361 below.]

A344 "The Man of Today and the Jewish Bible." Translated by Olga Marx. Pp. 1-13. [In item A343
above. Reprint of item A77.]

A345 "The Tree of Knowledge." Translated by Ronald
Gregor Smith. Pp. 14-21. [In item A343
above. Reprinted from item A130.]

A346 "Abraham the Seer." Translated by Sophie Meyer.
Pp. 22-43. [In item A343 above. Reprint of
item A139.]

A347 "The Burning Bush." Translated by I.M. Lask.
Pp. 44-62. [In item A343 above. Reprinted
from item A45.]

A348   "Holy Event." Translated by Carlyle Witton-
       Davies. Pp. 63-79. [In item A343 above.
       Reprinted from item A95.]

A349   "The Election of Israel: A Biblical Inquiry."
       Translated by Michael A. Meyer. Pp. 80-92.
       [In item A343 above.]

A350   "The Words on the Tablets." Translated by I.M.
       Lask. Pp. 93-117. [In item A343 above.
       Reprinted from item A45.]

A351   "What Are We to Do about the Ten Commandments?"
       Translated by Olga Marx. Pp. 118-21. [In item
       A343 above. Reprint of item A76.]

A352   "The Prayer of the First Fruits." Translated by
       Stanley Godman. Pp. 122-30. [In item A343
       above. Reprinted from item A125.]

A353   "Samuel and the Ark." Translated by Michael A.
       Meyer. Pp. 131-6. [In item A343 above.]

A354   "Biblical Leadership." Translated by Greta Hort.
       Pp. 137-50. [In item A343 above. Reprint of
       items A38 and A80.]

A355   "Plato and Isaiah." Translated by Olga Marx.
       Pp. 151-9. [In item A343 above. Reprint of
       item A78.]

A356   "Redemption." Translated by Stanley Godman.
       Pp. 160-5. [In item A343 above. Reprinted
       from item A125.]

A357   "False Prophets." Translated by Olga Marx.
       Pp. 166-71. [In item A343 above. Reprint of
       item A79.]

A358   "Prophecy, Apocalyptic, and the Historical Hour."
       Translated by Maurice Friedman. Pp. 172-87.
       [In item A343 above. Reprint of item A173.]

A359   "Job." Translated by Carlyle Witton-Davies.
       Pp. 188-98. [In item A343 above. Reprinted
       from item A95.]

A360 "The Heart Determines." Translated by Ronald Gregor Smith. Pp. 199–210. [In item A343 above. Reprinted from item A126.]

A361 "Biblical Humanism." Translated by Michael A. Meyer. Pp. 211-16. [In item A343 above. Another translation of item A91.]

1969

A362 "The Children." Translated by E. William Rollins and Harry Zohn. *Men of Dialogue: Martin Buber and Albrecht Goes* . Edited by E. William Rollins and Harry Zohn. New York: Funk and Wagnalls, 1969, pp. 225-8.

A363 "Elijah: A Mystery Play." Translated by Maurice Friedman. *Martin Buber and the Theater*. Edited by Maurice Friedman. New York: Funk and Wagnalls, 1969, pp. 114-64.

A364 "The End of the German-Jewish Symbiosis." Translated by E. William Rollins and Harry Zohn. *Men of Dialogue: Martin Buber and Albrecht Goes*. Edited by E. William Rollins and Harry Zohn. New York: Funk and Wagnalls, 1969, pp. 232-5. [Another translation of item A213.]

A365 *From the Treasure House of Hassidism*. Translated by Haim Shachter. Edited by David Hardan. Jerusalem: Cultural Division, Department for Education and Culture in the Diaspora, World Zionist Organization, 1969, 73 pp. [No subject index.]

A366 "On Polarity: Dialogue after the Theater." Translated by Maurice Friedman. *Martin Buber and the Theater*. Edited by Maurice Friedman. New York: Funk and Wagnalls, 1969, pp. 53-74. [Reprinted from item A222.]

A367 "Reach for the World, Ha-Bima!" Translated by Maurice Friedman. *Martin Buber and the Theater*. Edited by Maurice Friedman. New York: Funk and Wagnalls, 1969, pp. 88-91.

A368   "Silence and Outcry." Translated by E. William Rollins
       and Harry Zohn. *Men of Dialogue: Martin Buber and
       Albrecht Goes.* Edited by E. William Rollins and
       Harry Zohn. New York: Funk and Wagnalls, 1969, pp.
       244-8.

A369   "They and We." Translated by E. William Rollins and
       Harry Zohn. *Men of Dialogue: Martin Buber and
       Albrecht Goes.* Edited by E. William Rollins and
       Harry Zohn. New York: Funk and Wagnalls, 1969, pp.
       236-43.

                              1970

A370   *I and Thou.* Translated by Walter Kaufmann. New York:
       Charles Scribner's Sons, 1970, 185 pp. [No subject
       index. Another translation of item A17.]

A371   Preface to *Israel and the Arab World*, by Aharon Cohen.
       Translated by Aubrey Hodes, Naomi Handelman, and
       Mirian Shimeon. New York: Funk and Wagnalls, 1970,
       p. xi.

                              1972

A372   "The Dialogue Principle in Education." *Life-long
       Education in Israel.* Edited by Kalman Yaron.
       Jerusalem: Public Advisory Council on Adult Education
       at the Ministry of Education and Culture, 1972, pp.
       13-8. [No translator given. A reprint, in part, of
       item A97.]

A373   "In the Beginning: An English Rendition of the Book of
       Genesis: Based on the German Version of Martin Buber
       and Franz Rosenzweig." Translated by Everett Fox.
       Response, No. 14 (Summer 1972), 1-159.

                              1973

A374   *Meetings.* Translated and edited by Maurice Friedman.
       LaSalle, Ill.: Open Court Publishing Company, 1973,
       115 pp. [No subject index. Reprint of items A240
       and A325.]

A375   *On Zion: The History of an Idea.*   Translated by Stanley
       Godman.   New York: Schocken Books, 1973, 165 pp.
       [No subject index.   Reprint of item A125.]

                              1974

A376   "On Viennese Literature."   Translated by William M.
       Johnston.   *German Quarterly*, 47 (November 1974),
       559-66.

                              1975

A377   "Tribute to Chaim Weizmann."   *Chaim Weizmann: A Tribute
       on His Seventieth Birthday.*   Edited by Paul Goodman.
       London: Victor Gollancz Ltd., 1975, pp. 34-5.   [No
       translator given.]

Writings about Buber

1926

B1 Lewisohn, Ludwig. "Martin Buber." *Menorah Journal*, 12
     (February 1926), 65-70.

    An early overview based primarily on Buber's collections
of Hasidic tales. In Hasidism Buber found a "secret
Judaism," a fundamental Jewish psychology embodied in the
principles of unity, action, and the future. The concepts
of realization and unconditionedness are also briefly
discussed.

1927

B2 Van Der Hoop, J.H. "Religion as a Psychic Necessity."
     Psyche, 7 (April 1927), 102-19.

    A brief description of the I-Thou and I-It relationships
contained in a longer article.

B3 Weltsch, Robert. "A New Bible Translation." *New
     Palestine*, 20 May 1927, pp. 474-5.

    A positive review of the first four volumes of the
Buber-Rosenzweig translation.

1928

B4 Kohn, Hans. "The Personal Aspect of Zionism." *New
     Palestine*, 10 February 1928, pp. 165-6.

    In Buber the extremes of the enlightenment and Hasidism
are synthesized. Buber interprets the Jewish question in
terms of a personal effort by each individual Jew to
understand and realize the essence of Judaism.

1931

B5 Cohen, Lucy. Foreword to *Jewish Mysticism and the Legends
    of the Baalshem*, by Martin Buber. Translated by Lucy
    Cohen. London: J.M. Dent and Sons Ltd., 1931, pp. ix-xv

    Brief introduction to Buber's Hasidic writings.

1933

B6 "Raid Professor's Home." *New York Times*, 16 March 1933,
    p. 13.

    Brief report of the search of Buber's house by German
    political police.

1934

B7 Tepfer, John J. "Martin Buber and Neo-Mysticism."
    Central Conference of American Rabbis Yearbook, 44
    (1934), 203-19.

    An early overview of Buber's thought in which his work
    on Hasidism is considered his primary contribution and
    the starting point for many of his ideas. Through
    Hasidism Buber was able to return to his Jewish roots
    which he found in the records of everyday Hasidic life.
    His concept of the perfect community was derived from
    his study of Hasidic communities and later influenced
    his interpretation of Zionism. The Jewish task is to
    unite the concrete with the ideal. Thought must be syn-
    chronized with actual life. The supreme example of this
    occurs in the Hasidic tales. Buber's mysticism, like
    Hasidic mysticism, unites God, man, and the world.

1936

B8 "Picks 10 Greatest Jews." *New York Times*, 28 March 1936,
    p. 17.

    Buber included on list compiled by Ludwig Lewisohn.

1937

B9   Smith, Ronald Gregor. Introduction to *I and Thou*, by
     Martin Buber. Translated by Ronald Gregor Smith.
     Edinburgh: T. and T. Clark, 1937, pp. v-xii.

     Brief introduction to this first English translation.

1938

B10 Kohn, Hans. "The Religious Philosophy of Martin Buber."
     Menorah Journal, 26 (Spring 1938), 173-85.

     Another early overview emphasizing Hasidism and the
     I-Thou, I-It relationships.

1941

B11 Agus, Jacob Bernard. *Modern Philosophies of Judaism: A
     Study of Recent Jewish Philosophies of Religion*. New
     York: Behram's, 1941, pp. 213-79.

     An overview of the development of Buber's thought as
     influenced by Zionism, mysticism, Hasidism, and the
     philosophical climate of the time. The I-Thou relation
     is analyzed in terms of metaphysics, mysticism, and the
     practice of religion. For Buber this relationship is
     the ultimate metaphysical insight, and the author finds
     it capable of being expanded into a consistent meta-
     physics. The I-Thou relation is the direct apprehension
     of ultimate reality but lacks the qualities of self-
     mortification, purification, and union with God typical
     of classical mysticism. It is a mild form of mysticism
     based on a state of illumination but retaining the
     duality between man and God. The practical results of
     the I-Thou relation are compared to the extremes of
     individualism and collectivism. The danger of irrational
     subjectivism is also discussed. The I-Thou relation
     between man and God is a devotion uncontrolled by reason
     and lacks any rational method of interpreting the result-
     ing behavior.

B12 Oldhum, Joseph H. "All Real Life Is Meeting." *Christian
     News-Letter Supplement*, 24 December 1941, pp. 1-4.

     Early overview based on *I and Thou* (item A17). Finds
     similarities with John MacMurray. Both saw the solution

to society's problems in the reestablishment of the
world of true relationship.

1943

B13 Read, Herbert. *Education through Art.* London: Faber
       and Faber, 1943, pp. 279-89.

       Uses Buber's description of the role of the teacher
       in a discussion of the psychological development of the
       child in the classroom. The teacher is the mediator
       between the individual and society, helping the child to
       move from self-centeredness toward adaption to his social
       environment.

1944

B14 Liptzin, Solomon. *Germany's Stepchildren.* Philadelphia:
       Jewish Publication Society of America, 1944, pp. 255-69

       A review of Buber's concept of Zionism. He believed
       that the German Jew had to choose between being German
       and being Jewish. The Jewish role, when chosen, required
       the colonization of Palestine, forming not just another
       petty state, but communities in which the Jewish role
       could be lived. Buber's reply to Gandhi expressed the
       sentiments of many German and Palestinian Jews.

1945

B15 Werner, Alfred. "Jewish Lore in Fiction." *Christian
       Century*, 3 October 1945, pp. 1126-7.

       Review of *For the Sake of Heaven* (item A25), described
       as a failure as a novel but worth reading for the Hasidic
       wisdom.

B16 Wodehouse, Helen. "Martin Buber's 'I and Thou.'"
       Philosophy, 20 (April 1945), 17-30.

       Stresses the possibility of I-Thou relations with the
       non-human and with God, and the relationship between the
       I-Thou and I-It attitudes.

1946

B17 Hort, Greta. Introduction to *Mamre: Essays in Religion*,
    by Martin Buber. Melbourne: Melbourne University
    Press, 1946, pp. ix-xiii.

   Brief discussion of the difficulty of translating
   Buber's works, which are neither philosophy nor theology
   but a standing ground from which to view reality. Sees
   Buber's thought as applicable to all religions.

B18 Jarrett-Kerr, Martin. "Real Life is Being." *Theology*
    (S.P.C.K.), 47 (1946), 154-8.

   Weaknesses in Buber's dialogical thought include the
   lack of a precise statement of how one goes from the I-
   Thou world to the I-It world and back again, and the
   contradiction involved in talking about the I-Thou relation and thereby objectifying it. Further, the complete
   division Buber draws between the I-Thou language and the
   I-It language, the basis for his division of reality,
   does not seem logically possible. But if one does accept
   this dichotomy, one is led, despite Buber's denial, to a
   choice between the two worlds, either by the dismissal
   of the I-It world or by its transfiguration. Finally
   the author states that the only secure bridge between
   the two worlds is sacramental worship.

1947

B19 Oldham, Joseph H. "Life as Dialogue." *Christian News-
    Letter Supplement*, 19 March 1947, pp. 7-16.

   An overview of the philosophy of dialogue. Sees
   Buber's emphasis on the social nature of reality as a
   saving corrective for our age. Buber's social philosophy
   is an alternative to collectivism and individualism.
   Also explores Buber's interpretations of responsibility
   and the modern religious situation.

B20 Pfuetze, Paul E. "Martin Buber and Jewish Mysticism."
    Religion in Life, 16 (Autumn 1947), 553-67.

   Discusses three aspects of Buber's thought: (1) his
   interpretation of Hasidism and its active, natural mysticism, (2) his definition of the Jewish genius as expressed in the unity of monotheism, the cry for justice,
   and the hope for a future kingdom of God on earth, and
   (3) his concept of the personal in the I-Thou dialogue.

B21   Schwarzschild, Steven S.   "Martin Buber's Zionism--Its
      Bearing on Jewish Pacifism."   *Jewish Peace Fellowship
      Tidings*, 4 (September 1947), 417-38.

      (Not available for annotating.)

B22   Smith, Ronald G.   "Mr. Eliot's 'The Family Reunion' in
      the Light of Martin Buber's 'I and Thou.'"   *Theology*,
      50 (February 1947), 59-64.

      The salvation of Harry Lord Mountchesney in Eliot's
      play is a story of movement out of isolation into rela-
      tion, and can best be understood in terms of Buber's
      philosophy.

                              1948

B23   A.W.   "Tales of--and an Essay on--Hasidism."   *New York
      Times Book Review*, 14 November 1948, p. 52.

      Positive review of *Hasidism* (item A60) and *Tales of
      the Hasidim: The Early Masters* (item A55).   While Hasid-
      ism is at times reminiscent of Franciscan Christianity,
      the reviewer finds more similarity to Zen.

B24   Badt-Strauss, Bertha.   "Martin Buber."   *Jewish Spectator*,
      May 1948, pp. 22-3.

      Brief overview of Buber's life and thought.

B25   Blau, Joseph L.   "Martin Buber's Religious Philosophy:
      A Review Article."   *Review of Religion*, 13 (November
      1948), 48-64.

      In this overview the author relates Buber's under-
      standing of Hasidism, the Hasidic community, and the role
      of the Zaddik in this community, to his philosophy of
      dialogue.   Buber rejects the concept of the solitary
      individual as described in Kierkegaard's 'single one'
      and Stirner's 'unique one.'   Man exists in community
      and the mild mysticism of Buber does not lead to mystic-
      al absorption in God.   God is confronted so that man
      may be assured of meaning in this world.   The dialogue
      of religion has its starting point and culmination in
      the community.

B26   "Challenge and Response."   *Times Literary Supplement*,
      14 August 1948, p. 462.

A review of *Between Man and Man* (item A48). Criticizes Buber's interpretations of Kierkegaard's ethics and Christian messianism.

B27 Clarke, Fred. *Freedom in the Educative Society.* London: University of London Press, 1948, pp. 64-8.

Buber, like Rousseau, wanted to show that the formative influence of the teacher is compatible with the freedom of the student. He did this through his concept of the selection of the effective world.

B28 Fremantle, Anne. "Martin Buber." *Commonweal*, August 1948, pp. 404-5.

Overview, from a Christian viewpoint, of Buber as a religious thinker. Sees Buber's thought as providing a counterbalance to the Christian focus on the incarnation to the neglect of creation.

B29 Gruenthaner, Michael J. "'Tales of the Hasidim: The Early Masters.'" *Thought*, 23 (June 1948), 378-9.

A negative review of Buber's Hasidic message (item A55), which the reviewer sees as containing no significant revelation concerning God or the conduct of life.

B30 Gumbiner, Joseph H. "God and Man." *Commentary*, May 1948, pp. 482-3.

A review of *Between Man and Man* (item A48) in which the reviewer sees Buber's thought as a corrective to Kierkegaard's other-worldliness and Heidegger's solicitude and self-consciousness. Finds fault with Ronald Gregor Smith's translation.

B31 Minkin, Jacob S. "Buber Lifts Moses Out of the Mists." *Congress Weekly*, 13 February 1948, pp. 12-3.

A positive review of *Moses* (item A45) describing it as a dramatic but scholarly interpretation.

B32 Simon, Ernst. "Martin Buber: His Way between Thought and Deed--On His 70th Anniversary." *Jewish Frontier*, 17 (February 1948), 25-8.

An appreciation of Buber giving a brief overview of his thought and stressing his relationship with modern Judaism and Israel.

B33   Smith, Constance I. "The Single One and the Other."
      Hibbert Journal, 46 (July 1948), 315-21.

      A criticism of Kierkegaard's concept of the Single
      One in terms of Buber's thought. Discusses (1) the
      Single One's relation with God, (2) his relations with
      the other, and (3) his relations with the crowd. Man
      is seen, contrary to Kierkegaard, as standing in essen-
      tial relation to God only if he stands in essential re-
      lation to other men.

B34   Tanner, Eugene S. "'Tales of the Hasidim: The Early
      Masters.'" *Journal of Bible and Religion*, 16 (January
      1948), 128-30.

      In a positive review of item A55, the author suggests
      that the greatest weakness in the Hasidism of these early
      masters was the growth of blind adherence to their author-
      ity. This led to religious exploitation by their
      successors.

B35   Tillich, Paul. "Martin Buber and Christian Thought: His
      Three-fold Contribution to Protestantism." *Commentary*,
      June 1948, pp. 515-21.

      Buber's significance for Protestant theology is seen
      in three factors: (1) his existential interpretation of
      prophetic religion, (2) his rediscovery of mysticism as
      a factor within prophetic religion, and (3) his recogni-
      tion, through his Hasidic studies, of the relationship
      between prophetic religion and culture. However his
      rejection of the state as a contributor to I-Thou rela-
      tions within the community put him in disagreement with
      most religious socialists. History seems to show that
      without the shell of a state, community cannot exist.

B36   Werner, Alfred. "Buber at Seventy." *Congress Weekly*,
      13 February 1948, pp. 10-11.

      A brief overview emphasizing Buber's influence on
      German Jews and on Zionism.

B37   Witton-Davies, C. "Martin Buber." *Theology* (S.P.C.K.),
      51 (August 1948), 301-3.

      Appreciation on Buber's seventieth birthday.

1949

B38 Coates, J.B. *The Crisis of the Human Person: Some
     Personalist Interpretations*. New York: Longmans,
     Green, and Co., 1949, pp. 65-81.

     A sympathetic overview of Buber's thought, derived
     primarily from *I and Thou* (item A17).

B39 Kuhn, Helmut. "Book Review." *Journal of Philosophy*, 46
     (3 February 1949), 75-9.

     In a review of *Between Man and Man* (item A48), Buber's
     concept of the God-man relation is seen as in conformity
     with the Christian theory of love as well as Jewish
     teachings. Buber errs, however, in making the man-man
     relation the measure of the God-man relation instead of
     the other way around.

B40 Richards, V.W. "Buber on Education." *Parents Review*
     (England), November 1949, pp. 261-3.

     Brief overview of Buber's philosophy of education.

B41 Sandrow, Edward T. "'Israel and the World.'" *Jewish
     Education*, 21 (Winter 1949), 88-9.

     A positive review of item A69 emphasizing Buber's
     desire that Zionism and Jewish religious life not be
     divorced.

B42 Schulweis, Harold. "Crisis Theology and Martin Buber."
     Review of Religion, 14 (November 1949), 38-42.

     Argues that the similarity between Protestant crisis
     theology and Buber's thought has been exaggerated. Buber
     in fact is a critic of its emphasis on the otherness and
     transcendence of God, grace, other-worldly salvation,
     and acceptance of dogma.

B43 Smith, Ronald G. *The Thought of Martin Buber*. Burning
     Glass Paper No. 18. Shorne: Ridgeway House, 1949.
     19pp.

     (Not available for annotating.)

1950

B44   Coates, J.B. "The Purpose of the Existential School."
       Congregational Quarterly, July 1950, pp. 219-28.

       (Not available for annotating.)

B45   Fackenheim, Emil L. "In the Here and Now." *Commentary*,
       April 1950, pp. 393-5.

       A positive review of *The Prophetic Faith* (item A95).
       Buber's primary contribution to biblical study is his
       rejection of modern reductionism, the understanding of
       the Bible in terms of modern rational categories. He
       has engaged in a sustained polemic against contemporary
       beliefs in order to come to grips with biblical faith.
       The prophets do not speak in terms of an obligation to
       a timeless ideal, but of specific decisions to be made
       as the result of specific encounters with God.

B46   Lewis, H.D. "Revelation Without Content." *Hibbert
       Journal*, 48 (July 1950), 379-82.

       Argues that Buber's conception of the man-God relation-
       ship as pure relation, without content, is at variance
       with Christian revelation which includes specific knowl-
       edge of the nature and will of God. Buber's view stems
       from his belief that knowledge about God endangers God's
       transcendence. The author states that revelation with-
       out content is neither significant nor true to religious
       experience.

B47   May, Herbert G. "'The Prophetic Faith.'" *Journal of
       Bible and Religion*, 18 (April 1950), 131-2.

       Primarily a descriptive review of item A95. Feels
       Buber's interpretation of prophetic religion is tradition
       criticism, seeking to discover in the Hebrew Bible the
       influence of a primitive unity which was preserved de-
       spite editorial tendencies.

B48   Rylaarsdam, J. Coert. "Book Review." *Theology Today*,
       7 (October 1950), 399-401.

       In a positive review of *The Prophetic Faith* (item
       A95), the reviewer criticizes Buber for his failure to
       reconstruct the historical events of the Hebrew Bible
       and his reliance upon personal a priori assumptions.

B49 Spitz, David. "The Noble Dilemma." *New Republic*,
     31 July 1950, pp. 20-1.

     Brief review of *Paths in Utopia* (item A94) in which
the reviewer describes utopian hopes as futile.

B50 "Utopias Defended." *Social Justice Review*, 43
     (December 1950), 263-4.

     Brief review of *Paths in Utopia* (item A94) in which
the reviewer agrees that the only practical way of
building a socialistic society is from the bottom up, a
community of communities.

B51 Wodehouse, Helen. "The Threefold Work of Martin Buber."
     Fortnightly, May 1950, pp. 326-32.

     An overview of Buber's thought.

1951

B52 Assagioli, Roberto. "Discussion." *World Union for Pro-*
     gressive Judaism 25th Anniversary Conference, 1951,
     pp. 80-4.

     Response to Buber's address "Judaism and Civilization"
(item A104).

B53 "'Paths in Utopia.'" *Catholic Worker*, July-August 1951,
     pp. 3+.

     A positive review of item A94 linking Buber's thought
to radical Christian social-economic thought.

B54 Werner, Alfred. "A Talk with Martin Buber." *Jewish*
     Affairs, October 1951, pp. 21-4.

     Brief record of their conversation in which Buber
talked about the problems of the new state of Israel.

1952

B55 Berkovits, Elieser. "Martin Buber's Apology." *Congress*
     Weekly, 28 January 1952, pp. 8-9.

     Criticizes Buber for accepting the Goethe Prize.

B56 Cohen, Arthur A. "Revelation and Law: Reflections on
     Martin Buber's Views on Halakah." *Judaism*, 1 (July
     1952), 250-6.

Summarizes Buber's conception of revelation as dialogue and finds serious problems. Contrary to the dialogue model, God often treated the community of Israel as an object to be manipulated. In addition, revelation is in some sense independent of the structure of apprehension. Content is of primary significance. A further problem is Buber's concept of time. His emphasis on the fulfilled present tends to make the present static, a point of fixity before which God moves. It is too easy to draw God out of eternity and make him the Thou to our I in our subjective world. The author contends that to destroy the law is to lead man into mystical absorption or to render God submissive to man's needs.

B57   "Everyday Democracy Held Vital to Peace." *New York Times*, 21 April 1952, p. 21.

Mention of World Brotherhood Award given to Buber.

B58   Herberg, Will. "Philosopher of Israel." *Yale Review*, 42 (December 1952), 293-8.

A review of *Eclipse of God* (item A113), *At the Turning* (item A109), and *Israel and Palestine* (item A125). Although primarily positive, criticizes Buber's mystical strain as well as his "folkism," which the reviewer believes is not in harmony with biblical or rabbinical thinking about Israel.

B59   "Israeli Scholar Honored." *New York Times*, 7 April 1952, p. 23.

Brief report of a talk, "Hope for This Hour" (item A123), given by Buber in New York City.

B60   Kaplan, Mordecai. "Martin Buber: Theologian, Philosopher and Prophet." *Reconstructionist*, 2 May 1952, pp. 7-10.

Through the creation of a common frame of reference for the Jew and the non-Jew, based upon the Hebrew scriptures, Buber has done more than anyone to protect modern Judaism from the dangers of isolation and assimilation.

B61   Kehoe, R. "Book Review." *Blackfriars*, 33 (September 1952), 379-80.

Review of *Images of Good and Evil* (item A124). Althoug the reviewer believes that it is an important book, feels that it is obscure and doubts that its general thesis will find support.

B62 Meyerhoff, Hans. "The Paradox of Personalism." *Nation*,
   6 December 1952, p. 534.

   A review of *Eclipse of God* (item A113). Doubts that
   Buber has adequately explained the crisis of religion
   in the modern world.

B63 Schulweis, Harold. "Martin Buber: An Interview."
   Reconstructionist, 21 March 1952, pp. 7-10.

   Record of an interview in which Buber discussed the
   verifiability of the I-Thou relation with God, the mis-
   use of his works by the Nazis, and his views on the
   "biological transmission" of Jewish ethnic traits.

B64 Schulweis, Harold M. "The Personalism of Martin Buber."
   Personalist, 33 (Spring 1952), 131-4.

   Discussion of Buber's theological personalism.
   Describes I-Thou and I-It relationships and draws a
   parallel with the thought of Wilhelm Dilthey.

B65 Tillich, Paul. "Jewish Influence on Contemporary Christian Theology." *Cross Currents*, 2 (Spring 1952), 35-42.

   Sees Buber's thought as the strongest Jewish influence
   on current Protestant theology, particularly his doctrine
   of the I-Thou relation between man and God. Buber intro-
   duced the existentialist point of view into theology
   before Kierkegaard became known. He made it clear that
   without an encounter with God, God is an empty word.
   This was decisive for the reinterpretation of the meaning of revelation.

B66 Wheelwright, Philip. "On Being, Knowing, Saying."
   Sewanee Review, 60 (Spring 1952), 347-62.

   Review of Gabriel Marcel's *Mystery of Being*, Buber's
   I and Thou (item A17), and Nikolai Berdyaev's *Dream and
   Reality*. Sees each author as centrally concerned with
   defining reality using existentialist methodology.

B67 Wolf, Ernest M. "Martin Buber and German Jewry: Prophet
   and Teacher to a Generation in Catastrophe." *Judaism*,
   1 (October 1952), 346-52.

   Buber's place of leadership in the German Jewish community was based upon: (1) his involvement in the
   Zionist movement, (2) his rediscovery of Hasidism, which
   served as a corrective to the rationalistic tendencies
   in Judaism and a point of reconciliation for eastern and

western Jewry, (3) the Buber-Rosenzweig translation of
the Bible, and (4) Buber's involvement in Jewish
education.

1953

B68   Cohen, Arthur.   "'Eclipse of God.'"   *Judaism*, 2 (July
      1953), 280-3.

      In the *Eclipse of God* (item A113) Buber gives his
      answer to the hiddenness of God, the rediscovery of the
      power of encounter.   As Buber communicates this in the
      language of encounter, he can only address those who are
      already aware of its power.   He cannot open the closed
      heart with a language that presupposes openness.

B69   Conway, Pierre.   "New Philosophy."   *Commonweal*,
      21 August 1953, p. 494.

      A review of *Good and Evil* (item A130) from a Catholic
      point of view.   Sees Buber's interpretation as foreign
      to Catholic orthodoxy.

B70   Franquiz, J.A.   "'Eclipse of God.'"   *Journal of Bible
      and Religion*, 21 (July 1953), 195-7.

      The reviewer praises the book (item A113) for its em-
      phasis on the dignity of the human person and as a blow
      against materialism and religious naturalism.   He finds
      fault, however, with Buber's neglect of the social impli-
      cations of mysticism, his ignorance of the Christian
      faith, and his silence concerning the work of other
      writers.

B71   Friedman, Maurice.   "Martin Buber and Christian Thought."
      Review of Religion, 18 (November 1953), 31-43.

      A discussion of the differences between Buber's thought
      and that of the many Christian thinkers who have adopted
      his I-Thou, I-It philosophy.   The widespread influence
      of this philosophy does not imply an equally widespread
      understanding of it.   In many instances it has been
      serious distorted.

B72   Friedman, Maurice.   "Martin Buber's New View of Evil."
      Judaism, 2 (July 1953), 239-46.

      For Buber, evil is both the absence of direction and
      the absence of genuine relation.   This is seen clearly

in his treatment of conscience as the individual's awareness of what he really is, implying both dialogue and
direction. Guilt is the result of not taking the direction toward God. The structure of evil, which cannot be
explained by either the moral laws of society or the
self-analysis of psychology, is discovered in the meeting
with oneself, but only if one is aware of the voice of
conscience. Buber identifies two stages of evil as seen
in myths, decisionlessness and the decision to evil. In
later years, following the events of World War II, it
appeared that he was tending toward ascribing reality to
evil. However, he retained his belief that it was not
man's nature which is evil, but only his use of that
nature.

B73 "German Peace Prize for Prof. Buber." *Times* (London),
28 September 1953, p. 4.

Brief description of the ceremony.

B74 Griffiths, B. "'Eclipse of God.'" *Blackfriars*, 34
(December 1953), 70.

Brief review of item A113 in which the reviewer supports Buber's criticism of Jung as a gnostic.

B75 Herberg, Will. "'Eclipse of God.'" *Theology Today*, 10
(July 1953), 289-90.

In a generally positive review of item A113, finds too
many traces of Buber's earlier mysticism which are incom-
patible with his later personalist, existential, biblical
emphasis. Also disapproves of the echoes of folkism and
Buber's inadequate understanding of the Christian faith.

B76 "Rabbi Names Group to Work Out Peace." *New York Times*,
11 October 1953, p. 28.

Buber's name on list suggested for peace group by
Rabbi Israel Goldstein.

B77 "Religion and Philosophy." *Times Literary Supplement*,
8 May 1953, p. 305.

In a brief review of *Eclipse of God* (item A113), sees
Buber's chief omission to be an account of modern man's
preference for the world of It over the world of Thou.

B78 Riemer, Jack. "'Israel and Palestine.'" *Judaism*, 2
(April 1953), 186-8.

In a review of item A125, the reviewer sees Buber's
Zionism as a realistic approach to the ethics of state-
hood.

B79 "University News." *Times* (London), 11 July 1953, p. 3.

Buber among those given honorary degrees at Aberdeen
University.

1954

B80 Agus, Jacob B. *Guideposts in Modern Judaism.* New
York: Bloch Publishing Co., 1954, pp. 105-11.

Overview of Buber in a general discussion of modern
Jewish thought. Buber defines the Jewish elan as a
stream of consciousness that finds expression at various
times in folk-piety and in the prophetic-mystical experiences of saints. His three basic contributions are:
(1) the idea that the national soul of Israel is the
fundamental reality in the spiritual life of all Jews,
(2) his interpretation of the Hasidic movement, and
(3) his description of the I-Thou relationship.

B81 Fackenheim, Emil L. "'Israel and Palestine.'" *Jewish
Quarterly Review*, 45 (October 1954), 170-4.

A positive review of *Israel and Palestine* (item A125).
Discusses the intimate relationship between Buber's
philosophical outlook and his historical understanding.
Buber avoids the dilemma of either seeking truth and
value apart from Jewish historical tradition or becoming
a narrator of a dead Jewish past. He assumes that the
Jewish past is alive or at least capable of revival.
But the reviewer doubts that Buber's emphasis on the
spirit, as opposed to modern naturalism, nationalism,
and pragmatism, will find a receptive audience.

B82 Friedman, Maurice S. "'For the Sake of Heaven.'"
Journal of Bible and Religion, 22 (January 1954), 45-6.

Compares Buber's novel (item A25) with Dostoievsky's
The Brothers Karamazov in its dialectic between types of
religious figures and in its insights into the problems
of evil and human existence.

B83 Friedman, Maurice S. "Martin Buber at Seventy-five."
Religion in Life, 23 (Summer 1954), 405-17.

An overview covering Buber's interpretation of Judaism, his philosophy of dialogue, his concept of God, and the redemption of evil.

B84   Friedman, Maurice. "Martin Buber, Prophet and Philo-
      sopher." *Faith Today*, 1 (December-January 1954-55),
      30-40.

      Overview of Buber's life and work.

B85   Friedman, Maurice. "Martin Buber's Theory of Knowledge."
      Review of Metaphysics, 8 (December 1954), 264-80.

      Buber's I-Thou philosophy implies a theory of knowledge
      that cuts through the traditional subject-object approach
      and establishes an entirely different way of knowing.
      Through the concreteness of the meeting with the other,
      Buber avoids idealism as well as abstracting the subject
      into an isolated consciousness. This social conception
      of knowledge reverses the direction of thought which de-
      rived knowledge of other selves from analogy. Although
      the knowledge of others is direct, it is not unmediated.
      The mediation of signs, everything we meet that addresses
      us, does not, however, detract from the presentness of the
      I-Thou relation. It is this presentness which makes it
      logically impossible to criticize I-Thou knowing on the
      basis of an I-It system and is fatal to the logical
      positivist's attempt to relegate ethics and religion to
      subjective emotion. Presentness is also the key to
      understanding the I-Thou relation with nature.

B86   Friedman, Maurice. "Martin Buber's View of Biblical
      Faith." *Journal of Bible and Religion*, 22 (January
      1954), 3-13.

      Buber sees the dialogue between God and the people of
      Israel as the central aspect of Jewish religion. This
      dialogue finds its most significant expression in the
      concept of the kingship of God. Buber's work of biblical
      interpretation is primarily devoted to tracing the
      development of this concept from its earliest expression
      in terms of a tribal god to its later development as the
      God of sufferers. At this latter stage, God is seen as
      taking part in man's suffering. To help the sufferers
      is to know God. Among the sufferers God finds his
      special agent, a hidden servant, who takes on the suffer-
      ings of his people. Jesus cannot be identified with this
      suffering servant because he stepped out of concealment.

B87   Friedman, Maurice S.   "Revelation and Law in the Thought
       of Martin Buber."   *Judaism*, 3 (Winter 1954), 9-19.

       Revelation for Buber imparts presence as power rather
       than specific content.   Revelation is a dialogue between
       man and God and thus man helps determine its form.   Each
       prophet was part of a unique historical situation and
       each transmitted what his revelation meant for his par-
       ticular situation.   Differences between prophets are
       also expressions of the progressive revelation of God
       through history.   Law resulting from this dialogue may
       be accepted by the individual only to the extent that it
       is real for him.   Criticisms of this view by Arthur Cohen
       and Franz Rosenzweig are discussed and found to be based
       on misunderstandings of Buber's position.

B88   Friedman, Maurice.   "Symbol, Myth, and History in the
       Thought of Martin Buber."   *Journal of Religion*, 34
       (January 1954), 1-11.

       In discussing God and man's relationship with God,
       Buber walks a narrow line between the mystical and the
       nonmystical.   He denies that God is merely immanent or
       transcendent.   The relationship is described in terms of
       the meeting of two persons.   The meaning of a symbol is
       found in the fact that it points to this meeting with
       the Absolute.   Myth is the most concrete and dramatic
       form of a symbol, a memory of the man-God meeting.   The
       author discusses several criticisms of Buber's position.

B89   Pfuetze, Paul E.   "The Concept of the Self in Contemporary
       Protestant Theology."   *Journal of Religious Thought*,
       12 (Autumn-Winter 1954-55), 5-16.

       The concept of the social self as a self-other system,
       as seen in the writings of George Herbert Mead and Buber,
       has had a strong influence on Protestant theology.
       Discusses the God-man relationship, faith, religion,
       ethics, the image of God, sin, and repentance in terms
       of the I-Thou philosophy.

B90   Pfuetze, Paul E.   *The Social Self*.   New York: Bookman
       Associates, 1954, 392 pp.

       An overview and comparison of the philosophical anthro-
       pology and social philosophy of George Herbert Mead and
       Buber.   The author supports Buber's theocentric personal-
       ism over Mead's naturalism because it provides a better
       understanding of the human condition.   Suggests a

reconstruction of Mead's thought along these lines. The
last six pages contain a recapitulation and summary of
the main points of the book in outline form. There is a
subject index.

B91   Simon, M. Raphael. "'Eclipse of God.'" *Thomist*, 17
          (July 1954), 403-6.

   In a review of *Eclipse of God* (item A113), faults
Buber for inaccurate statements about Christianity and
his ignorance of Aristotelian and scholastic philosophy.

1955

B92   Brown, James. "Subject-Object and I-Thou: Martin Buber."
          Subject and Object in Modern Theology. London: SCM
          Press, 1955, pp. 107-39.

   A somewhat unsympathetic analysis of Buber's thought
emphasizing the I-Thou and I-It relationships. The
Kantian dichotomy between these two attitudes is expanded
by Buber from the sphere of ethics into religion. In
Buber's hands it becomes existential in that he analyzes
human existence phenomenologically. Existence is brought
into being by the subject, and the I by the Thou. The
author feels that Buber has not adequately resolved the
question of the objectivity of the I-Thou experience, or
the reciprocity of the I-Thou relation between man and
nature. He also feels that the religion of *I and Thou*
(item A17) is pantheistic. He suggests that in the end
Buber's thought is merely an "existential veneer" upon
Hegel.

B93   Bruns, J. Edgar. "Martin Buber: 'Two Types of Faith.'"
          Bridge: A Yearbook of Judaeo-Christian Studies, 1
          (1955), 322-5.

   A generally sympathetic review of item A107. Two major
criticisms are made: (1) Buber is overly dependent upon
liberal Protestant biblical scholarship, and (2) the
lines between emunah (trust in) and pistis (belief that)
are drawn too sharply and without regard for objectivity.

B94   Friedman, Maurice. "Healing Through Meeting: Martin
          Buber and Psychotherapy." *Cross Currents*, 5 (Fall
          1955), 297-310.

   An exploration of Buber's conception of man as a whole
person in relation with others, as applied to

psychotherapy and psychosis. Criticizes Freud and Jung
for neglecting this aspect of the human psyche and shows
similarities between Buber's views and many current
psychological theories.

B95   Friedman, Maurice S. *Martin Buber: The Life of Dialogue*.
      Chicago: University of Chicago Press, 1955. 301 pp.

      This has long been the standard work on Buber's life
      and thought. It contains a systematic exploration of
      his major ideas and commentary on all of his works. It
      was written by a disciple of Buber and is almost com-
      pletely lacking in critical comment. The major sections
      of the book deal with Buber's early thought, the nature
      of evil, the relationship between man and man, and the
      relationship between man and God. The author pays par-
      ticular attention to the influence of Buber's thought on
      other thinkers. There is an extensive index.

B96   Friedman, Maurice. "Martin Buber and Judaism." *CCAR
      Journal*, 11 (1955), 13-8+.

      Stating that Buber's impact on modern Judaism has
      been profound, gives an overview of the philosophy of
      dialogue and its importance to Buber's interpretation of
      the Bible, his relationship to Zionism, his Hasidic
      thought, and his position on the halakah.

B97   Friedman, Maurice. "Martin Buber on Peace." *Jewish
      Peace Fellowship Tidings*, 9 (Winter 1955), n.p.

      One-page article in which Buber is described as a
      peacemaker but not a pacifist.

B98   Halevi, Jacob L. "Kierkegaard and the Midrash."
      Judaism, 4 (Winter 1955), 13-28.

      Briefly criticizes Buber's interpretation of
      Kierkegaard.

B99   Infield, Henrick. *Utopia and Experiment: Essays in the
      Sociology of Cooperation*. New York: Praeger, 1955,
      pp. 9-17.

      A discussion of the defense of utopian socialism made
      by Buber and David Riesman.

B100 Paton, H.J. "I and Thou." *The Modern Predicament: A
      Study in the Philosophy of Religion*. London: George
      Allen and Unwin, 1955, pp. 162-73.

An explanation of the I-Thou and I-It relationships,
and how the former leads to God. Buber's philosophy
contains two principles crucial to religion today.
First, religion and science are not rival, mutually exclusive systems but two attitudes man takes toward the
world. Second, religion is an expression of the whole
man and is not based upon a special religious faculty.

B101 Rosenzweig, Franz. "The Builders: Concerning the Law."
      On Jewish Learning. Edited by N.N. Glatzer. New
      York: Schocken Books, 1955, pp. 72-92.

A letter to Buber centering on their disagreement
over Jewish law and the practice of Judaism, Rosenzweig
taking the more orthodox position.

B102 Smith, Ronald Gregor. "The Religion of Martin Buber."
      Theology Today, 12 (July 1955), 206-15.

Buber's philosophy forms a convergence of several
streams of current thought, including Judaism, Christianity, and sociology.

1956

B103 Altmann, Alexander. "Theology in Twentieth-Century
      German Jewry." *Leo Baeck Institute Year Book*, 1
      (1956), 193-216.

Discusses the contributions of Buber and others.
Buber brought a deep religious faith to cultural
Zionism and forced German Jewry to re-think its theology. He was an anti-romantic, emphasizing Jewish
prophecy and messianic outlook. He saw the Jew as
living face to face with the absolute, and called for
an inner awakening of the contemporary Jewish spirit.
As he developed his philosophy of dialogue, he emphasized the everyday aspect of religion. This philosophical outlook helped form the Buber-Rosenzweig translation of the Bible.

B104 Farber, Leslie H. "Martin Buber and Psychiatry."
      Psychiatry, 19 (May 1956), 109-20.

Objecting to the lack of conceptual wholeness in the
scientific definition of man in current psychiatry,
the author suggests the substitution of Buber's I-Thou
philosophy. Buber's stress on the importance of meeting
and relationship can surmount the division between those
therapists emphasizing the inner person, subjectivity,

and feeling, and those emphasizing the outer world, objectivity, and the intellect. The stress on relation-ship also corrects both Freud's and Sullivan's reductive interpretations of human behavior. Sullivan's inter-personal theory is compared with Buber's I-Thou philoso-phy. There follows a lengthy discussion of psychosis in terms of this I-Thou framework. For a revision of this article, see item B349.

B105   Farber, Leslie. "Secrets of the Universe?" *Psychiatry*, 19 (November 1956), 408-15.

A reply to Mullahy's article (item B114). Defends his criticism of Sullivan's theories and scientific psychiatry's view of human beings. Reiterates his reasons for recommending Buber's philosophy to the field of psychiatry but little actual discussion of Buber.

B106   Friedman, Maurice S. "Discussion." *Pastoral Psychology*, 7 (December 1956), 51-3.

Buber's concept of the one-sided dialogical relation-ship as applied to psychotherapy. Psychological illness is an illness of the patient's relations with the world. The roots of neurosis lie both in the patient's closing himself off from the world and the world's rejection and nonconfirmation of the patient. The therapist helps restore this direct meeting.

B107   Friedman, Maurice. "Martin Buber and the Social Problems of Our Time." *Yivo Annual of Jewish Social Science*, 11 (1956-57), 235-46.

The basis of social problems in our time is the decay of the organic community in favor of associations that provide no real contact between man and man. Buber's solution is rooted in Hasidism, Zionism, and socialism, as well as in his philosophy of dialogue. His social philosophy rejects both individualism and collectivism in favor of true community based on the interhuman. To replace capitalism and communism, Buber proposes a federalism of socialist communities.

B108   Friedman, Maurice. "Martin Buber's Philosophy of Education." *Educational Theory*, 6 (April 1956), 95-104.

The teacher educates the pupil by building a mutuality
between them. This mutuality is achieved through trust
and the act of inclusion, the teacher's experiencing
the pupil from the pupil's point of view. The teacher
selects out of the world and presents those elements
which the child needs for growth. The student pro-
gresses through his encounters with the Thou of the
teacher and the writer, and the reality they present to
him. This reality is made concrete through these
relationships. Buber contrasts propaganda, imposing an
opinion on another, with education. In the latter one
nourishes in the other what one has recognized in oneself as the right.

B109 Glatzer, Nahum N. "The Frankfort Lehrhaus." *Leo Baeck*
      Institute Year Book, 1 (1956), 105-22.

      Buber's work in the Frankfurt Lehrhaus briefly dis-
      cussed. He started lecturing in the winter of 1921-22
      while writing *I and Thou* (item A17). He used this
      material as the basis for his first lectures, and later
      gave a seminar on Hasidism. He became one of the lead-
      ers of the Lehrhaus.

B110 Herberg, Will. Introduction to *The Writings of Martin*
      Buber, by Martin Buber. Edited by Will Herberg.
      Cleveland: World Publishing Co., 1956, pp. 11-39.

      An introductory overview to this collection of ex-
      cerpts from previously translated material by Buber.
      Sees Buber's thinking as falling within the general
      movement of religious existentialism.

B111 Howe, Reuel L. "Discussion." *Pastoral Psychology*, 7
      (December 1956), 48-51.

      Brief statement on Buber's contribution to viewing
      the psychotherapeutic situation from a religious
      perspective.

B112 "I and Thou." *Time*, 23 January 1956, pp. 39-40.

      Brief overview inspired by the publication of
      Friedman's *Martin Buber: The Life of Dialogue* (item
      B95).

B113 Liebeschutz, Hans. "Jewish Thought and Its German Back-
      ground." *Leo Baeck Institute Year Book*, 1 (1956),
      217-36.

Briefly describes Buber's criticism of Hermann Cohen's
concept of Judaism. Buber felt that Cohen's Judaism
was too theoretical and did not call for a radical
change in life. He also objected to Cohen's allocation
of the function of education to the state. Cohen overlooked the fundamental fact of Jewish existence: exile.
The state, motivated by power politics, could not be
trusted.

B114 Mullahy, Patrick. "Interpersonal Psychiatry Versus
      the Philosophy of I-Thou and I-It." *Psychiatry*, 19
      (November 1956), 401-8.

A criticism of Farber's article (item B104). Primarily a defense of scientific psychiatry and the
theories of Freud and Sullivan. Buber's concepts, as
used by Farber, are criticized for their vagueness.
The author sees little reason for accepting Buber's
definition of man over the definitions of other
philosophers. There is little direct discussion of
Buber's theory of dialogue.

B115 Niebuhr, Reinhold. "Faith Is the Key." *New York Times
      Book Review*, 10 June 1956, p. 6.

A positive review of Friedman's *Martin Buber: The
Life of Dialogue* (item B95). However, Niebuhr feels
that Friedman was not critical enough of Buber's in-
ability to deal with the problem of political institutions in the modern world.

B116 Simon, Ernst. "Jewish Adult Education in Nazi Germany
      as Spiritual Resistance." *Leo Baeck Institute Year
      Book*, 1 (1956), 68-104.

In a general article, briefly describes Buber's part
in this educational movement. Buber believed that the
foundation of this education had to be an inner sprit-
ual resistance based upon the concept of the Jews as
the eternal people of God.

1957

B117 Ben-Horin, Meir. "Martin Buber's 'Absolute Personal-
      ity.'" *Judaism*, 6 (Winter 1957), 22-30.

A highly critical evaluation of Buber's concept of
God as Absolute Personality and 'Super-Good.' Buber's

rejection of God as idea or moral ideal is seen as an
attempt to separate the concept of God from the process
of human reason. Flaws seen in Buber's point of view
are discussed and the author concludes that a reliance
upon religion as loyalty to a transcendent personality,
or as a dialogue between man and this personality, de-
tracts man from the search for human self-fulfillment.

B118   Cohen, Arthur A. *Martin Buber*. London: Bowes and
          Bowes, 1957. 110 pp.

An overview of Buber's life and thought emphasizing
his pursuit of the holy. The author divides Buber's
work into three major areas of concentration: the problem of being, the critical examination of Jewish literature for historical examples to support his insights
into this problem, and his translation of these insights
into a program for modern man. In dealing with Buber's
interpretation of Hasidism, the author criticizes his
outbursts of "romantic exaggeration." He also argues
that Buber does not understand the tragedy of failure.
There is no index.

B119   Cousins, Norman. "Talk, Write, Act." *Saturday Review
          of Literature*, 23 March 1957, p. 20.

Brief report of Cousins' meeting with Buber in
Jerusalem. At that time Buber felt that man's separation from his fellows had been growing and hardening.
He expressed little faith in the world's leaders to
meet this problem.

B120   Diamond, Malcolm. "Martin Buber and Contemporary
          Theology." *Union Seminary Quarterly Review*, 12
          (January 1957), 17-24.

An overview emphasizing Buber's influence on
Christian thought.

B121   Friedman, Maurice. "Martin Buber's Concept of Educa-
          tion: A New Approach to College Teaching." *Christian
          Scholar*, 40 (June 1957), 109-16.

Contrasts Buber's concept of education with Robert
Hutchin's Great Books theory and John Dewey's prag-
matic education. Buber rejects both the emphasis on
the uniform content of education in the former, and the
education of character as defined in the latter.
Buber's approach is based upon his philosophy of dialogue as seen in the teacher-student relationship.

B122   Goes, Albrecht. "Martin Buber, the Support." *Jewish Affairs*, October 1957, pp. 19–23.

An appreciation of Buber's work given as an address during the presentation of the German Peace Prize. Reprinted in *Men of Dialogue* (item B421).

B123   Levin, Meyer. "'The Legend of the Baal-Shem.'" *Judaism*, 6 (Winter 1957), 88–90.

A positive review of item A133. Finds prefigurations of Kafka, existentialism, and psychoanalytic thought in these legends.

B124   McPherson, Thomas. "The Second Great Commandment: Religion and Morality." *Congregational Quarterly*, 35 (July 1957), 212–27.

Tries to establish the relationship between morality and the religious life. Contrasts Kierkegaard's rejection of this relationship with Buber's view that what is essential to the moral life, the I-Thou relation, is also essential to the religious life. Sees the I-Thou relation as an obscure rendition of Kant's categorial imperative. Author rejects Buber's stand because he doubts the possibility of an I-Thou relation with God.

B125   Mendelsohn, Jack. "Between Man and Man." *Congress Weekly*, 18 November 1957, pp. 7–9.

Record of an interview with Buber.

B126   "Of Man into Man." *Newsweek*, 1 April 1957, p. 82.

Brief review of Buber's four "esoteric" lectures at the Washington School of Psychiatry (items A101, A145, and A146). The I-Thou concept is seen as a link between psychiatry and religion. Draws a parallel between the importance Buber and Harry Stack Sullivan place upon interpersonal communication.

B127   "School Here Cites Philosopher." *New York Times*, 17 April 1957, p. 33.

Brief mention of an honorary degree conferred on Buber by the New School for Social Research.

B128 Schulweis, Harold. "Myth and Existentialism." *Judaism*, 6 (Fall 1957), 302-10.

Compares Buber and Rudolph Bultmann on their approaches to the interpretation of the Bible, and finds great similarity. Both are critical of fundamentalist literalism and the methods of religious modernism. Their position is seen as a third alternative. They rely on the existential character of the religious experience, first demythologizing the event and then giving an existential translation of the literal myth. Thus they seek to salvage the piety of orthodoxy without the literal supernatural beliefs on which it depends. In doing so, both commit what the author calls the "fallacy of figurativism," the error of reading current sophisticated interpretations into articles of belief originally taken literally.

1958

B129 Fischoff, Ephraim. Introduction to *Paths in Utopia*, by Martin Buber. Translated by R.F.C. Hull. Boston: Beacon Press, 1958, pp. ix-xxv.

An introduction to the 1958 edition of *Paths in Utopia* (item A94). States that the central concept of Buber's social thought, as well as his philosophy and theology, is that of community.

B130 Friedman, Maurice. "I-Thou and I-It." *Handbook of Christian Theology*, edited by Marvin Halverson and Arthur A. Cohen. New York: Meridian Books, 1958, pp. 173-6.

A brief review of Buber's I-Thou and I-It relations, and the many Christian thinkers who have been influenced by these concepts.

B131 Friedman, Maurice. Introduction to *Hasidism and Modern Man*, by Martin Buber. Edited and translated by Maurice Friedman. New York: Horizon Press, 1958, pp. 10-18.

Brief introduction to the essays contained in this book.

B132 Friedman, Maurice. "Religious Symbolism and 'Universal' Religion." *Journal of Religion*, 38 (October 1958), 215-25.

In a general article on religious symbolism, briefly discusses Buber's views as opposed to those of the idealist and the mystic.

B133   Gilman, Richard.   "Martin Buber."   *Jubilee*, 5 (January 1958), 46-50.

A positive review of *Pointing the Way* (item A148). Buber is described as a teacher or guide rather than a theologian or critic.

B134   Heller, Arthur D.   "Martin Buber at Eighty."   *Jewish Quarterly*, 5 (Summer 1958), p. 70.

Reminisces about Buber's talks on Judaism given in Prague around 1912.

B135   Herberg, Will.   "Martin Buber."   *Four Existential Theologians*.   New York: Doubleday and Co., 1958, pp. 171-6.

A brief overview as an introduction to selections from Buber's works.

B136   Jones, Edgar.   "Man in Society."   *Congregational Quarterly*, 36 (June 1958), 155-61.

Briefly outlines the concepts of I-Thou and I-It relations and then just as briefly relates them to technology, the individual's relationship to the group, and communication in education and industry.

B137   Kaufmann, Walter.   "The Stature of Martin Buber." *Commentary*, October 1958, 355-9.

Reviews of *Hasidism and Modern Man* (item A178), *Pointing the Way* (item A148), *To Hallow This Life* (item A190), and *Moses* (item A45). Believes that Buber, more than anyone else, has pointed the way toward a non-Hegelian, non-Greek, biblical religion.

B138   Kokotek, J.J.   "Martin Buber--An Interpreter of Judaism."   *Our Congregation* (London), March 1958.

(Not available for annotating.)

B139   McDermott, John.   "Martin Buber's I-Thou Philosophy." *Bridge: A Yearbook of Judaeo-Christian Studies*, 3 (1958), 187-208.

Contrasts Kierkegaard's belittling of the nonsubjective
with Buber's realistic balance between subjective and
objective reality. Gives an overview of Buber's philosophy of dialogue and its application to education.
Finds in Buber's vision of the concrete a vestige of
abstraction, such as when he speaks of 'the child.'

B140   Maybuam, Ignaz. "Martin Buber: The Master of the
       Dialogue." *Jewish Chronicle*, 31 January 1958, pp. 1+.

       Brief overview on Buber's eightieth birthday. Buber
       endeavored to hear the voice of God in the dialogue
       between God and his people.

B141   Murchland, Bernard G. "Buber's Pursuit of the Holy."
       Commonweal, 8 August 1958, pp. 469-71.

       A review article of Arthur Cohen's *Martin Buber*
       (item B118) giving an overview of Buber's thought.
       Agrees with Cohen that Buber, by playing down the tragic
       dimension of existence, failed to rise to the heights of
       true prophetic indignation. Draws parallels to the
       thought of Giambattista Vico, Gabriel Marcel, and other
       Christian thinkers.

B142   Niebuhr, Reinhold. "Essays on Man." *New York Times
       Book Review*, 13 April 1958, pp. 36-7.

       A primarily positive review of *Pointing the Way*
       (item A148). However, the reviewer believes that Buber's
       perfectionist view of man creates problems in his politi-
       cal outlook. Buber's argument with Gandhi was the result
       of his misunderstanding of Gandhi's position.

B143   Osterreicher, John M. "Introduction." *Bridge: A Year-
       book of Judaeo-Christian Studies*, 3 (1958), 19-24.

       An introduction to a volume of articles dealing with
       Buber's thought. Objects to Buber's views on Jesus and
       his rejection of traditional Jewish beliefs.

B144   Pfuetze, Paul E. "The Concept of Self in Contemporary
       Psychotherapy." *Pastoral Psychology*, 9 (February
       1958), 9-19.

       Discusses the importance of the concept of the social
       self in the fields of counseling and psychotherapy.
       Shows the influence of Buber and G.H. Mead, among others.

B145   Schall, James V. "Buber and Huxley: Recent Developments
       in Philosophy." *Month*, 19 (February 1958), 99-102.

       Contrasts Buber and Aldous Huxley on the route to
       self discovery. For Huxley language hides the true
       self in abstractions. We must turn to methods that
       allow us to go beyond language to experience 'isness.'
       For Buber, the self is fully discovered in communica-
       tion with others.

B146   Simon, Ernst. "Martin Buber and German Jewry." *Leo
       Baeck Institute Year Book*, 3 (1958), 3-39.

       Buber's development as a spokesman of German Jewry
       for both Jews and the German gentile intelligentsia
       began with his Hasidic writings. They not only rescued
       the movement for Jews but made Hasidism an essential
       part of the Christian cultural consciousness. The
       author analyzes these writings and their appeal to the
       educated German reader. As Buber developed, he was
       influenced by Nietzsche, Meister Eckhart, and Max Weber.
       The direction of his development was apparent from his
       public opposition to Theodor Herzl's secular Jewish
       nationalism, Hermann Cohen's German-Jewish synthesis,
       and Franz Rosenzweig's desire to return to Jewish
       traditions.

B147   Sloyan, Gerald S. "Buber and the Significance of
       Jesus." *Bridge: A Yearbook of Judaeo-Christian
       Studies*, 3 (1958), 209-33.

       The key to Buber's view of Jesus is his conviction
       that contact between God and man takes place through
       direct encounter, not through intermediaries, symbols,
       or images. The early Church made a mediator of Jesus,
       distorting his teaching of direct encounter with God.
       After they deified Jesus, they substituted adherence
       to propositions about Jesus for the Jewish faith which
       is perfect trust in God. For Buber, to think that
       the single event of Jesus exhausts the Jewish messianic
       hope is to distort it. Jesus was a leader lost to the
       Jews because of his exaggerated conception of himself
       as the unique fulfillment of the Torah. After discuss-
       ing these views, the author defends Catholicism's use
       of dogma, and the messianic consciousness of Jesus.

B148   Spicehandler, Ezra. "Ben-Gurion and Dr. Buber."
       Journal of the Central Conference of American Rabbis,
       No. 20 (January 1958), 29-31.

Ben Gurion and Buber on the uniqueness of Israel.

B149   Trapp, Jacob.   Introduction to *To Hallow This Life*, by
       Martin Buber.   New York: Harper and Brothers Publish-
       ers, 1958, pp. ix-xiv.

       Brief overview as an introduction.

B150   Ulanov, Barry.   "Job and His Comforters."   *Bridge: A
       Yearbook of Judaeo-Christian Studies*, 3 (1958), 234-68.

       Buber's views on the Book of Job discussed as part of
       a larger article.   Buber saw Job as an analogue of the
       believing man who accepts the world as it is.   The re-
       ward for this is God's pity, participation in the work
       of salvation, and personal revelation.   In the present
       age of the hiddenness of God, this dialogue between man
       and God is broken.   The responsibility is both with God
       and with man.   The author believes that Buber's concep-
       tualization contributes to the eclipse of God.   Buber
       leaves us struggling in despair because God and the
       good seem at variance.

B151   Weiss-Rosmarin, Trude.   "Martin Buber at Eighty."
       Jewish Spectator, March 1958, pp. 6-10.

       To mark Buber's eightieth birthday, scores his ob-
       scurity of style, the unintelligibility of his ideas,
       his mystically-tinged affectations, his plagiarism,
       his lack of Jewish sensitivity, and his predilection
       for Christianity.   Sees Buber as an embarrassment to
       Jews.

B152   Weltsch, Robert.   "The Grand Old Man of Jewry."   *AJR
       Information*, February 1958, pp. 4-5.

       Brief overview of Buber's influence upon Jewish life
       on the occasion of his eightieth birthday.

B153   Wiest, Walter E.   "Martin Buber."   *Ten Makers of Modern
       Protestant Thought*.   Edited by George L. Hunt.   New
       York: Association Press, 1958, pp. 114-22.

       States Buber's three primary contributions to Protes-
       tant thought are his interpretation of prophetic reli-
       gion, his understanding of human relations, and his
       concept of the human-object relationship.

1959

B154   Baillie, John. *Our Knowledge of God.* New York:
       Charles Scribner's Sons, 1959, pp. 221-4.

       Brief discussion of Buber's concept of God as the
       Eternal Thou who can be related to but not expressed.

B155   Borowitz, Eugene B. "Existentialism's Meaning for
       Judaism." *Commentary*, November 1959, pp. 414-20.

       In a discussion of several existentialists, sees
       Buber's thought as existential in method if not in
       content. Feels Buber can provide a basis for the
       liberal traditions of Judaism. However, liberal Jews
       are bothered by Buber's return to older Jewish theo-
       logical concepts such as that of a personal God, prayer
       as a dialogue with God, and revelation as communication
       between God and man.

B156   Fackenheim, Emil L. "Some Recent Works by and on Martin
       Buber." *Religious Education*, 54 (September-October
       1959), 413-7.

       Brief comments on Buber's *Tales of Rabbi Nahman* (item
       A143), *Hasidism and Modern Man* (item A178), *The Way of
       Man According to the Teachings of Hasidism* (item A100),
       Pointing the Way (item A148), *Eclipse of God* (item A113)
       and on Friedman's *Martin Buber: The Life of Dialogue*
       (item B95) and Cohen's *Martin Buber* (item B118). The
       reviewer isolates three developments in Buber's thought
       evident in these volumes: (1) Buber has come more deeply
       to grips with the concrete reality of the lived life,
       (2) his epistemology is clearly based upon dialogue,
       and (3) contrary to *I and Thou* (item A17), God may now
       be seen unaccountably silent.

B157   Friedman, Maurice. "Liberal Judaism and Contemporary
       Jewish Thought." *Midstream*, 5 (Autumn 1959), 16-28.

       In an article on several Jewish thinkers, gives an
       overview of Buber's religious thought and its relation-
       ship to Reform Judaism. While both tend to regard the
       observance of Jewish law as unessential to the practice
       of Judaism, they do so for different reasons. Reform
       Jews tend to see the law as less important than ritual
       and moral principles, while Buber rejects the law as a
       separate objective reality existing outside of the God-
       man dialogue. Buber's personalism also makes it diffi-
       cult to relate his thought to an institutional program.

B158 Friedman, Maurice. "Martin Buber's Biblical Judaism."
    CCAR Journal, No. 24 (January 1959), 21-7.

    An overview of Buber's interpretation of Judaism.
Buber saw the biblical God as Absolute Person who enters
into dialogue with man. The Bible is the historical
record of this dialogue as seen through man's eyes.
Its most significant expression is found in the concept
of the kingship of God. The author analyzes this concept in terms of Buber's interpretation of the Sinai
covenant, Isaiah's messiah, the suffering servant in
the Jewish and Christian traditions, and Hasidism.

B159 Friedman, Maurice. "Martin Buber's 'Theology' and
    Religious Education." *Religious Education*, 54
    (January-February 1959), 5-17.

    The primary goal of religious education, according to
Buber, is to point man toward a dialogue with God. This
is accomplished through an I-Thou relationship between
teacher and student. The objective content of religion
is important only in that it points the way toward this
God-man meeting. Revelation is the presence of God
rather than information about God's essence.

B160 Halevi, Jacob L. "Kierkegaard's Teleological Suspen-
    sion of the Ethical: Is It Jewish?" *Judaism*, 8
    (Fall 1959), 291-302.

    Briefly criticizes Buber's understanding of the
"teleological suspension of the ethical."

B161 Judges, A.V. "Martin Buber." *The Function of Teaching*.
    London: Faber and Faber, 1959, pp. 89-108.

    An overview of Buber's philosophy of education
stressing its redemptive nature and its basis in relationship. Unique in that the author does not use the
I-Thou terminology.

B162 McDonough, Sheila. "Martin Buber." *Pakistan Philo-
    sophical Congress*, 6 (1959), 266-78.

    An overview stressing the I-Thou and I-It relation-
ships and his interpretation of Judaism.

B163 Rexroth, Kenneth. "The Hasidism of Martin Buber."
    Bird in the Bush. New York: New Directions, 1959.
    pp. 106-42.

Sees Buber as a romantic traditionalist whose thought
is aesthetic rather than religious, and similar to the
English Hegelians. Take away his writings about God,
and nothing important has been changed in his philosophy
The crux of his thought is Hasidism, divested of its
Gnosticism, and his idea of community. His efforts to
interpret the Torah for modern man are an exercise in
futility. He is an artist who has responded to the most
ordinary facts of life, the presence of others and the
possibility of love. His errors are the result of
'metaphysical greed.'

B164 Rotenstreich, Nathan. "Buber's Dialogical Philosophy:
      The Historical Dimension." *Philosophy Today*, 3
      (Fall 1959), 168-75.

The philosophical roots of Buber's thought lie in
Lebensphilosophie and intuitionism. His ties to the
former can be seen in his rejection of abstract philosophy and his desire to remain within the stream of
life. His intuitionism is expressed in his realism and
in the non-cognitive attitude which forms the basis of
his I-Thou relation. Buber avoids the terms intuition
and empathy, but uses 'inclusion' and 'real imagining'
which strongly suggest these terms. Philosophical opti-
mism is apparent in his belief that dialogue can overcome both man's cosmic and social homelessness.
Reprinted in item B374.

B165 Rotenstreich, Nathan. "Some Problems in Buber's
      Dialogical Philosophy." *Philosophy Today*, 3 (Fall
      1959), 151-67.

Buber's analysis of the dialogical life and the pri-
macy of mutuality is here seen as his main contribution
to an ontology of human life. When Buber identifies
the focus of this dialogue as responsibility, he
grounds responsibility in ontology or anthropology.
Dialogue becomes the basis for man's relationship with
man and with God. Yet Buber never states whether
these two mutualities are independent or are two real-
izations of a general mutuality. His later thought
also leaves doubt as to whether relationship is actually primary within the human sphere. The notion of
setting at a distance is presupposed by mutuality. To
set at a distance requires a reflective attitude, implying this attitude is required for mutuality. Further
granted the importance of mutuality on a factual level,
does this necessarily imply a similar importance on an

ontological level? Related to this is the question of whether Buber was describing the human situation as it is or as it should be. Was ontology replaced by imperatives? Reprinted in item B374.

B166 Tillich, Paul. "An Evaluation of Martin Buber: Protestant and Jewish Thought." *Theology of Culture.* Edited by Robert C. Kimball. New York: Oxford University Press, 1959, pp. 188-99.

Tillich sees three significant elements in Buber's thought for Protestant theology: (1) his existential interpretation of prophetic religion, (2) his rediscovery of the mystical element in that religion which may help overcome the Protestant ambiguity towards mysticism, and (3) the relationship he draws between prophetic religion and the social and political realms of culture.

B167 Wieman, Henry N. "The Problem of Mysticism." *Mysticism and the Modern Mind.* Edited by Alfred P. Stiernotte. New York: Liberal Arts Press, 1959, pp. 30-5.

A brief discussion of the I-Thou relationship with God in terms of the mystical experience. Contrasts Buber's view with that of Zen and Karl Jaspers.

1960

B168 Bowman, Clarice M. "Martin Buber and the Voluntary Turning." *Religion in Life*, 30 (Winter 1960-61), 81-91.

A discussion of the I-Thou relationship in terms of an existential willingness to turn from a distorted, inadequate mode of perceiving others to authentic communication with other selves. This turning is possible through grace.

B169 Diamond, Malcolm L. *Martin Buber: Jewish Existentialist.* New York: Oxford University Press, 1960. 240 pp.

An introduction to Buber's thought covering all of its major aspects: the philosophy of dialogue, the relationship between man and God, Hasidism and the hallowing of everyday life, the mission of Judaism, and his interpretation of Christianity. The author places Buber within the general category of existentialism.

While positive toward his thought, he discusses what he
sees as Buber's tendency toward obscurity and selec-
tivity in dealing with Judaism and Hasidism. There is
a subject index.

B170   Friedman, Maurice. "Dialogue and the 'Essential We':
       The Basis cf Values in the Philosophy of Martin
       Buber." *American Journal of Psychoanalysis*, 20
       (1960), 26-34.

       Places psychotherapy within the framework of the
       philosophy of dialogue. Values exist only in a con-
       crete reciprocal relationship between two persons. No
       abstract code is valid prior to actual meeting. Meeting
       is possible because of the two basic movements in human
       life, distancing and relationship. Through these move-
       ments a relationship is established where mutual confir-
       mation may take place. In psychotherapy this mutuality
       is not equal. However, it is still an I-Thou relation-
       ship. In group psychotherapy the I-Thou relationship
       takes place in the We of community. Within this We,
       guilt, the result of the failure of a person to respond
       to the address of the world, may be alleviated.

B171   Friedman, Maurice. Introduction to *The Origin and Mean-
       ing of Hasidism*, by Martin Buber. Edited and trans-
       lated by Maurice Friedman. New York: Horizon Press,
       1960, pp. 7-19.

       A brief introduction to the essays contained in the
       volume.

B172   Glatzer, N.N. Preface to *The Way of Responses: Martin
       Buber*. New York: Schocken Books, 1960, pp. 9-14.

       An introduction to this selection of Buber's
       writings which focuses on the theme of response.

B173   "Hadassah Presents Five Szold Awards." *New York Times*,
       16 December 1960, p. 24.

       Mention of Buber as one of the recipients.

B174   Kurzweil, Zvi E. "Three Views on Revelation and Law."
       Judaism, 9 (Fall 1960), 291-8.

       According to Buber, the communicable results of reve-
       lation are human in meaning and form, and cannot be seen
       as infallible. In this way Buber rejects traditional
       Judaism. He sees a difference between the Judaism of

the patriarchs and that of Sinai. The first is characterized by faith and the second by law. He stresses
the importance of faith as the basis of the law. The
views of Franz Rosenzweig and Raphael Hirsch are also
discussed.

B175   Rioch, Margaret J. "The Meaning of Martin Buber's
       'Elements of the Interhuman' for the Practice of
       Psychotherapy." *Psychiatry*, 23 (May 1960), 133-40.

A psychotherapist must participate to some extent in
genuine dialogue. Three processes and their opposites,
presented by Buber, either foster or hinder this dialogue: (1) being versus seeming in terms of the therapist's view of himself and his function, (2) personal
'making present' versus the inadequate perception of
the other as an object to be classified by symptom, and
(3) unfolding versus imposition in terms of the therapist's basic assumptions and values as imparted to the
patient.

B176   Schachter, Zalman S. "Hasidism and Neo-Hasidism."
       Judaism, 9 (Summer 1960), 216-21.

Discusses the 'neo-Hasidism' of Buber and Abraham
Heschel and finds that the actual cosmology and psychology of the Hasidim are broader than those pictured
by these writers. Also feels that relationship between
man and man cannot serve as a model for the relationship
between man and God. Perhaps Buber and Heschel can
bring a Jew to the verge of God's kingdom, but the
spiritual direction of the Hasid must come from his
rebbe.

B177   Schatz-Uffenheimer, Rivkah. "Review Essay--Martin
       Buber, Master of Hasidic Teaching." *Judaism*, 9
       (Summer 1960), 277-81.

A review of *The Origin and Meaning of Hasidism* (item
A193). Sees Buber's interpretation as a selective process in which, because of his background, he determines
a priori the main principles to emphasize. The greatness of Hasidism for Buber lies in its relation to the
concrete, placing man's everyday life at the center of
concern. The author sees this as a reduction of the
prominent tension that exists in Hasidism between God
and the world. He also disagrees with Buber's eleva-
tion of the ethical motif to a place equal to that of
the religious motif, and the downplaying the mystical
element.

B178   Stace, W.T. *Mysticism and Philosophy*. Philadelphia:
       J.B. Lippincott Company, 1960, pp. 155-60.

       Briefly criticizes Buber's mystical dualism as an
       expression of the Jewish rejection of the concept of
       mystical union.

B179   Zeigler, Leslie. "Personal Existence: A Study of Buber
       and Kierkegaard." *Journal of Religion*, 40 (April
       1960), 80-94.

       Compares Buber and Kierkegaard on the nature of per-
       sonal existence by investigating their positions on the
       relationship of man to God, the relationship of thought
       to being, the nature of the individual's decision to
       act out his beliefs, the concept of human authenticity,
       and the nature of truth. The author supports Kierke-
       gaard over Buber and suggests that Buber is not con-
       cerned with actual persons but with abstractions. His
       concept of the eternal Thou is seen as the ultimate
       abstraction.

                              1961

B180   Balthasar, Hans Urs Von. *Martin Buber and Christianity:
       A Dialogue between Israel and the Church*. Translated
       by Alexander Dru. London: Harvill Press, 1961.
       127 pp.

       A study of Buber's interpretation of Judaism and
       Christianity. The author feels that Buber's version
       of Christianity is dominated by liberal Protestant
       theology, to the neglect of Catholic tradition. He is
       also critical of the lack of allowance for chance in
       Buber's thought. When discussing any issue, Buber
       gives such a strong sense of direction inherent in the
       issue that nothing is left to the movement of change
       and becoming. Also, within Buber's view of history
       there is no room for events which may lead to an essen-
       tial change in the God-man relation. In comparing
       Judaism and Christianity, Buber concludes that they are
       irreconcilable. The author agrees that this may be so
       among men, but not in terms of the grace of God.
       There is no index.

B181   Barth, Karl. "Liberal Theology: Some Alternatives."
       Hibbert Journal, 59 (April 1961), 213-9.

Briefly discusses Buber as one of several theologians who present viable lines of development for liberal Christian theology.

B182 "Casals on Atom Plea." *New York Times*, 15 November 1961, p. 18.

Lists Buber as a signer of an appeal to stop nuclear testing.

B183 Crane, A.R. "The Educational Thought of Martin Buber." *Australian Journal of Education*, 5 (July 1961), 91-9.

An overview emphasizing the nature of the teacher-pupil relationship and the goals of education.

B184 De Rosis, Louis. "Discussion of the Papers of Drs. Friedman and Farber." *Review of Existential Psychology and Psychiatry*, 1 (Fall 1961), 243-8.

A response to Friedman's paper (item B186). Feels Buber's thought has been worked out through contact with non-neurotic, non-psychotic, fairly well-integrated persons. Takes some of Buber's concepts and interprets them in psychoanalytic terms. Sees evil urges as compulsive drives and the unconscious as the agent of these urges. Objects to Friedman's implication that an outside-the-person agency is responsible for the person's knowledge of his uniqueness. The idealized self and the authentic self are discussed in terms of I-Thou relationships.

B185 Friedman, Maurice. "Martin Buber and the Covenant of Peace." *Fellowship*, 27 (January 1, 1961), 4-7.

Buber's peacemaking was founded on the concepts of dialogue and reconciliation, as seen in his work to improve Jewish-Arab relations.

B186 Friedman, Maurice. "Will, Decision and Responsibility in the Thought of Martin Buber." *Review of Existential Psychology and Psychiatry*, 1 (Fall 1961), 217-28.

Buber views the will as the wholeness of the person, the unification of passion and direction. An individual's unique way is found through knowledge of his essential quality. He may know this quality only as undirected passion. Decision is the process of giving direction to this passion, of bringing the individual's whole being into dialogue. Good is the conversion of

passion into the substance of real life, into relationship. Thus Buber's will-decision is similar to subli-
mation except that it functions between man and man
rather than within man. Evil is directionless passion
left decisionless, or, in a more radical form, a decision to bring undirected passion into undirected reality.
Responsibility is the need to respond to that circle of
creation in which a person stands. The responsible man
responds with his wholeness to each unique situation.
Guilt is the result of the failure to respond. See
item B184.

B187   Helen James John, Sr. "Variations on a Theme."
       Commonweal, 21 April 1961, pp. 100-2.

       A brief comparison of human relationships in the
thought of Buber, Jean-Paul Sartre, and Gabriel Marcel.

B188   Holmer, Paul L. *Theology and the Scientific Study of*
       Religion. Minneapolis: T.S. Denison and Company,
       1961, pp. 92-103.

       An exploration of the I-Thou relation between man and
God. Buber correctly rejects the usual religious language that makes God an object and the knower a subject.
Even if men could know God as an object, this awareness
would not adequately describe the mode of religious
knowing or the characteristic of being religious. It is
another matter, however, to insist, as Buber does, that
religious man knows nothing by virtue of his faith.
Buber wants to discard religious dogmas. More properly
they should be turned into a personal expression of
faith.

B189   Leifer, Daniel L. "Buber and Rosenzweig: Two Types of
       Revelation." *Mosaic*, 2 (Winter 1961), 43-63.

       While Buber accepted the possibility of revelation,
he saw it as contentless and refused to commit himself
to the halakah. Rosenzweig took the more traditional
view, accepting the contents of Jewish revelation and
the necessity of observing the halakah. The author
attempts to explain this difference in terms of the two
thinkers' concepts of Judaism, and in their evaluation
of the importance of history to these concepts.

B190   Levin, Meyer. "Sage Who Inspired Hammarskjold." *New*
       York Times Magazine, 3 December 1961, pp. 43+.

An overview of Buber's thought and his life in Germany
and Israel.

B191   Scholem, Gersham. "Martin Buber's Hasidism: A Critique."
       Commentary, October 1961, pp. 305-16.

Argues that the spiritual message Buber reads into
the Hasidic movement is too bound up with the assumptions of his own philosophy to give an understanding
of the actual phenomenon of Hasidism. Of the two categories of Hasidic literature, the early theoretical
writings and the legendary literature developed later,
Buber ignored the former and based his interpretation
on the latter, making the primary source secondary and
the secondary, primary. His emphasis on the simple
Hasidic man of faith ignores the fact that the truly
spiritual man was always seen as a gnostic initiate.
While Buber believed that the concrete here and now is
crucial to Hasidic thought, the actual goal was communion
with the hidden reality behind the here and now. Finally,
Buber, being a religious anarchist, does not acknowledge any teaching about what should be done, putting
the whole emphasis on how whatever is done, is done.
References to the Torah, which for the Hasidism was
the focus of life, became nebulous in Buber's presentation. Reprinted in item B484.

B192   "Translation of Work by Buber Was Planned by Hammar-
       skjold." *New York Times*, 1 October 1961, p. 31.

Relates that prior to his death, Dag Hammarskjold
had planned to translate *I and Thou* (item A17) into
Swedish.

B193   Trapp, Jacob. "Buber and Jewish-Christian Exchange."
       Christian Century, 8 November 1961, 1328-31.

Buber's thought seen as a meeting place for Christians and Jews. Discusses Buber's understanding of
Jesus and his concept of redemption, and their relationship to Christian beliefs.

B194   Weiner, Herbert. *The Wild Goats of Ein Gedi* . Garden
       City, N.Y.: Doubleday and Co., 1961, pp. 269-77.

Brief report of a conversation with Buber in which
the author tries to discover the reasons for Buber's
lack of influence in Israel.

B195   Bar-On, Zvie A.   "In Quest of Fundamentals."   *Ariel*, 1
       (Spring 1962), 52-65.

       Brief overview of the I-Thou and I-It relationships.

B196   Berkovits, Eliezer.   *A Jewish Critique of the Philosophy
       of Martin Buber*.   New York: Yeshiva University,
       1962.   107 pp.

       An analysis of Buber's thought in terms of Torah
       Judaism.   Criticizes Buber's subjectivity and argues
       that his thought cannot be supported on the strength of
       its own internal evidence.   Also faults Buber's descrip-
       tion of dialogue which excludes content from revelation.
       If revelation lacks content, where is man's obligation
       to respond?   All ethics become essentially relativistic.
       Buber's attempt to establish community through I-Thou
       relations also fails because he provides no way to go
       beyond the exclusiveness of this relationship.   How
       could the multitude of Israel encounter the eternal Thou
       as a people?   The singularity of the I-Thou relation
       cannot account for Judaism.   The biblical encounter is
       not an I-Thou relation.

B197   Blau, Joseph L.   "Realization through Dialogue."   *The
       Story of Jewish Philosophy*.   New York: Random House,
       1962, pp. 295-305.

       A short overview emphasizing I-Thou and I-It relations
       and the concept of community.   Sees Buber's philosophy
       as a search for what has been missing in western Judaism
       since the emancipation.

B198   Breisach, Ernst.   *Introduction to Modern Existentialism*.
       New York: Grove Press, 1962, pp. 160-71.

       An overview emphasizing Buber's life of dialogue and
       its social consequences.   Believes a knowledge of Fer-
       dinand Toennies' thought is necesary to understand
       Buber's social philosophy.

B199   Brunner, Emil.   "Excursus: Martin Buber's Teaching on
       the Apostles' Misunderstanding of Faith."   *The Christi-
       Doctrine of the Church, Faith, and the Consummation:
       Dogmatics III*.   Philadelphia: Westminster Press, 1962,
       pp. 159-62.

Rejects Buber's distinction between Jewish 'trust in'
and Christian 'belief that.' Peter's confession of
Christ preceded any instruction about Jesus the Christ.
Thus, faith in Jesus stands within Buber's concept of
faith as trust and obedience.

B200 Cohen, Arthur A. *The Natural and the Supernatural Jew.*
New York: Pantheon Books, 1962, pp. 149-78.

A discussion of the modern eclipse of God, the accom-
panying eclipse of man, and the resulting alienation.
Describes Buber as an existential humanist whose
philosophy is centered in God. For the Jewish community there are many problems connected with Buber and
his thought, particularly the fact that he was not a
practicing Jew. But the real danger in Buber's humanism is that God is made a respondent of man in an essentially ahistorical universe. Thus he has divested Jewish
tradition of its two authorities, God and the command
of history. The author concludes with a comparison of
the attempts of Franz Rosenzweig, Hermann Cohen, Leo
Baeck, and Buber to recover Judaism within the framework of western culture.

B201 Fellows, Lawrence. "Buber Calls Eichmann Execution
Great 'Mistake.'" *New York Times*, 5 June 1962, p. 15.

Buber believed that it was pointless to seek retri-
bution for crimes of the magnitude represented by Eichmann. He also feared that the execution might expiate
the guilt beginning to be felt by young Germans.

B202 Fellows, Lawrence. "Group of Israelis Aids Arab
Rights." *New York Times*, 28 January 1962, p. 15.

Buber mentioned as one member of the Ihud protesting
the treatment of Arabs in Israel.

B203 Fellows, Lawrence. "Philosopher Assails Ben-Gurion for
Calling Israel Arabs a Peril." *New York Times*,
18 January 1962, p. 2.

Quotes at length a statement signed by Buber and other
members of the Ihud criticizing Ben-Gurion's approach
to the Arabs in Israel.

B204 Fingarette, Herbert. "Real Guilt and Neurotic Guilt."
Journal of Existential Psychiatry, 3 (Fall 1962),
145-58.

Argues against Buber's distinction between neurotic
and authentic guilt. Buber's approach creates a radical
split between psychotherapy and the human encounter.
While the author agrees that guilt is a fundamental
reality of normal human existence, he objects to the
two-part human world thus created and the fact that the
psychotherapist is left to function only in the restric-
ted psychological realm. All guilt is real guilt. The
distinctive characteristic of neurotic guilt is not its
unreality but its unacknowledged source within the individual. Inauthenticity is the result refusing to
acknowledge this source.

B205   Helen James John, Sr. "Eichmann and Buber: A Message of
       Responsibility." *Commonweal*, 6 July 1962, 374-6.

       Although Buber's plea for mercy for Adolf Eichmann
       cited scriptural commandments and reasoning reminiscent
       of natural law morality, it must be understood in terms
       of Buber's handling of the question of evil. Evil and
       guilt are realities in man but they are not irredeem-
       able. God "wills not the death of the sinner, but that
       he be converted and live on."

B206   Horowitz, David. "Buber and Hasidism." *Commentary*,
       February 1962, pp. 161-2.

       Criticism of Scholem's critique of Buber's Hasidism
       (item B191). Briefly discussed are Buber's selection
       of Hasidic legendary literature over the more theoreti-
       cal writings, the concept of the here and now in Buber
       and in Hasidic thought, and the charge of religious
       anarchism.

B207   Kurzweil, Zvi E. "Buber on Education." *Judaism*, 11
       (Winter 1962), 44-55.

       The outstanding feature of Buber's philosophy of edu-
       cation is that it centers around the teacher-pupil
       relationship. This relationship, like the therapist-
       patient and pastor-parishioner relationships, is denied
       the full mutuality of inclusion. The teacher repre-
       sents to the pupil a world of ordered experience, a
       scale of values, and an embodiment of purpose. Buber
       is not particularly concerned with the technicalities
       of school instruction such as normal disciplinary
       measures or the choice of subjects to be taught. How-
       ever, his concept of freedom for the pupil does not
       exclude the teacher's rights in these areas. While the

goals of education are determined by the general spirit
of the age, Buber characterizes the spirit of our age
in negative terms. When the culture does not supply
proper goals, education should point toward the imita-
tion of God and a spiritual perception of the universe.
The author feels that education cannot teach this
supreme aim, but can help prepare the student to move
toward it.

B208   Lask, Israel Meir. "Reb Leib Sarah's Explains."
       Menorah Journal, 49 (Autumn-Winter 1962), 130-5.

       (Not available for annotating.)

B209   Mailer, Norman. "Responses and Reactions." *Commen-
       tary*, December 1962, pp. 504-6; February 1963, pp.
       146-8; April 1963, pp. 335-7; June 1963, pp. 517-8;
       August 1963, pp. 164-5.

       Mailer's reactions to Buber's Hasidic tales. Little
       about Buber.

B210   "Philosopher's Plea." *Time*, 23 March 1962, p. 28.

       Brief item about Buber's plea to Ben-Gurion to com-
       mute Adolf Eichmann's death sentence.

B211   Scholem, Gersham. "Buber and Hasidism." *Commentary*,
       February 1962, pp. 162-3.

       A response to Horowitz's criticism (item B206).

B212   Schwarzschild, Steven S. "Directions for Contemporary
       Jewish Philosophy: To Recast Rationalism." *Judaism*,
       11 (Summer 1962), 205-9.

       In a general article on Jewish philosophy, cites
       Buber and Franz Rosenzweig to illustrate the rebellion
       against rationalism. Objects to their subjectivity as
       a dead end and pleads for a return to the Cartesian
       search for a basis of rational thinking.

B213   "Soviet Scored on Jews." *New York Times*, 7 April 1962,
       p. 3.

       Brief mention of a message to Khruschchev, signed by
       Buber and others, about Russian Jews sentenced to death
       for economic crimes.

1963

B214   Beek, M.A. "The Mediator at His Task." *Leo Baeck
        Institute Year Book*, 8 (1963), 258-9.

        A review of Buber's accomplishments given as an
        address when he was awarded the Erasmus Prize in 1963.

B215   Bentwich, Norman. "Martin Buber, Educator and Philo-
        sopher." *Views*, No. 1 (Spring 1963), 85-7.

        (Not available for annotating.)

B216   Bergman, Samuel Hugo. *Faith and Reason: An Intro-
        duction to Modern Jewish Thought*. Edited and trans-
        lated by Alfred Jospe. New York: Schocken Books,
        1963, pp. 81-97.

        An overview.

B217   Bernhard, Prince of the Netherlands. "Praemium Eras-
        mianum Address." *Leo Baeck Institute Year Book*, 8
        (1963), 255-6.

        Address given on the presentation of the Erasmus
        Prize to Buber for his contribution to the spiritual
        and cultural life of Europe.

B218   Biser, Eugin. "Martin Buber." *Philosophy Today*, 7
        (Summer 1963), 100-14.

        Buber believes that modern man is suffering from God-
        darkness, a loss of immediacy between man and God. He
        saw the historical condition for this loss in the
        Christian concept of sonship. What for Judaism was
        the legacy of everyone born within the covenant became
        in Christianity the exclusive right of Jesus. The
        placement of a mediator between man and God destroyed
        the immediacy in this relationship. The author argues
        that this is a rehash of Nietzsche and a misinterpre-
        tation of Christianity. The dialogical principle, the
        most original aspect of Buber's thought, is an intense
        expression of his desire for immediacy. Within this
        framework the author discusses Buber's criticism of
        rationalism, subjectivism, existentialism, Marxism,
        and psychoanalysis.

B219   Borowitz, Eugene B. "2 Modern Approaches to God."
        Jewish Heritage, 6 (Fall 1963), 10-6.

Buber's approach to God is seen as diametrically opposed to that of Mordecai Kaplan. Kaplan maintains that modern man finds it difficult to believe in God because God cannot be explained scientifically. For Buber the difficulty is that modern man thinks that he *can* treat the problem of God scientifically. God is cut down to human size and turned into an object. The author believes that Buber has helped rediscover the God-man relationship that lies at the heart of Jewish tradition.

B220 "Buber Joins in Sobell Plea." *New York Times*, 27 June 1963, p. 8.

Brief mention of Buber's part in a plea for clemency for Morton Sobell.

B221 "Erasmus Prize Won by Theologian." *Times* (London), 28 March 1963, p. 10.

Brief notice of Buber's award.

B222 Friedman, Maurice. "Martin Buber." *Great Jewish Thinkers of the Twentieth Century.* Edited by Simon Noveck. [Washington]: B'nai B'rith, 1963, pp. 183-209.

An overview of Buber's development and philosophy.

B223 Friedman, Maurice. "Sex in Sartre and Buber." *Review of Existential Psychology and Psychiatry*, 3 (Spring 1963), 113-24.

Similarities and differences of Jean Paul Sartre and Buber in conceptualizing sexual relations. Both have, in contrast to most existentialist thinkers, an essentially positive attitude toward sex, Buber's being the more positive. For him sexuality represents an evil urge or passion, the proper response to which leads to essential relationships. Giving direction to these evil urges brings man into the interhuman. But nowhere are the I-Thou and I-It attitudes so intermingled and confused as in the sphere of sex. True mutuality must be present, a recognition of otherness and the experiencing of this otherness.

B224 Gerson, Manachem. "Encounter with Martin Buber." *AJR Information*, February 1963, p. 8.

Buber's influence on German youth in the late 1920s,
particularly his emphasis upon the communal life, led
to overly optimistic expectations in the early kibbutz
movement. Disappointed in the reality of communal
living, the settlers blamed Buber. The rift was widened
by Buber's disapproval of their Marxist and Freudian
ideas. In later years, Buber and the kibbutzim met as
allies in trying to solve Israel's political and social
problems.

B225 Goldberger, Emanuel. "A Dialogue with Martin Buber."
Congress Bi-Weekly, 30 December 1963, pp. 10-2.

Brief report of a 1961 interview with Buber.

B226 Halio, Jay L. "The Life of Dialogue in Education."
Journal of General Education, 14 (January 1963),
213-9.

Feels that Buber's primary writings on education
dealt with the education of young children, nursery
school to junior high. This is why Buber omits mention
of the student's responsibility and how it may alter
the dialogical relationship at the higher levels. The
student at this age is ready to experience inclusion,
and thus the dialogue becomes two-sided.

B227 Hammer, Louis Z. "Lyric Poetry as Religious Language."
Monist, 47 (Spring 1963), 401-16.

Uses Buber's philosophy of dialogue to support the
thesis that the poet stands in a religious dimension.
If religion is everything that is lived in its possibility of dialogue, then lyric poetry may be religious
language. The lyric poem, with its single speaker,
can represent a withdrawal into the personal center,
from which genuine dialogical speech must emanate.

B228 Heiman, Leo. "God Is My Telephone Operator." *Jewish
Digest*, July 1963, pp. 9-11.

Brief report of an interview with Buber.

B229 Jacob, Walter. "The Inter-religious Dialogue."
Jewish Heritage, 6 (Fall 1963), 31-5.

In an article discussing several Jewish writers,
Jacob briefly describes Buber's attitude towards
Christianity and sees his position as a basis for inter-
faith dialogue.

B230 "Judaism: I-Thou and I-It." *Time*, 12 July 1963, pp.
      49-50.

      Overview at the time of Buber's Erasmus Prize.

B231 Jude Michael, Bro. "The Divine Indwelling and the
      Adolescent." *LaSalle Catechist*, 29 (Autumn 1963),
      257-60.

      Briefly argues that Buber's theology can be recon-
      ciled with Catholic theology and therefore there is
      merit in translating him into the Catholic theological
      and pedagogical idiom.

B232 Macquarrie, John. *Twentieth-Century Religious Thought*.
      London: SCM Press, 1963, pp. 195-7, 208.

      A brief overview of Buber's thought and a discussion
      of his influence on Karl Heim.

B233 Schoeps, Hans Joachim. *The Jewish-Christian Argument:
      A History of Theologies in Conflict*. Translated by
      David E. Green. London: Faber and Faber, 1963, pp.
      146-58.

      In 1933 the Jewish Academy of Stuttgart sponsored a
      dialogue between Buber and the Christian theologian
      Karl Ludwig Schmidt. While the latter saw the Jews as
      losing their spiritual center by rejecting Jesus as
      the messiah, Buber countered by affirming that the
      faith-reality of someone else is a mystery which we
      cannot judge because we cannot know it from inside.
      While this view facilitates a dialogue between Chris-
      tianity and Judaism, it separates Buber from the tra-
      ditional Jewish and Christian positions of the
      exclusive and ultimate nature of their own revelations.

B234 Slusher, Howard S. "A Philosophical Foundation for
      Motivation of Community Health Education." *Journal
      of School Health*, 33 (October 1963), 353-60.

      Health educators must avoid the choice between indi-
      vidualism and collectivism and concern themselves with
      the nature of man's existence within the community.
      Buber's thought provides a framework for the teacher-
      student relationship and the individual-community
      relationship. Through this framework the teacher can
      motivate the student to live a healthy life for his
      own good as well as for the good of society.

B235   Stevenson, W. Taylor. "I-Thou and I-It: An Attempted
       Clarification of Their Relationship." *Journal of
       Religion*, 43 (July 1963), 193-209.

       Argues that there is ambiguity in Buber's conceptions
       of the I-Thou and I-It relations. While his definition
       of the I-Thou relation renders it highly exclusive, he
       frequently implies an intimate union between it and the
       realm of the I-It. If the I-Thou spirit determines how
       man apprehends and enters into relationship with the
       world of I-It, then they must be capable of the closest
       union. Buber's description of a sacramental existence
       also implies a close union between the two, as does his
       concept of the original relational event.

B236   Thieme, Karl. "Martin Buber and Franz Rosenzweig's
       Translation of the Old Testament." *Babel: Inter-
       national Journal of Translation*, 9, Nos. 1-2 (1963),
       83-6.

       Their translation has placed them in a position of
       honor next to the translators of the Septuagint, Jerome,
       Luther, and men of the King James Bible. They have
       succeeded in incorporating into an Indo-European lan-
       guage as much of the original Hebrew as possible. The
       author discusses in particular the rhythmical rendering
       of the breath phrases, the extensive preservation of
       word-root relationships, and their method of indicating
       the name of God.

B237   Thomas, W. Stephen. "Thought of Martin Buber on Henry
       Thoreau." *Thoreau Society Bulletin*, No. 85 (Fall
       1963), 1.

       Brief record of a conversation in which Buber dis-
       cussed Thoreau. Buber felt that Thoreau's concept of
       civil disobedience was a generalization lacking speci-
       fic principles of application.

B238   Weltsch, Robert. "Tribute to Martin Buber: On His
       85th Birthday." *AJR Information*, February 1963, p. 6.

       Briefly discusses various publication efforts then
       in progress, including Buber's complete writings in
       German, and critical works.

B239   Winetrout, Kenneth. "Buber: Philosopher of the I-Thou
       Dialogue." *Educational Theory*, 13 (January 1963),
       53-7.

An overview stressing Buber's concept of the I-Thou,
I-It relations and his educational philosophy.

1964

B240   Aiken, Henry David.   "Right-Wing Existentialists."
       New York Review of Books, 20 August 1964, pp. 9-11.

       A review of *Daniel* (item A222) and two books by
       Gabriel Marcel. Finds similarities in their thought,
       labeling both religiously conservative anti-rational-
       ists with similar philosophical backgrounds. Describes
       Daniel as a romantic period piece suggestive of Hegel
       and Nietzsche.

B241   Diamond, Malcolm L.   "Faith and Its Tensions: A Criti-
       cism of Religious Existentialism." *Judaism*, 13
       (Summer 1964), 317-27.

       Discussion of Buber's distinction between "belief in"
       and "belief that." Feels that the immunity to epistemo-
       logical inquiry provided by Buber's position is pur-
       chased at a great price. The traditional theological
       problems remain and must be argued in metaphysical terms.

B242   Friedman, Maurice, ed.   "Interrogation of Martin Buber."
       Philosophical Interrogations. Edited by Sydney Rome
       and Beatrice Rome. New York: Holt, Rinehart and
       Winston, 1964, pp. 13-117.

       Questions submitted to Buber by various philosophers
       and his replies. Taken together they cover most major
       aspects of his thought and serve to clarify many points.
       The editor has arranged the material in seven major
       subject areas: the philosophy of dialogue, the theory
       of knowledge, education, social philosophy, the philo-
       sophy of religion, the Bible and biblical Judaism, and
       evil. Unfortunately there is no index. However, a
       detailed table of contents helps to find material by
       particular topics.

B243   Friedman, Maurice.   Introduction to *Daniel: Dialogues
       on Realization*, by Martin Buber. Edited and trans-
       lated by Maurice Friedman. New York: Holt, Rinehart
       and Winston, 1964, pp. 3-44.

       Traces the intellectual background of this work.
       Reviews the themes of each of the five dialogues, and

briefly discusses the relationship between this book
and Buber's later thought.

B244   Friedman, Maurice. "The Transmoral Morality." *Journal*
          for the Scientific Study of Religion, 3 (Spring 1964),
          174-80.

       In a discussion of the ground of moral philosophy in
       modern thought, includes Buber's concept of conscience,
       the person's awareness of what he is uniquely intended
       to be. It is the conscience that summons us to rela-
       tionship and it is the relationship with the Absolute
       that is the source of the ethical.

B245   Gittelsohn, Roland B. "A World to Make Real." *Saturday*
          Review, 1 August 1964, pp. 26-7.

       A review of *Daniel* (item A222). Suggests part of the
       difficulty in understanding Buber is the confusion
       within his thinking.

B246   Kaplan, Mordecai M. "A Modern Esoteric Rationale."
          The Purpose and Meaning of Jewish Existence.
          Philadelphia: Jewish Publication Society of America,
          1964, pp. 255-86.

       Buber saw himself as a religious thinker rather than
       a creator of a philosophical system. The key to Buber's
       writings is his belief that the divine message contained
       in the Jewish religious tradition is necessary to human
       unity. Salvation of mankind depends upon a commitment
       to faith in the living God. This faith, according to
       Buber, cannot come through philosophy. Philosophy be-
       gins with a false premise, the existence of a self-
       enclosed mind on the one hand and a completely separate
       outside world on the other. The author feels that
       Buber has overstated his case against philosophy, and
       tries to show how philosophy has arrived at conclusions
       similar to Buber's concerning its own shortcomings and
       the relational nature of reality. Item B360 is a
       slightly revised version of this paper.

B247   Kingsley, Ralph P. "The Buber-Rosenzweig Translation
          of the Bible." *CCAR Journal*, 11 (January 1964),
          17-22.

       Argues that their translation of the Hebrew Bible was
       not successful because their basic assumptions were in-
       correct. The unity of style in biblical language, on
       which they based their efforts, is problematic, and

they were thus unable to achieve the consistency in translation they desired. But even if they had been successful in translating the original biblical language into German, the average reader would probably not recognize the subtle effects they were trying to achieve. They should have aimed for a modern idiomatic translation.

B248 Koo, Gladys Y. "The Structure and Process of Self." *Educational Theory*, 14 (April 1964), 111-7+.

A comparison of Buber and George Herbert Mead on the structure of the self. Feels Buber's I-Thou concept best describes the process of becoming a person and the attitudinal states of separation and relation so crucial to this process. Buber complements Mead's work in language by showing that symbols merely point to original experiences and may present or hide the self. To Mead's description of consciousness as the reflexive movement between the symbolic I and Me, Buber adds the necessity to test the content of this consciousness in the interpersonal encounter. Buber's description of the ontological nature of the I corrects the lack of structure in Mead's I.

B249 Roubiczek, Paul. "Personal Relationship--Martin Buber." *Existentialism: For and Against*. Cambridge: Syndics of the Cambridge University Press, 1964, pp. 139-60.

A positive overview concentrating on the philosophy of dialogue.

B250 Scholem, Gersham. "Buber's Hasidism." *Commentary*, February 1964, pp. 18-20.

A continuation of the discussion of Buber's interpretation of Hasidism (items B191, B206, and B212). The author again criticizes Buber's selection of the legendary literature over the theoretical writings. He also objects to the parallels drawn by Buber between Hasidic anecdotes and Zen stories. Reprinted in item B484.

B251 Wingeier, Douglas E. "Some Implications of the Philosophy of Martin Buber for Christian Education." *South East Asia Journal of Theology*, 6 (July 1964), 34-50.

An overview of Buber's thought applied to the Christian religious congregation, and the educational process

which takes place within this congregation. Describes
what a congregation would be like if it took Buber's
thought seriously.

1965

B252 Armstrong, C.B. "Thou." *Church Quarterly Review*, 166
      (October–December 1965), 494-8.

      Objects to the influence of *I and Thou* (item A17) on
      current Christian theology. Buber's fundamental error
      consisted in reducing the significance of objectivity
      in favor of the supposedly greater reality of meeting.
      Any relationship becomes more fertile in proportion to
      the objectivity by which the other is viewed.

B253 Bentwich, Norman. "Buber in Israel." *Jewish Woman's
      Review*, 1965, pp. 8-9.

      (Not available for annotating.)

B254 Borowitz, Eugene B. *A Layman's Introduction to Reli-
      gious Existentialism*. Philadelphia: Westminster
      Press, 1965, pp. 160-87.

      An overview of Buber's thought in terms of the act of
      knowing, drawing the distinction between the knowing of
      objects and the knowing of persons. Stresses the I-
      Thou and I-It relations, as well as Buber's relation-
      ship to Judaism and his concept of faith.

B255 Cahnman, Werner J. "Martin Buber: A Reminiscence."
      Reconstructionist, 15 October 1965, pp. 7-12.

      The author recalls the importance of Buber's thought
      to German Jews between the world wars.

B256 Cohen, Arthur A. "Martin Buber: An Appreciation."
      American Judaism, 15 (Fall 1965), 11.

      Brief memorial.

B257 Cox, Harvey. *The Secular City*. New York: Macmillan
      Co., 1965, pp. 48-9.

      Briefly suggests that the danger of the I-Thou, I-It
      typology is that all relationships which are not in-
      tensely personal are shoved into the latter category.
      Additional categories are needed to describe urban life.

B258 "Dr. Buber Buried Near Jerusalem." *New York Times*,
      15 June 1965, p. 38.

      Report on Buber's funeral.

B259 Dugan, George. "Rabbis in City Pay Homage to Buber."
      New York Times, 20 June 1965, p. 72.

      Memorial service in New York.

B260 Frankel, Ernst S. "Martin Buber--The European Years."
      Jewish Woman's Review, 1965, pp. 8-9.

      (Not available for annotating.)

B261 Friedman, Maurice. "The Existential Man: Buber." *The
      Educated Man: Studies in the History of Educational
      Thought.* Edited by Paul Nash, Andreas M. Kazamias,
      and Henry J. Perkinson. New York: John Wiley and
      Sons, 1965, pp. 363-87.

      An overview of Buber's philosophy of dialogue and its
      application to the process of education. The teacher's
      task is seen as the selection of the effective world
      and imparting this selection through mutuality to the
      pupils. This requires, on the teacher's part, the act
      of inclusion or experiencing the relationship from the
      pupil's point of view. Buber's philosophy of education
      is seen as an alternative to the authoritarian and per-
      missive philosophies current today. His views are com-
      pared to those of John Dewey and Robert M. Hutchins.

B262 Friedman, Maurice. Introduction to *Between Man and
      Man*, by Martin Buber. New York: Macmillan Company,
      1965, pp. xiii-xxi.

      A new introduction for this edition. Discusses the
      relationship of these papers to Buber's philosophical
      anthropology and *I and Thou* (item A17).

B263 Friedman, Maurice. Introduction to *The Knowledge of
      Man*, by Martin Buber. Translated by Maurice Friedman
      and Ronald Gregor Smith. New York: Harper and Row,
      Publishers, 1965, pp. 11-58.

      Summarizes Buber's philosophical anthropology and
      then analyzes each essay in this collection for its
      contribution to this anthropology.

B264 Friedman, Maurice. "Martin Buber's Challenge to Jewish
      Philosophy." *Judaism*, 14 (Summer 1965), 267-76.

Buber did not apply an alien philosophy to Judaism
but developed both the content and the approach of his
philosophy through his interaction with Judaism. The
whole of Judaism is not necessarily represented in a
balanced fashion in his philosophy. He drew more from
biblical and Hasidic Judaism than from Talmudic sources,
medieval Jewish philosophy, or modern liberal Judaism.
His interpretation of biblical Judaism as well as his
philosophy in general is illuminated by his interpretation of creation, revelation, and redemption as
"stages, actions, and events" in God's interaction with
the world.

B265   Friedman, Maurice. "Martin Buber's Final Legacy: 'The
       Knowledge of Man.'" *Journal for the Scientific Study
       of Religion*, 5 (Fall 1965), 4-9.

       The Knowledge of Man (item A229) contains the final
       stage of Buber's philosophical anthropology. His
       philosophy of dialogue is not just a phenomenological
       description of man's twofold attitude, but an ontology.
       In this book he deepens the ontological base of his
       anthropology by describing man's two basic movements,
       distancing and relation. From these movements is
       derived the twofold principle of human life, and through
       these movements dialogue is possible. Self-realization
       is a by-product of this dialogue, rather than a dimensio
       of the self. Mysticism is a flight from the inter-human
       world, and guilt is the result of harm done to this
       world.

B266   "From Vienna to Jerusalem: Journey of a Teacher."
       Jewish Observer and Middle East Review, 18 June 1965,
       p. 7.

       Brief eulogy.

B267   Gotshalk, Richard. "Buber's Conception of Responsibil-
       ity." *Journal of Existentialism*, 6 (Fall 1965), 1-8.

       A critical consideration of responsibility as re-
       sponse. Buber fails to distinguish clearly between the
       attitude within which one acts, and the activity itself.
       This obscures the responsiveness involved in objective
       thinking. Responsibility becomes a dimension of activit
       as such, and its presence or absence the basis of speak-
       ing of activity as responsible. Yet responsibility by
       itself is no guarantee of the adequacy of a response
       and no guide for understanding what the relevant form

of activity is for any given situation. Means of over-
coming this problem are discussed.

B268   "'The Greatest Jew of Our Time.'" *Jewish Observer and
       Middle East Review*, 18 June 1965, p. 6.

       Brief report of Buber's funeral.

B269   "He Made the Universe Transparent." *Christian Century*,
       23 June 1965, p. 796.

       Brief eulogy.

B270   Herberg, Will. "Martin Buber, RIP." *National Review*,
       29 June 1965, pp. 539-40.

       Eulogy.

B271   "Israel Mourns Martin Buber." *Tablet*, 26 June 1965,
       pp. 727-8.

       Brief tribute stressing Buber's influence on Christian
       thought and his Orthodox Jewish opposition.

B272   J.G.W. "The Search for the Truth." *Jewish Observer
       and Middle East Review*, 18 June 1965, p. 5.

       Eulogy which characterizes Buber as the Jewish out-
       sider par excellence.

B273   "Jews: 'All Life is a Meeting.'" *Time*, 25 June 1965,
       p. 82.

       Eulogy.

B274   "Jews Here Mourn Death of Buber." *New York Times*,
       14 June 1965, p. 29.

       American tributes to Buber on his death.

B275   Kappler, Frank. "Wise Old Teacher of I-Thou." *Life*,
       25 June 1965, pp. 97-8.

       Eulogy.

B276   Kloman, William. "Aspects of Existential Communication."
       Journal of Existentialism, 6 (Fall 1965), 59-68.

       In a general discussion of human communication, sug-
       gests that it is impeded by placing it in a comological
       framework. Criticizes the contentions of both Jaspers
       and Buber that communication illuminates the nature of

God. This denies individuals their essential independence and indicates a lack of trust in the possibilities
of man. Not only does man perceive meaning in relatedness, he in fact creates it.

B277   Logan, J.C. "Martin Buber: A Voice Outside the Camp."
       Christian Advocate, 9 September 1965, p. 9.

       (Not available for annotating.)

B278   "Martin Buber." *New York Times*, 14 June 1965, p. 32.
       Editorial on Buber's death.

B279   "Martin Buber." *Commonweal*, 2 July 1965, pp. 461.
       Short eulogy.

B280   *Martin Buber: An Appreciation of His Life and Thought.*
       New York: American Friends of the Hebrew University,
       1965.

       Contributors: Judah Nadich, Maurice Friedman, Seymour
       Siegel, Paul Tillich, Henry Sonneborn. (Not available
       for annotating.)

B281   "Martin Buber, 87, Dies in Israel; Renowned Jewish
       Philosopher." *New York Times*, 14 June 1965, pp. 1+.

       Brief overview of Buber's life and thought.

B282   "Martin Buber Is Gathered to His Fathers." *Israel
       Digest*, 18 June 1965, p. 3.

       Eulogy.

B283   Nadelmann, Ludwig. "Tradition and Nationalism in the
       Thought of Martin Buber." *Reconstructionist*,
       15 October 1965, pp. 12-6.

       Discussion of Buber's view of Jewish tradition as
       related to the modern Jew and the state of Israel.
       Buber reinterprets Jewish tradition in order to trans-
       mit it to today's Jews. He sees the values within
       this tradition as the result of the interaction between
       a people and a faith. There can be no Jewish national-
       ism without Jewish faith. This is the basis of Buber's
       criticism of the secular Israeli state.

B284   Niebuhr, Reinhold. "Martin Buber: 1878-1965."
       Christianity and Crisis, 12 July 1965, pp. 146-7.

A eulogy in which Niebuhr argues that Buber lacked an understanding of the moral nature of human collectives such as race, class, and nation.

B285   Niebuhr, Reinhold. "Martin Buber: In Memoriam." *Saturday Review*, 24 July 1965, p. 37.

Eulogy, slightly revised from item 284.

B286   "A Noble Jew--A Great Man: Paying Homage to Martin Buber." *Jewish and Middle East Review*, 19 July 1965, p. 25.

Brief report on a memorial service held in London.

B287   "Obituary: Dr. Martin Buber." *Times* (London), 14 June 1965, p. 12.

Brief overview of Buber's life and thought.

B288   "Presence of Greatness." *Newsweek*, 28 June 1965, pp. 76-7.

A brief overview and eulogy.

B289   Rosenberg, Harold. "'I' and 'Thou' in a Closet." *Herald Tribune Book Week*, 17 January 1965, pp. 4+.

A review of *Daniel* (item A222). Finds that in this book the 'I' has met no 'Thou' and thus dramatic confrontation is entirely lacking. Daniel himself is not a character but a puppet of the author. The book's primary weakness is the poverty of experience expressed. Experiences are almost always experiences of looking, followed by the dawning of comprehension. Events become abstractions.

B290   Schwarzschild, Steven S. "Mordecai Martin Buber." *Judaism*, 14 (Summer 1965), 259.

Brief memorial.

B291   Simon, Ernst. "From Dialogue to Peace--Martin Buber: In Memoriam." *Conservative Judaism*, 19 (Summer 1965), 28-31.

Brief overview.

B292   Singer, Isaac Bashevis. "Rootless Mysticism." *Commentary*, January 1965, pp. 7-8.

A negative review of *Daniel* (item A222) and Buber's thought in general. Sees Buber as an unclear thinker who fails to elucidate a means of achieving an I-Thou relation, the duties of a man toward the Thou, or whether the I-Thou relation is anything more than a kind of spiritual indulgence. When Buber separated his system from Hasidism and Judaism, he lost his spiritual home and created a mysticism for a cosmopolitan intellectual elite.

B293 Smith, Robert C. "Buber: Philosopher of Living Dialogue." *Reconstructionist*, 15 October 1965, pp. 17-21.

An overview of the philosophy of dialogue.

B294 Smith, Robert C. "Magic, Gnosis, and Faith." *Christian Scholar*, 48 (Winter 1965), 304-8.

According to Buber, magic and gnosis are enemies of the dialogical way of life. In the guise of religion, both negate the necessity for dialogue; magic does so by obtaining results without entering into relation, gnosis by creating a false sense of security. Both arise today because of the inaccessibility of a sure and solid faith.

B295 Smith, Robert C. "Martin Buber: Philosopher of Living Dialogue." *Theology and Life*, 8 (Fall 1965), 203-20.

An overview stressing that Buber's greatness lies not only in his philosophical achievements, but also in his lived ideological concern about man with man.

B296 Smith, Ronald G. "Martin Buber: Philosopher of Living Dialogue." *Covenant Companion*, 19 November 1965, pp. 6+.

(Not available for annotating.)

B297 Sullivan, K. "Book Reviews." *Jubilee* (April 1965), 51.

Review of *Daniel* (item A222). (Not available for annotating.)

B298 Tillich, Paul. "Martin Buber--1878-1965." *Pastoral Psychology*, 16 (September 1965), 52-4+.

An address given by Tillich at a memorial service held shortly after Buber's death. Reminisces about their relationship, which he feels was never a Jewish-Christian dialogue but rather a dialogue between a Jew and a Protestant who had transcended the limits of Judaism and Protestantism.

B299   "Two Great Men." *America*, 10 July 1965, p. 38.

     Brief eulogy.

B300   Walker, Roy. "Religion and the Theatre." *Listener*,
       29 April 1965, pp. 632-3.

     Buber's seven stages of theater-going, as discussed
in "On Polarity: After the Theater" (item A366).

B301   Weiss-Rosmarin, Trude. "Martin Buber." *Jewish Spec-*
       tator, September 1965, pp. 3-5.

     A highly critical discussion of Buber's relationship
to Judaism. Buber drew on Jewish tradition but gave it
an un-Jewish interpretation. He refused to follow the
halakah or involve himself in the prayer community of
the synagogue, ignoring the bond between Jewish consciousness and Jewish religious faith. His interpretation of Hasidic piety pictured it incorrectly as a
protest against normative Jewish life. Buber personi-
fied the modern Jew who is more at home in the non-
Jewish Christian culture.

B302   Weltsch, Robert. "Martin Buber and the Bible." *AJR*
       Information, February 1965, p. 10.

     Brief discussion of the importance of biblical
themes in Buber's works.

B303   Weltsch, Robert. "Zionism's Wider Context: A New
       Image of Judaism." *Jewish Observer and Middle East
       Review*, 18 June 1965, pp. 6-7.

     Eulogy emphasizing Buber's interpretation of
Judaism.

B304   Winocour, Jack. "Martin Buber 1878-1965." *World
       Jewry*, July/August 1965, p. 11.

     Brief eulogy.

1966

B305   Baker, Bruce F. "Existential Philosophers on Education."
       Educational Theory, 16 (July 1966), 216-24.

     In an attempt to find a basis for an existential
philosophy of education, the author explores the thought
of Nietzsche, Ortega y Gasset, and Jaspers, as well as

Buber. Finds that only Buber treats education as a
serious topic for philosophical inquiry. The essence
of education is the I-Thou relationship developed
through authentic communication between teacher and
student. Through this process, academic subject matter
is brought from the abstract impersonal realm of objective knowledge into a personally meaningful reality.

B306   Borowitz, Eugene B. "The Legacy of Martin Buber."
       Union Seminary Quarterly Review, 22 (November 1966),
       3-17.

Sees four major results of Buber's thought: (1) a new
defense of the person in an age that reduces the person
to. a cipher, (2) an analysis of reality which makes it
possible to accept religious faith as part of man's
being, (3) an understanding that we must speak of religious reality in a language different from the language
of things, and (4) by use of this language a new relevance is given to traditional religious categories.
Buber's thought is marred by the imprecision of the I-
Thou category, particularly in terms of ethics, and the
unclear relationship between the realms of I-Thou and
I-It.

B307   Borowitz, Eugene. "On the Commentary Symposium: Alter-
       natives in Creating a Jewish Apologetics." *Judaism*,
       15 (Fall 1966), 459-65.

Franz Rosenzweig's path to the Jewish faith leads
through German idealism, a path not possible for modern
men. Buber's thought supplies an alternative approach
to Rosenzweig's Judaism.

B308   Bruggeman, A. "The Cosmic Christ: Some Recent Inter-
       pretations." *Indian Journal of Theology*, 15 (1966),
       130-42.

(Not available for annotating.)

B309   Cohen, Aharon. "Buber's Zionism and the Arabs." *New
       Outlook: Middle East Monthly*, September 1966, pp. 5-9.

A brief history of Buber's Zionism. From the very
beginning the problems of Jewish-Arab relations and
nationalism occupied a central position in his thinking.
His belief in the special spiritual quality of the
Jewish people required him to struggle throughout his
life against its loss through conventional Western
nationalism.

B310   Cohn, Bernhard N. *Martin Buber: The Life in Dialogue.*
       Filmstrip. 47 frames. New York: Union of American
       Hebrew Congregations, 1966.

       Biography and overview of Buber's philosophy.

B311   Feron, James. "Work Advances on Buber's MSS." *New
       York Times*, 15 June 1966, p. 44.

       Report of the work in progress on Buber's papers.

B312   Friedman, Maurice, and Chaim Potok. "Dialogue."
       Commentary, September 1966, pp. 22-8.

       Letters discussing Potok's article (item B327).
       Friedman attacks Potok's position on Buber's interpre-
       tations of Jesus and Hasidism, and Potok responds.

B313   Gerson, Menahem. "Not to Sit and Wait." *New Outlook:
       Middle East Monthly*, October-November 1966, pp. 45-8.

       Discusses two aspects of Buber's political activities
       in Israel. Buber refused to join any political party
       for fear that his ideas, when expressed within the
       party, would be turned into propaganda. He also argued
       that discussions with the Arab governments on repatriat-
       ing Arab refugees should begin prior to peace negotia-
       tions.

B314   Gittelsohn, Ronald B. "Hosannas from a Hallowed Few."
       Saturday Review, 4 June 1966, pp. 16-7.

       Review of *The Origin and Meaning of Hasidism* (item
       A193). Primarily positive but thinks Buber fails to
       see that Hasidism's correctives to the extremes of
       Jewish intellectualism can become extremes themselves.
       Also, the position of the Zaddik, as mediator between
       God and the community, has a strangely un-Jewish ring.

B315   Glatzer, Nahum N. *Baeck-Buber-Rosenzweig Reading the
       Book of Job.* Leo Baeck Memorial Lecture No. 10.
       New York: Leo Baeck Institute, 1966, pp. 9-15.

       In his interpretation of Job, Buber attempts to solve
       the problem of evil and the remoteness of God for modern
       man by defining evil as aimlessness within man. He thus
       tries to restore our faith in a benign creator. The
       author feels that Buber's reduction of Job's extrange-
       ment from God, and the intimacy he reads into God's
       answer to Job, are not justified by the text.

B316 Gregory, T.S. "A Christian Reads Martin Buber."
      London Quarterly and Holburn Review, April 1966,
      pp. 121-5.

      An analysis of Buber's concepts of Christianity and
      Judaism, concluding that Christianity is closer to
      Buber's Judaism than he admits. Faults Buber for ignor-
      ing the modern irreligious aspects of the everyday.
      Feels he is so aware of the sacredness of the secular
      that he does not understand its secularity.

B317 Harper, Ralph. "The Implicit Love of God." *Human Love:*
      Existential and Mystical. Baltimore: Johns Hopkins
      Press, 1966, pp. 79-82.

      Briefly discusses Buber's idea of approaching God
      through attentiveness to other persons.

B318 Himmelfarb, Milton. Introduction to *The Condition of*
      Jewish Belief: A Symposium Compiled by the Editors of
      Commentary Magazine. New York: Macmillan Co., 1966,
      pp. 1-6.

      In discussing the results of a questionnaire submitted
      to a group of rabbis, mentions Buber's lack of influence
      upon Jewish thought in America.

B319 LeFevre, Perry. *Understanding of Man*. Philadelphia:
      Westminster Press, 1966, pp. 107-20.

      An overview of Buber's thought stressing the philoso-
      phy of dialogue, the man-God relationship, and the
      choice between community and collectivity.

B320 McCarthy, Charles R. "Personal Freedom and Community
      Responsibility." *Catholic World*, June 1966, pp. 165-8

      Uses Buber's conception of community as formed
      through I-Thou relations between men and between man
      and God to reconcile the stress in Vatican II on per-
      sonal freedom on the one hand, and responsibility within
      the community of believers on the other.

B321 McNeill, John J. "Martin Buber's Biblical Philosophy
      of History." *International Philosophical Quarterly*,
      6 (March 1966), 90-100.

      Buber's I-Thou philosophy is a valuable contribution
      to the philosophy of history. Every great culture
      rests on an original response to the address of the

Absolute Thou. Theophany begets history, and history
in turn is a record of man's response to this encounter.
Thus a supreme principle, both religious and narrative,
is constructed by each great civilization. All spheres
of life are determined by their relation to this principle. However, as a civilization develops, it strives
to become independent of this principle. This takes
the form of reducing the principle from a living mode
of I-Thou relation to a static I-It relation, and then
to a mere human convention. Redemption for a civilization as well as for an individual is to open again to
the Absolute.

B322　Martin, Bernard.　"Martin Buber and Twentieth-Century
　　　　Judaism." *Central Conference of American Rabbis
　　　　Yearbook*, 76 (1966), 149-64.

　　　　Examines some of the factors that have led to the
neglect of Buber's thought among Jews; namely the anti-
theological and anti-philosophical bias in Judaism,
Buber's existential interpretation of biblical faith,
his rejection of traditional teachings on Jewish law,
his views on Jesus, and his protest against Jewish
nationalism. Then argues that Buber made three major
contributions to modern Judaism. His philosophy gives
a compelling image of man and the redemptive value of
dialogue. His view of the Bible, as a record of encounter between the Jewish people and God, gives Jews a
third alternative to traditional literalism and modern
relativism. Finally, he has re-affirmed the personal
living God of classical Jewish spirituality.

B323　"Martin Buber's Books." *Jewish Observer and Middle East
　　　　Review*, 24 June 1966, p. 11.

　　　　Briefly notes the disposition of Buber's personal
records. His library is to go to the Harry Truman
Centre for the Advancement of Peace in Jerusalem, his
archives and his collection of books on Hasidism and
the Kabala to the Jewish National and Hebrew University
Library, and his papers on Zionism to the Zionist
archives.

B324　Meserve, Harry C.　"Buber, Schweitzer, Tillich."
　　　　Journal of Religion and Health, 5 (January 1966),
　　　　3-6.

　　　　Brief eulogy.

B325   Misrahi, Robert. "The Dialogue in Practice." *New
       Outlook: Middle East Monthly*, October-November 1966,
       pp. 25-34.

       Argues that we cannot separate Buber's philosophy
       from his political ideas. His concepts of community
       and intercommunity relations are applied to Israel-Arab
       relations. Three conditions are seen as necessary for
       authentic dialogue between peoples; openness and the
       absence of reservation, a true confrontation, and a
       rejection of propaganda.

B326   Petras, John W. "God, Man and Society: The Perspectives
       of Buber and Kierkegaard." *Journal of Religious
       Thought*, 23 (1966-67), 119-28.

       A comparison of man's relationship with man and with
       God as seen in the works of Buber and Kierkegaard.
       Conceptualizes Buber's philosophy in terms of three
       relationships, I-It, I-Thou, and I-Absolute Thou (God).
       These are viewed as three different planes of existence,
       or levels of self-realization, which may be attained by
       man. He then draws parallels to Kierkegaard's three
       stages: the aesthetic, the ethical, and the religious.

B327   Potok, Chaim. "Martin Buber and the Jews." *Commentary*,
       March 1966, pp. 43-9.

       Buber, the most influential Jewish philosopher of our
       time, has been largely rejected by his own people. In
       the 1920s and 1930s he had a considerable audience among
       liberal European Jews but this audience was annihilated
       by Hitler. He has been ignored by Orthodox Jews and
       the Hasidim because of his ambivalence toward Jewish
       law. Conservative and Reform Jews who identify with
       the rationalist stream of western culture reject his
       religious subjectivism. His views on Jesus are also
       an impediment to Jews. Finally, his view of Judaism
       has been strongly influenced by Christian mysticism.

B328   Siegel, Seymour. "Martin Buber: An Appreciation."
       American Jewish Year Book, 67 (1966), 37-43.

       An overview of Buber's thought stressing his influ-
       ence on the Jewish community.

B329   Silverman, David. "Religion as Adventure." *Conserva-
       tive Judaism*, 20 (Winter 1966), 65-71.

Comments briefly upon Buber's insistence on the openness of the human encounter at the expense of any set
norms, including Jewish law.

B330   Simon, Ernst. "Buber or Ben Gurion?" *New Outlook:*
       Middle East Monthly, February 1966, pp. 9-17.

A pro-Buber, anti-Ben-Gurion analysis of their re-
spective positions on the Arab question, the Aharon
Cohen case, the attempt to make the Middle East a
nuclear-free zone, and the political processes in
Israel.

B331   Simon, Akiva Ernst. "Buber's Legacy for Peace." *New*
       Outlook: Middle East Monthly, October-November 1966,
       pp. 14-24.

A discussion of Buber's interpretation of Zionism
and his hope for a binational state in Palestine. He
saw this state as an interim solution leading towards
a larger regional confederation. He accepted the
establishment of the state of Israel with a heavy heart
and continued to work to promote Jewish-Arab peace.

B332   Smith, Ronald Gregor. *Martin Buber*. London: Carey
       Kingsgate Press, 1966. 45 pp.

An introduction to Buber describing the main thrust
of his work as anthropological. Despite his writings
about God, Buber looked for an understanding of man in
man's everyday existence. The substance and style of
all of Buber's work was provided by the Hasidic movement. He tried to express a unity of the world, man,
and God in terms of communion rather than mysticism.
His social thought avoids both individualism and collectivism. One fourth of the book is devoted to an analysis
of Buber's relation to Christianity. The author questions Buber's distinction between two types of faith,
seeing Christ as the consummation of the dialogical
meaning of history. There is no index.

B333   Smith, Ronald F. "Martin Buber's View of the Inter-
       human." *Jewish Journal of Sociology*, 8 (June 1966),
       64-80.

Buber's philosophy of the interpersonal is difficult
to apply to the social sciences because it tends to
disrupt previously held theories. It forces the student to consider man in his totality, to go beyond the
divisions between traditional fields of study. Buber

was interested in the inner structure of human groups
and was critical of all associations which fell short
of I-Thou relations. He attempted to establish an
ontology of the personal based on the fact that man is
fully man only in relation with others. He also brought
transcendence back into the study of man, not in the
traditional metaphysical sense, but in the I-Thou relation where spirit becomes the mode of man's being, the
vehicle of man's historical existence.

B334   Weiss-Rosmarin, Trude. "Buber and the Dialogical Prin-
       ciple." *Jewish Spectator*, May 1966, pp. 5-6.

       Again berates Buber for his failure to properly
acknowledge his indebtedness to other thinkers, particularly Hermann Cohen, for the basic concepts of his
philosophy of dialogue. Sees this as an example of
Buber's un-Jewish life style.

B335   Williams, Daniel Day. "Martin Buber and Christian
       Thought." *Central Conference of American Rabbis
       Yearbook*, 76 (1966), 165-78.

       Three phases of Buber's influence on Christian theo-
logy are discussed: (1) the early widespread acceptance
of the philosophy of *I and Thou* (item A17), (2) a period
of exploration and criticism of this philosophy, and
(3) the response to Buber's critique of Christianity
and its relationship with Judaism. Buber became a
critic as well as an interpreter of Christianity. The
author argues that current trends in theology are in
the direction suggested by his criticism.

B336   Zolo, Danilo. "The Religious Commitment." *New Outlook:
       Middle East Monthly*, October-November 1966, pp. 34-6.

       Stresses the religious factor in Buber's quest for
peace.

                              1967

B337   Ames, Van Meter. "Buber and Mead." *Antioch Review*,
       27 (Summer 1967), 181-91.

       A comparison of the thought of George Herbert Mead
and Buber with particular emphasis upon Paul Pfuetze's
criticism (item B90) that Mead, as opposed to Buber,
does not adequately explain the genesis of the self.

Since Mead derives the self only from a biological and social process, Pfuetze felt his thought needed to be amended in the direction of Buber's God-centered personalism. In defense of Mead's position the author states that his dialogic account of the self has much in common with Buber's I-Thou duality and his conception of the physical as an abstraction from the social approximates Buber's distinction between I-Thou and I-It relationships. Further, Mead's concept of the generalized other can be seen as the equivalent of Buber's Ultimate Thou or God. The divergence of conceptualization between the two thinkers is discussed in terms of their intellectual background, biblical Judaism and Hasidism for Buber, and modern science, Whitehead, and Einstein for Mead.

B338 Auerback, Charles. "Reflections on Martin Buber." *CCAR Journal*, 14 (April 1967), 28-64.

A wide-ranging overview of Buber's thought. Considers Buber's unique contribution to be his synthesis of three forces in modern Jewish life: biblical faith, Hasidic piety, and the needs of modern times.

B339 Balthasar, Hans Urs Von. "Martin Buber and Christianity." *The Philosophy of Martin Buber*. Edited by Paul Arthur Schlipp and Maurice Friedman. La Salle, Ill.: Open Court, 1967, pp. 341-59.

Buber's formulation of the Jewish Idea must be dealt with by the Christian because of the relationship between the two faiths. The author finds fault with several aspects of Buber's formulation including the reduction of the essence of Jewish faith to the I-Thou relationship with God, the unity of religion and civil society expressed in this relationship, and the synthesis proposed between the particular structure and the universal mission of Judaism. The author also rejects Buber's contention that the two modes of faith are mutually contradictory, and sees Judaism and Christianity, as expressed in the Catholic Church, as two witnesses to a mandate from God to the world.

B340 Ben-Shlomo, Zeev. "Clandestine Buber in U.S.S.R." *Jewish Chronicle*, 29 September 1967, p. 20.

Brief report of the illegal circulation of Buber's works in the Soviet Union.

341.   Bergman, Hugo. "Martin Buber and Mysticism." *The
       Philosophy of Martin Buber*. Edited by Paul Arthur
       Schilpp and Maurice Friedman. La Salle, Ill.: Open
       Court, 1967, pp. 297-308.

   Buber early rejected world-negating mysticism and
insisted that the way to God is through the world.
This position left the danger of a merger of the divine
and the human, and he later sharpened the distinction
between God and man. His writings on Hasidism imply a
realistic mysticism in which the immediacy of the relationship is balanced by the concreteness of the par-
ticipants. However, while Buber showed us the goal of
man's spiritual life and the necessity of true dialogue,
he did not show how these goals were to be realized.
Buber's attitude toward gnosticism is also discussed,
and his distinction between devotion and gnosis is
criticized.

B342   Birnbaum, Ruth. "Buruch Spinoza--Martin Buber: Dia-
       lectic and Dialogue." *Personalist*, 48 (Winter 1967),
       119-28.

   While recognizing major antithetical features in the
philosophies of Spinoza and Buber, the author feels
that they converge at several points. Both see man's
highest good as the knowledge of God, knowledge attain-
able by all men. Both believe that this knowledge can
best be expressed in human relationships. Good and evil
are interpreted as internal forces which may either help
or hinder man in his path to God. Good and evil, however, are not diametrically opposed. Evil is a chaotic
state not yet channeled in the direction of God. External factors can contribute to this chaos: for Spinoza
the laws and abrasions of the natural world, for Buber
the lack of mutuality.

B343   Brod, Max. "Judaism and Christianity in the Work of
       Martin Buber." *The Philosophy of Martin Buber*.
       Edited by Paul Arthur Schilpp and Maurice Friedman.
       La Salle, Ill.: Open Court, 1967, pp. 319-40.

   The author views Buber's books on Judaism and Christianity, as well as his translation of the Hebrew
Bible, as a record of the history of a faith. The
heart of this faith was the bringing into reality of
the kingship of God. His works on Christianity centered on his distinction between the Hebrew word
emunah or 'trust in' and the Greek word *pistis* or

'belief that.' Buber saw Paul's emphasis on the belief
that Jesus was God as separating Christianity from the
traditional Jewish man-God relationship of trust. While
Jesus remained within the Jewish tradition, Paul created
a new religion based upon a pessimistic and unbiblical
doctrine of original sin. To Paul's dangerous world of
the unredeemed, Buber contrasted Kafka as a Jew who,
because he retained his primal roots, was safe.

B344 Brunner, Emil. "Judaism and Christianity in Buber."
      The Philosophy of Martin Buber. Edited by Paul
      Arthur Schilpp and Maurice Friedman. La Salle, Ill.:
      Open Court, 1967, pp. 309-18.

Buber's basic ideas are common to both Christianity
and Judaism. When he contrasts the two approaches to
God, his purpose is to clarify the religious message of
Judaism and show that the Jesus of history belongs to
this same Jewish world. When he claims, however, that
the theology of the apostles, particularly Paul, diver-
ges from this Jewish world by making obedience to an
historical event the object of faith, he is ignoring
the importance of historical revelation in the Jewish
faith. The author feels that justifiable faith can be
understood only from a conception of sin which is not
found in Buber's thought.

B345 Carson, Saul. "Buber's Influence on Dag Hammarskjold:
      One Channel of Spiritual Thought." *Australian Jewish
      Herald*, 21 April 1967.

(Not available for annotating.)

B346 Diamond, Malcolm L. "Dialogue and Theology." *The
      Philosophy of Martin Buber*. Edited by Paul Arthur
      Schilpp and Maurice Friedman. La Salle, Ill.: Open
      Court, 1967. pp. 235-47.

Three major criticisms of Buber's philosophy are discussed. First, contrary to Buber, historical continuity
can only be attained in those areas not concerned with
fundamental problems of human nature and destiny. Further, at a time in history when man most needs to apply
his reason to human affairs, Buber seems to be espousing
a philosophy of emotional commitment. Finally, if the
"I" of the I-It attitude is characterized by excessive
self-absorption and a utilitarian approach to beings,
how can it be the ground of an objectively verifiable,
transobjective knowledge? The author contrasts Buber's

dialogical approach to theology with the ontological
approach of Paul Tillich. While Tillich established
being-itself as an objective starting point, Buber sees
no similar point of reference that stands outside of
dialogue. His mistrust of theological categories leads
him to use evocative and paradoxical language.

B347   Dusen, Henry P. van. *Dag Hammarskjold: The Statesman
       and His Faith.* New York: Harper and Row Publishers,
       1967, pp. 186-7, 215-9.

       Briefly discusses Hammarskjold's relationship with
       Buber.

B348   Fackenheim, Emil L. "Martin Buber's Concept of Revela-
       tion." *The Philosophy of Martin Buber.* Edited by
       Paul Arthur Schilpp and Maurice Friedman. La Salle,
       Ill.: Open Court, 1967, pp. 273-96.

       Buber's concept of revelation is an attempt to com-
       bine the principle of rational inquiry with faith in a
       self-revealing God. It is an extension of the doctrine
       of I-Thou, I-It relations. He first demonstrates that
       religion is an I-Thou relation, distinct from other I-
       Thou relations in that God is a Thou that cannot become
       an It. The content of revelation is a translation of
       this experience into human form. It thus becomes a
       mixture of the divine and the human. The question that
       remains unanswered in Buber's writings is whether the
       doctrine of I and Thou is derived exclusively from I-
       Thou knowledge, and thus can only be accepted through
       commitment, or if it is a philosophy that mediates be-
       tween I-It and I-Thou knowledge.

B349   Farber, Leslie H. "Martin Buber and Psychotherapy."
       The Philosophy of Martin Buber. Edited by Paul
       Arthur Schilpp and Maurice Friedman. La Salle, Ill.:
       Open Court, 1967, pp. 577-601.

       A revision of an earlier article (item B104). Most
       of the added material concerns psychotherapy and does
       not apply specifically to Buber.

B350   Fox, Marvin. "Some Problems in Buber's Moral Philo-
       sophy." *The Philosophy of Martin Buber.* Edited by
       Paul Arthur Schilpp and Maurice Friedman. La Salle,
       Ill.: Open Court, 1967, pp. 151-70.

Buber believes that moral values must be absolute, and that these absolute values are derived from revelation. However, his view of revelation as having no absolute content leaves man with no guide by which to judge the content of his specific revelation. In addition, each moral situation is, for Buber, so unique that only the individual experiencing it can decide what to do. Thus we are also left unable to make judgments of other men's moral values. These positions seem to contradict Buber's view that moral values must be absolute. Buber, however, does not always follow his own rules. He often speaks of revelation as having a content, as when he discusses Hasidism or the role of the teacher. He also makes judgments on the moral worth of specific men and moral pronouncements which he seems to intend as universally binding. The author calls upon Buber to clarify his position.

B351 Friedman, Maurice. "The Bases of Buber's Ethics." *The Philosophy of Martin Buber*. Edited by Paul Arthur Schilpp and Maurice Friedman. La Salle, Ill.: Open Court, 1967, pp. 171-200.

Buber's ethics are grounded in his philosophical anthropology and his philosophy of religion. The "ought" in his philosophical anthropology is contained in his conception of authentic existence, and, in his philosophy of religion, in the command of God. But authenticity implies finding, through the unique concrete situation, one's personal direction to God. The choice for Buber is not between religion and morality as in Kierkegaard, but between a religion and morality which is wedded to the universal or to the concrete. One can identify an autonomous ethic within Buber's thought only if we define religion as a sphere separate from the concrete, an idea which Buber rejects.

B352 Friedman, Maurice. "Martin Buber--A Modern Bridge Between Judaism and Christianity." *Search for Identity in a Changing World*. Woman's Division, Board of Missions, The Methodist Church, 1967.

(Not available for annotating.)

B353 Friedman, Maurice. "Martin Buber's Biblical Judaism." *Bible Today*, No. 30 (April 1967), 2114-20.

Slight revision of his 1959 article (item B158).

B354   Friedman, Maurice. "Martin Buber's Credo." *A Believ-*
        ing Humanism. By Martin Buber. Translated by Maurice
        Friedman. New York: Simon and Schuster, 1967,
        pp. 21-6.

        In this introduction to item A261, stresses existen-
        tial trust as the heart of Buber's teaching.

B355   Friedman, Maurice. *To Deny Our Nothingness*. New York:
        Delacorte Press, 1967, pp. 108-14, 287-304.

        In a general discussion of the modern philosophical
        situation, contrasts T.S. Eliot's mystical dualism with
        Buber's mysticism of the everyday as seen in Hasidism.
        Also presents Buber's philosophy of dialogue and the
        six stages toward authentic personhood derived from
        Hasidism.

B356   Glatzer, Nahum N. "Buber As an Interpreter of the
        Bible." *The Philosophy of Martin Buber*. Edited by
        Paul Arthur Schilpp and Maurice Friedman. La Salle,
        Ill.: Open Court, 1967, pp. 361-80.

        Buber saw the Bible as a product of Israel's encoun-
        ter with the Absolute. To understand its teachings
        Buber tried to go back to the original language, taking
        his clues from the choice of words and images, key
        phrases, and the structure and rhythm of the stories.
        Scholarly investigation, however, cannot be an end in
        itself. Buber was primarily concerned with relating
        these teachings to the present day reader. The author
        discusses some of the concepts used by Buber, including
        the kingship of God, the central position of the pro-
        phets, creation, the Sinai event, revelation, and
        Jewish law.

B357   Glatzer, Nathum N. Editor's postscript to *On Judaism*,
        by Martin Buber. New York: Schocken Books, 1967,
        pp. 237-42.

        Places the writings collected in this work in their
        historical context, as having created a third alterna-
        tive to orthodoxy and assimilation for early twentieth-
        century European Jews.

B358   Hammer, Louis Z. "The Relevance of Buber's Thought to
        Aesthetics." *The Philosophy of Martin Buber*. Edited
        by Paul Arthur Schilpp and Maurice Friedman. La
        Salle, Ill.: Open Court, 1967, pp. 609-28.

For Buber, the artist is one who remains faithful,
within the spheres of the senses and language, to what
he meets in the world. Art, along with knowledge, love,
and faith, brings man into relation with his world.
Beauty is not the response of the viewer, nor a quality
of the object, but a dialogue between the senses of man
and the world. The author contrasts Buber's view of
art with that of Susanne Langer and R.G. Collingwood,
and then applies this view to an analysis of music and
poetry.

B359   Hartshorne, Charles. "Martin Buber's Metaphysics."
       The Philosophy of Martin Buber. Edited by Paul
       Arthur Schilpp and Maurice Friedman. La Salle, Ill.:
       Open Court, 1967, pp. 49-68.

The author attempts to find metaphysical principles
in Buber's thought. The primary principle is seen as
relatedness. A thing said to be relative depends for
its being upon some relation to another. God can only
be a Thou and therefore cannot be non-relative. However, to identify God with what is absolute, as Buber
does, creates an idea of God as formless, unconditioned,
wholly independent reality. The author suggests that a
better concept of divine nature is supreme relatedness,
a mode of self-relating to others which is perfect and
unsurpassable.

B360   Kaplan, Mordecai M. "Buber's Evaluation of Philosophic
       Thought and Religious Tradition." *The Philosophy of
       Martin Buber.* Edited by Paul Arthur Schilpp and
       Maurice Friedman. La Salle, Ill.: Open Court, 1967,
       pp. 249-72.

Slight revision of item B246.

B361   Kaufmann, Fritz. "Martin Buber's Philosophy of Reli-
       gion." *The Philosophy of Martin Buber.* Edited by
       Paul Arthur Schilpp and Maurice Friedman. La Salle,
       Ill.: Open Court, 1967, pp. 201-33.

Buber rejects any philosophical approach which objec-
tifies God and sees his own thought as pointing to,
rather than encompassing, God. The author finds a similar understanding of purpose running through western
philosophy. He compares certain ideas in Buber's religious thought with similar ideas in Plato, Saint Augustine, Pascal, Descartes, and Kant. These ideas have
come together in Buber. The author discusses the modern

experience of the eclipse of God and Buber's concept of
the infinite flashing out in the finite, of God stepping
into life and giving it infinite significance. This
consecration of the world is best seen in Buber's Hasidic stories. The contradiction between this experience
of God in the world and God's transcendence is brought
together in Buber's idea of absolute personality.

B362   Kaufmann, Walter. "Buber's Religious Significance."
       The Philosophy of Martin Buber. Edited by Paul
       Arthur Schilpp and Maurice Friedman. La Salle, Ill.:
       Open Court, 1967, pp. 665-85.

       The author finds Buber's major contributions to reli-
       gious thought in his approach to critical religious
       questions, his translation of the new Hebrew Bible, and
       his interpretation of Hasidism. In approach, Buber's
       method of exposition is contrasted with that of Jaspers
       and Heidegger. The Buber-Rosenzweig translation of
       the Bible is seen as unique in its dependence upon orig-
       inal sources and its faithfulness to those sources.
       Finally, Buber's interpretation of Hasidism, through
       their stories, has given us one of the great religious
       books of all time.

B363   Kerenyi, Carl. "Martin Buber as Classical Author."
       The Philosophy of Martin Buber. Edited by Paul
       Arthur Schilpp and Maurice Friedman. La Salle, Ill.:
       Open Court, 1967, pp. 629-38.

       The danger of religion is that it steps between man
       and God, destroying the immediacy and openness of this
       relationship. Buber's Hasidic works move toward restor-
       ation of this immediacy, evoking great fighters of the
       spirit. This places Buber among the ranks of classical
       authors whose works form world literature.

B364   Kuhn, Helmut. "Dialogue in Expectation." *The Philo-
       sophy of Martin Buber*. Edited by Paul Arthur Schilpp
       and Maurice Friedman. La Salle, Ill.: Open Court,
       1967, pp. 639-64.

       For Buber, the human approach to reality is through
       encounter. The established rituals and dogmas of reli-
       gion and philosophy pale beside the desire for the
       immediate manifestation of the spirit in the here and
       now. Buber sought to redefine the relationship between
       the spirit and the world, retaining the openness of the
       one to the other. The locus of epiphany is the

community, the actuality of the common life. The spirit
is found through commitment to our fellow creatures.
This idea of the dependence of the I on the Thou became
common philosophic property through Buber.

B365 Levians, Emmanuel. "Martin Buber and the Theory of
      Knowledge." *The Philosophy of Martin Buber.* Edited
      by Paul Arthur Schilpp and Maurice Friedman. La
      Salle, Ill.: Open Court, 1967, pp. 133-50.

      The I-Thou encounter is both a knowing relationship
      and an ontological event. Through it the I becomes com-
      mitted to a transcendent reality that tells it something.
      Truth may not be approached by a dispassionate spectator.
      It is found in this fundamental relation to being.
      Problems with Buber's view include the difficulty of
      abscribing an ethical meaning to the I-Thou relation
      and still maintaining reciprocity, and the ignoring of
      philosophy as a source of truth.

B366 McGuire, Walter. "Martin Buber and the Covenantal
      Faith." *Dominicana*, 52 (March 1967), 52-9.

      A discussion of Buber's notion of covenantal faith in
      Judaism and Christianity. Sees Buber's distinction
      between Jewish trusting faith and Christian object faith
      as artificial. The Old Testament faith is founded upon
      an object faith, a belief that God made certain promises
      to Abraham.

B367 Marcel, Gabriel. "I and Thou." *The Philosophy of
      Martin Buber.* Edited by Paul Arthur Schilpp and
      Maurice Friedman. La Salle, Ill.: Open Court, 1967,
      pp. 43-8.

      Outlines Buber's concept of the I-Thou relation.
      Cites parallels in his own thought but admits that
      Buber went further in exploring this basic aspect of
      human existence. In an era of collectivism versus
      individualism, Buber purposes a philosophy of relation-
      ship.

B368 Muilenburg, James. "Buber as an Interpreter of the
      Bible." *The Philosophy of Martin Buber.* Edited by
      Paul Arthur Schilpp and Maurice Friedman. La Salle,
      Ill.: Open Court, 1967, pp. 381-402.

      When translating the Hebrew Bible, Buber attempted to
      recover the speech of the original Hebrew. He stressed

the key words, rhythms, and internal structure of each
section. Buber also employed other Near Eastern materials to help him understand the faith of ancient Israel.
He rejected the widely held belief that the Jews first
worshipped Yahweh at Sinai, and argued for the historical reality of an earlier relationship. Buber's most
significant contribution to biblical interpretation was,
according to the author, his analysis of the role of
the kingship of God in the ancient Jewish community.

B369 Mullins, James. "The Problem of the Individual in the
      Philosophies of Dewey and Buber." *Educational Theory*,
      17 (January 1967), 76-82.

      Believes that Buber's emphasis on the individual and
      the importance of dialogue in the educational process
      counterbalances John Dewey's stress on the social com-
      ponents of this process.

B370 Oliver, Roy. "Martin Buber: The Poetry of Living."
      Jewish Quarterly, 15 (Summer 1967), 7-12+; 15 (Winter
      1967-68), 39-42.

      Buber as a poet in terms of his response to the
      immediacy of the world. Reviews his concept of encoun-
      ter as he applied it to nature, animals, the land, and
      men.

B371 Orlinsky, Harry M. "Book Review." *Library Journal*,
      92 (September 1967), 2928.

      A short negative review of *Kingship of God* (item
      A326). Feels Buber's biblical works cannot be taken
      seriously because he was not a biblical scholar.

B372 Pfuetze, Paul E. "Martin Buber and American Pragmatism."
      The Philosophy of Martin Buber. Edited by Paul
      Arthur Schilpp and Maurice Friedman. La Salle, Ill.:
      Open Court, 1967, pp. 511-42.

      A comparison of the pragmatism of George Herbert Mead
      and the existentialism of Buber, stressing similarities
      in their anthropologies and social philosophies. Both
      conceive of man as a self-other system involving the
      mechanism of speech. Both attempt to establish an ethi-
      cal system which preserves genuine community and yet
      frees ethics from social patterns. Each is criticized
      for his vague metaphysics. The author believes that
      the religious basis of Buber's thought, as opposed to
      Mead's naturalism, allows a more complete understanding
      of man.

B373 Rosenbloom, J. "A 'Way' from Martin Buber." *Pulpit*,
      38 (February 1967), 26-7.

      Brief overview.

B374 Rotenstreich, Nathan. "The Right and the Limitations
      of Buber's Dialogical Thought." *The Philosophy of
      Martin Buber*. Edited by Paul Arthur Schilpp and
      Maurice Friedman. La Salle, Ill.: Open Court, 1967,
      pp. 97-132.

      Reprint of two earlier articles by the author (items
      B164 and B165).

B375 Rudavsky, David. "The Neo-Hasidism of Martin Buber."
      Religious Education, 62 (May-June 1967), 235-44.

      An overview of Buber's thought stressing his writings
      on Hasidism and his philosophy of dialogue.

B376 Schatz-Uffenheimer, Rivkah. "Man's Relation to God and
      World in Buber's Rendering of the Hasidic Teaching."
      The Philosophy of Martin Buber. Edited by Paul
      Arthur Schilpp and Maurice Friedman. La Salle, Ill.:
      Open Court, 1967, pp. 403-34.

      While acknowledging the importance of Buber's work on
      Hasidism, the author believes that many problems arise
      when comparing his interpretations with the original
      Hasidic sources. Buber saw the goal of Hasidism as the
      reduction of the gulf between God and the everyday world.
      The original sources indicate that the Hasidim did wish
      to redeem the world, but the world as it ought to be,
      in a state of primordial creation. They retained the
      dualism between God and the everyday world, drawing
      back from their early emphasis upon service to God in
      this world. Contact with the world became a test of
      man's ability to cleave to God. Buber's concept of
      hallowing the everyday must also be limited by the
      Hasidic division between the permitted and the forbidden,
      the clean and the unclean. Not everything was capable
      of being hallowed. Buber ignored the Hasidic desire to
      climb upward to encounter God, to transcend the encoun-
      ter with this world. The author believes that part of
      Buber's problem was his reliance on anecdotal Hasidic
      tales.

B377 Schilpp, Paul Arthur, and Maurice Friedman, eds. *The
      Philosophy of Martin Buber*. La Salle, Ill.: Open
      Court, 1967. 811 pp.

A collection of articles by and about Buber which,
in the present work, are entered by author under the
year 1967 (see items B339, B341, B343-B344, B346, B348-
B351, B356, B358-B365, B367-B368, B372, B374, B376,
B378-B379, B381-B385). There is an extensive index.

B378 Schneider, Herbert W. "The Historical Significance of
      Buber's Philosophy." *The Philosophy of Martin Buber*.
      Edited by Paul Arthur Schilpp and Maurice Friedman.
      La Salle, Ill.: Open Court, 1967, pp. 469-74.

      Discusses Buber's contribution to religious empiri-
      cism and socialism. Buber's work is in the tradition
      of empiricism's attempt to explain the meaning of God.
      He avoids the introspective search for a sense of the
      divine and places the religious experience in the inter-
      personal sphere, subject meeting subject. This emphasis
      on the interpersonal is also important in his interpre-
      tation of socialism. His is the socialism of personal
      sharing in a community.

B379 Simon, Ernst. "Martin Buber, the Educator." *The
      Philosophy of Martin Buber*. Edited by Paul Arthur
      Schilpp and Maurice Friedman. La Salle, Ill.: Open
      Court, 1967, pp. 543-76.

      A wide-ranging discussion of Buber's philosophy of
      education. The ideals of Jewish education for Buber
      are found in Hasidism and the early Kubbutz movement.
      The goal of education is to create a true community of
      individuals who stand together in their fullness before
      God. Aspects of this philosophy discussed here include
      the rise and the role of educational elites, the role
      of the teacher, the teacher-student relationship, the
      teacher's selection of the effective world, and the
      relationship between ethical education and civil edu-
      cation in an unredeemed world.

B380 Streiker, Lowell D. "Martin Buber." *Modern Theolo-
      gians: Christians and Jews*. Edited by Thomas E. Bird.
      Notre Dame, Ind.: University of Notre Dame Press,
      1967, pp. 1-17.

      Overview stressing Buber's interpretations of the I-
      Thou relationship, community, Hasidism, and Christianity.

B381 Taubes, Jacob. "Buber and Philosophy of History."
      The Philosophy of Martin Buber. Edited by Paul Arthur
      Schlipp and Maurice Friedman. La Salle, Ill.: Open
      Court, 1967, pp. 451-68.

Hegel, according to Buber, destroys the dialogical
meaning of history by reducing human decisions to sham
struggles. Buber traces Hegel's view to Paul's theology
of history. He compares Paul's closed apocalyptic
vision to the Jewish prophetic experience which pre-
serves the God-man dialogue and a history open to alternatives. The messianic figure of Deutero-Isaiah retains
this openness which Paul's Christology rejects. Buber
finds in history a series of charismatic experiences
which are transformed into routine by institutions. He
judges the course of history by these transformations.
The author contends that each charismatic experience
has added new forms of fellowship among men and endur-
ance and cohesion to social institutions.

B382   Wahl, Jean. "Martin Buber and the Philosophies of
       Existence." *The Philosophy of Martin Buber*. Edited
       by Paul Arthur Schilpp and Maurice Friedman. La
       Salle, Ill.: Open Court, 1967, pp. 475-510.

Buber is placed within the existentialist tradition
and his thought is compared with that of Kierkegaard,
Heidegger, Sartre, and, to a lesser extent, Jaspers and
Marcel.

B383   Weizsacker, Carl F. von. "I-Thou and I-It in the Con-
       temporary Natural Sciences." *The Philosophy of Martin
       Buber*. Edited by Paul Arthur Schilpp and Maurice
       Friedman. La Salle, Ill.: Open Court, 1967, pp. 603-7.

Suggests two ways the I-Thou relation enters modern
physics. A 'rudimentary' I-Thou relation exists between
the theoretical and experimental aspects of the physi-
cist's work. The I-Thou relation may also come into
play in the teamwork required in modern physics.

B384   Weltsch, Robert. "Buber's Political Philosophy." *The
       Philosophy of Martin Buber* Edited by Paul Arthur
       Schilpp and Maurice Friedman. La Salle, Ill.: Open
       Court, 1967, pp. 435-49.

In this century the pursuit of political goals has
been seen as the highest human duty for which men will
sacrifice everything, including traditional values.
There is no social activity which cannot become political. The danger is that political struggle leads to a
distortion and overriding of moral issues. The historical basis for this distortion is found in ancient
Judaism's idea of the chosen people exempt from moral

objections when its own destiny was at stake. To oppose
this, Buber suggests a conception of political activism
determined by social motives and moral ideas.

B385 Wheelwright, Philip. "Buber's Philosophical Anthro-
      pology." *The Philosophy of Martin Buber*. Edited by
      Paul Arthur Schilpp and Maurice Friedman. La Salle,
      Ill.: Open Court, 1967, pp. 69-95.

      Describes the lineage of philosophical anthropology
      from Kant through Ernst Cassirer to Buber. Buber de-
      fines man as a single one, in company with other single
      beings, whose vocation is to enter into relationship
      with these others. This is the antithesis of mysticism
      and egoism. Later Buber makes the category of person-
      hood twofold, involving both distancing and relation-
      ship. While they are mutually implicative, distancing
      is prior to relationship and may be in conflict with it.
      Relationship between persons also implies a divine-human
      relationship, discussed by Buber in terms of dialogue
      and the imitation of God. The author also discusses
      the possibility of more than two types of relationships,
      and what he considers Buber's overstatement of the case
      for the realm of the between.

B386 Wyschogrod, Michael. "Martin Buber." *Encyclopedia of
      Philosophy*. Vol. 1. New York: Macmillan Company
      and the Free Press, 1967, pp. 409-11.

      Brief overview.

                              1968

B387 Barker, E.T., and M.H. Mason. "Buber Behind Bars."
      Journal of the Canadian Psychiatric Association, 13
      (February 1968), 61-72.

      A description of a treatment program at a maximum
      security hospital which was based upon Buber's concepts
      of mental illness as a failure in communication and
      therapy as an attempt to recover wholeness through
      relationship. Very little about Buber.

B388 Beckerk, Ernest. *The Structure of Evil*. New York:
      George Braziller, 1968, pp. 259-64.

      Buber seen as continuing the thought of Charles
      Fourier and Ludwig Feuerbach, allowing for a fusion of
      idealist estehtics and self-psychology. Similarities
      also found between Buber and Max Scheler.

B389   Beek, M.A., and J. Sperna Weiland. *Martin Buber: Per-
        sonalist and Prophet.* New York: Newman Press, 1968.
        104 pp.

        An overview stressing Buber's interpretation of
        Judaism, and his views on man's relationships to man
        and to God. Buber's discovery of Hasidism was the be-
        ginning of a new way. The day-to-day Hasidic existence
        expressed for Buber the meaning of life, namely man's
        opportunity to collaborate with God's coming into the
        world. Buber was the first European thinker to devise
        an anthropology based upon dialogue and humanity in
        fellowship. The authors feel that the unity of Buber's
        work lies in his desire to build a truly human society.
        For Buber, humanism meant socialism, the structuring of
        society in such a way as to foster I-Thou relations.
        There is no index.

B390   Borowitz, Eugene B. *A New Jewish Theology in the Making.*
        Philadelphia: Westminster Press, 1968, pp. 123-46.

        Buber's accomplishment was that he identified a limit
        to technical reasoning, with its subordination of the
        personal to the impersonal, without denying its legiti-
        macy and usefulness. He defended the unique person
        against forces that would submerge him. His analysis
        of I-Thou relationships with man and God allows man to
        accept a reality beyond the realm of I-It. He developed
        a new language to describe this reality and with this
        language gave a new relevance to traditional religious
        categories. Although Buber speaks in terms of Jewish
        universalism, his devotion to the Bible and to Israel
        allowed him to set forth the particular Jewish calling.
        Three problems with Buber's thought are discussed:
        (1) the apparent lack of a firm basis for ethical stan-
        dards, (2) the relationship between the realms of I-
        Thou and I-It, and (3) Buber's rejection of Jewish reli-
        gious law.

B391   Campbell, Edward F., Jr. "Book Reviews." *Interpreta-
        tion,* 22 (April 1968), 226-7.

        Positive review of the *Kingship of God* (item A326)
        contrasting the views of Gerhard Von Rad and Buber on
        the Sinai covenant. The reviewer is critical of the
        translation and typographical errors contained in the
        book.

B392   Cook, Daniel J. "Buber in Translation." *Dimensions
        in American Judaism,* 2 (Summer 1968), 56-7.

In a review of *On Judaism* (item A327), argues that
Buber's views suffer from appeals to feelings and questionable facts. The worth of the book is in its illumi-
nation of Buber's cultural and intellectual origins.

B393 Downing, Christine. "Theology as Translation."
      Religion in Life, 37 (Autumn 1968), 401-16.

In translating the Hebrew Bible into German, Buber
was for the first time doing theology in the conventional sense of explicating scripture. Buber and Rosenzweig
saw their task as bringing the word of God to speaking-
ness so that it could be heard again. It must address
us, be experienced as revelation. For this encounter
the Bible must be taken out of the commonplace and be
made unfamiliar. This required the translators to
renew and reshape the German language. Buber wanted to
return to the original oral quality for which the
written Bible is only the preserving form. He recognized the theological basis for the inseparability of
form and content.

B394 Fair, Bryan J. "Martin Buber and Some Theologians of
      'Encounter.'" *Scottish Journal of Theology*, 21
      (March 1968), 27-36.

In a discussion of several encounter theologians,
states that many interpreters of Buber err in assuming
that his use of the term 'Thou' is similar to its use
by Christian theologians. They ignore the fact that
Buber's 'Thou' is applied to both personal and non-
personal beings. Further, the author denies that Buber
claims a knowledge of other persons independent of a
knowledge about them.

B395 Frankenstein, Carl. "Buber's Theory of Dialogue: A
      Critical Re-Examination." *Cross Currents*, 18 (Spring
      1968), 229-41.

The author rejects the view that the partner in a
dialogue is a Thou. Rather he sees him as another independent I. The dichotomy is I and Non-I, not I and
Thou. This separate I has an existence regardless of
whether I address him or not. Responsibility is not,
as Buber claims, identical with the response demanded
from another, but rather the readiness to transcend my
I-position to help the other become a fuller I. A
true dialogic relationship exists only when I am willing
to become the object of another. It is an act of

conscious awareness on the part of both the I and the
non-I, and does not exist in some "between" realm. The
authenticity of the relationship is demonstrated by what
each I gets out of it. Buber also overlooks man's relation to his own inner life. He rejects the necessary
dialogue between the I and the inner non-I. The early
development of the child and the therapeutic process
are discussed in Jungian terms, as opposed to the I-Thou
framework. Finally the author objects to Buber's use
of the God-man relationship as the prototype of dialogue.

B396 Friedman, Maurice. "Martin Buber and Pacifism."
      Shalom, December 1968.

      (Not available for annotating.)

B397 Glatzer, Nahum N. "Editor's Postscript to *On the Bible:*
      Eighteen Studies, by Martin Buber. New York:
      Schocken Books, 1968, pp. 233-40.

      An overview of Buber's studies of the Hebrew Bible.
      Focuses on the Buber-Rosenzweig translation of the
      Bible, the theme of the kingdom of God, and the role of
      the prophets.

B398 Gordon, Rosemary. "Transference as a Fulcrum of Analy-
      sis." *Journal of Analytical Psychology*, 13 (July
      1968), 109-17.

      Suggests the I-It attitude corresponds to a trans-
      ference relationship.

B399 Hodes, Aubrey. "Arab-Jewish Rapprochement: Buber's
      Plea for Arab-Jewish Understanding." *Wiener Library*
      Bulletin, 23 (Winter 1968-69), 16-23.

      From his first major public stand on Jewish-Arab
      cooperation in 1921 until his death, Buber worked for
      rapprochement between the two peoples. He rejected
      Gandhi's suggestion that the Jews stay in Germany be-
      cause without the land of Israel, Jewish dispersion
      would lead to dismemberment. While he saw that parti-
      tion would lead to war, and objected to the growing
      militaristic trend in the Jewish community, he was not
      a pacifist. After the establishment of Israel until
      his death, he took an active role in defending the civil
      rights of Israel's Arab citizens.

B400 Lelyveld, Arthur J. *Atheism Is Dead: A Jewish Response to Radical Theology*. Cleveland: World Publishing, 1968, pp. 143-55.

Compares the thought of Buber and John MacMurray. For both the starting point is the individual human being in relationship with others and with God. But while MacMurray's personalism leads to a morality based upon interpersonal relationships, for Buber the proper basis is dialogue with the Eternal Thou. The author argues that MacMurray's stress on relationships between agents restricts the area of the personal, and his cognitive approach to philosophy results in talk about God rather than addressing God in a lived relationship.

B401 Lewis, Theodore N. "Buber in Translation." *Dimensions in American Judaism*, 2 (Summer 1968), 56+.

A brief review of *Kingship of God* (item A326) in which the reviewer criticizes the literal translation of the German which resulted in difficult and often unintelligible English.

B402 Marty, Martin. "The Man Who Passed through Gateways." *New York Times Book Review*, 14 April 1968, pp. 6-7+.

Positive reviews of *On Judaism* (item A327) and *A Believing Humanism* (item A261) containing a brief overview of Buber's thought. Feels that Buber is not immediately accessible to many readers today because of the nonspiritual and dehumanizing direction of both eastern and western society.

B403 Murti, V.V. Ramana. "Buber's Dialogue and Gandhi's Satyagraha." *Journal of the History of Ideas*, 29 (October-December 1968), 605-13.

In correspondence between Gandhi and Buber prior to the Second World War, Gandhi suggested satyagraha methods, non-violent resistance and voluntary suffering, be used by the Jews in Nazi Germany and Palestine. Buber replied that these methods were inappropriate in the two situations. The author discusses the similarities between the goals of satyagraha and Buber's philosophy of dialogue. The methods practiced by Gandhi in India may be a means of implementing dialogue between peoples in conflict.

B404 Oliver, Roy. *The Wanderer and the Way: The Hebrew
        Tradition in the Writings of Martin Buber*. Ithaca,
        N.Y.: Cornell University Press, 1968. 168 pp.

      The Hebrew Bible is used as a base from which to
      understand Buber's Hasidic writings and his philosophy
      of dialogue. Seven personalities, Adam, Noah, Abraham,
      Moses, the Psalmist, Isaiah, and Isaiah's servant-
      messiah, are studied in terms of themes appearing in
      Buber's interpretation of each personality, the treat-
      ment of these themes in his other writings, and reflec-
      tion of these themes in the major events in Buber's
      life. There is no index.

B405 Reines, Alvin J. "Book Review." *Jewish Social Studies*,
        30 (April 1968), 122-4.

      A negative review of *The Knowledge of Man* (item A229)
      and *The Origin and Meaning of Hasidism* (item A193).
      Finds fault with Buber's 'thoroughgoing subjectivity,'
      suggesting that it may have led him to overemphasize
      the importance of the Hasidic movement and the I-Thou
      relation. The reviewer also objects to Buber's criti-
      cism of the Freudian concept of the unconscious.

B406 Santmire, H. Paul. "I-Thou, I-It, and I-Ens." *Journal
        of Religion*, 48 (July 1968), 260-73.

      Conceiving of the I-Thou relation as occurring exclu-
      sively between persons creates difficulties when talking
      about an individual's relations with his body, the
      natural world, and God. If these are considered I-Thou
      relations, we come to a limit of our knowledge. One
      solution, rejected by the author, is pan-psychism. A
      better solution is to speak of a third type of relation,
      termed the I-Ens relation. It describes an aspect of
      human relatedness not covered by Buber or other con-
      temporary thinkers.

B407 Scudder, John R., Jr. "Freedom with Authority: A
        Buber Model for Teaching." *Educational Theory*, 18
        (Spring 1968), 133-42.

      Buber's model for education achieves a balance
      between authority and freedom. His philosophy of dia-
      logue is contrasted with the "rule model" of Israel
      Scheffler. This model presupposes generally accepted
      fundamental principles by which we judge experience.
      Teaching involves transmitting these principles. The

author believes that there are no such principles accepted today by the intellectual community. In the dialogue model the teacher presents his own relationship with the truth along with alternatives gained through his own dialogue with the academic world. The teacher is not an objective oracle but one who enters into an I-Thou relationship with the world, his discipline, and his students. Thus the teacher may function as an authority, based upon this dialogue with his discipline, while allowing each student the freedom to develop as an individual.

B408   Stahmer, Harold. *"Speak that I May See Thee!" The Religious Significance of Language*. New York: Macmillan, 1968, pp. 183-212, 251-78.

A book on the religious significance of the spoken word. An overview of Buber's thought is included, emphasizing the central position he gives to the relational aspect of the spoken word. The author traces the development of this position from Buber's earlier philosophical interests through his major writings, and its influence upon his interpretation of Judaism, the Hebrew Bible, Hasidism, and his philosophy of dialogue. Buber's position is then compared with that of Franz Rosenzweig, Ferdinand Ebner, Søren Kierkegaard, and Eugen Rosenstock-Huessy.

B409   Troy, Philip. "Buber in the Secular City." *Listening*, 3 (Winter 1968), 56-61.

Harvey Cox, in his book *The Secular City* (item B257), stated that Buber's I-Thou, I-It typology was not suitable for urban man. Cox posited an area between these poles where it would be possible to be completely human without being intimate. An I-You category would recognize that urban man cannot have deep personal relationships with everyone he meets and yet does not want to reduce them to objects. However, as Buber defined these relationships, one either responds with one's whole being or with part of his being. Thus Cox's third category has no meaning.

B410   Van Til, Cornelius. *Christ and the Jews*. Philadelphia: Presbyterian and Reform Publishing Company, 1968, pp. 25-61.

An evaluation of Buber's theology, particularly that concerning Jesus and Paul, from an exclusively Christian point of view. "He who is not a Christian is not, properly speaking, a theist." "The true nature of dialogue between God and man can be understood only by those who know God through Jesus Christ...." Reviews five modern interpreters of Buber who see his philosophy, together with that of modern Protestant followers of Kant and Kierkegaard, as a foundation for the church of the future. Argues that basic to the Christian interpretation of Buber must be his denial of Jesus as messiah.

1969

B411 Agassi, Joseph. "Can Religion Go Beyond Reason?" *Zygon*, 4 (June 1969), 128-68.

Argues that true religion is the quest of scientific research. There are, however, attempts being made to retain traditional religious outlooks in forms compatible with science, and to revive ritual and faith in an effort to find meaning. Buber's thought is seen as one example of religion revived as a way of life. The author feels that his efforts have been unsuccessful. He criticizes Buber's belief that commitment is a precondition of rationality. He also finds fault with Buber's approach to faith, prayer, and interpretation of the Bible.

B412 Beerman, Rene. "Soviet-Jewish Philosophers, Existentialism, and Buber." *Bulletin on Soviet and East European Jewish Affairs*, No. 3 (January 1969), 20-4.

Reviews one negative overview of Buber's thought by the Soviet writer G.L. Bakanurskii.

B413 Bettis, Joseph D., ed. *Phenomenology of Religion*. New York: Harper and Row, 1969, pp. 219-23.

In a brief introduction to excerpts from *I and Thou* (item A17), the editor relates Buber's thought to that of Ludwig Feuerbach.

B414 Bridges, William E. "Transcendentalism and Psychotherapy: Another Look at Emerson." *American Literature*, 41 (May 1969), 157-77.

Briefly finds similarities in Emerson's concepts of self-reliance and friendship, and Buber's I-Thou relations. Believes the transcendental movement prefigured positions taken by Buber.

B415   Downing, Christine R. "Guilt and Responsibility in the
       Thought of Martin Buber." *Judaism*, 18 (Winter 1969),
       53-63.

       For Buber guilt is the result of the failure to re-
       spond to a legitimate address or claim upon us. This
       may come from another person or from our true potential,
       our true selves. Guilt is ontological as well as patho-
       logical. Existential guilt occurs when one injures the
       order of the human world. Responsibility is learned
       from this failure to relate.

B416   Etscovitz, Lionel. "Martin Buber's Challenge to Educa-
       tional Philosophy." *Philosophy of Education Proceed-
       ings: 1969.* Edwardsville, Ill.: Philosophy of
       Education Society, 1969, pp. 113-9.

       For Buber, the contemporary educational situation
       reflects a crisis in life as a whole, the split between
       the rational and the irrational view of man. It is a
       dialogical crisis which involves not only a loss of
       relation but also a loss of valuation. Education today
       does not encourage or provide the opportunity for
       choice. This is reflected in an emphasis upon the past
       in the form of facts, ignoring the present and the
       future. An exploration of the implications of Buber's
       philosophy of dialogue for education will lead to a
       reconciliation of rationalism and irrationalism.

B417   Etscovitz, Lionel. "Religious Education as Sacred and
       Profane: An Interpretation of Martin Buber." *Reli-
       gious Education*, 64 (July-August 1969), 279-86.

       Buber's concepts of relation and separation discussed
       in terms of their use in developing values. The dialogi-
       cal crisis of our time results in man's separation from
       God and from man. Without meeting God in the everyday,
       man is left without a center of valuing. There is a
       failure to unite the religious and the ethical dimen-
       sions of his relationships with his fellow men. The
       goal of religious education has become the teaching of
       timeless truth and isolated spirituality rather than
       the sacredness of existence. Buber's educational thought
       is contrasted with that of Plato, whose prophetic empha-
       sis on the future lacks relevancy to life, and John
       Dewey, whose therapeutic emphasis lacks a sense of mis-
       sion beyond the present. Buber's thought unites these
       prophetic and therapeutic aspects of education.

B418   Friedman, Maurice. *Martin Buber and the Theater*. New
       York: Funk and Wagnalls, 1969, 170 pp.

       Three essays by Friedman and four by Buber. The first
       two essays by Friedman are an historical approach to
       Buber's involvement with the theater, starting with
       his student days in Vienna through his relation with
       the playwright Hugo von Hofmannsthal. The third of
       Friedman's essays is an introduction to "Elijah" and a
       discussion of the play's relationship to various aspects
       of Buber's thought.

B419   Goes, Albrecht. "In Memoriam Martin Buber." *Men of
       Dialogue: Martin Buber and Albrecht Goes*. Edited by
       William Rollins and Harry Zohn. New York: Funk and
       Wagnalls, 1969, pp. 276-7.

       Brief eulogy.

B420   Goes, Albrecht. "Martin Buber, A Living Legend."
       Men of Dialogue: Martin Buber and Albrecht Goes.
       Edited by William Rollins and Harry Zohn. New York:
       Funk and Wagnalls, 1969, pp. 185-203.

       In an address given on Buber's eightieth birthday,
       Goes gives an overview of Buber's life and thought.

B421   Goes, Albrecht. "Martin Buber, Our Support." *Men of
       Dialogue: Martin Buber and Albrecht Goes*. Edited by
       William Rollins and Harry Zohn. New York: Funk and
       Wagnalls, 1969, pp. 12-9.

       Reprint of item B122.

B422   Goes, Albrecht. "The 'Patriarch' from Jerusalem."
       Men of Dialogue: Martin Buber and Albrecht Goes.
       Edited by William Rollins and Harry Zohn. New York:
       Funk and Wagnalls, 1969, pp. 204-14.

       A 1962 address describing the author's encounters
       with Buber's works and with Buber himself.

B423   Goes, Albrecht. "A Solid House." *Men of Dialogue:
       Martin Buber and Albrecht Goes*. Edited by William
       Rollins and Harry Zohn. New York: Funk and Wagnalls,
       1969, pp. 217-9.

       Briefly recounts the circumstances of the death of
       Buber's wife.

B424   Granatstein, Melvin. "Are the Ikkarim Intelligible?"
       Tradition, 10 (Fall 1969), 15-21.

       Uses Buber's concept of the I-Thou relation to show
       that man's meeting with God may be intelligible and
       verifiable, thus making it possible to talk about reli-
       gious claims.

B425   Haberman, Joshua O. "Franz Rosenzweig's Doctrine of
       Revelation." *Judaism*, 18 (Summer 1969), 320-36.

       In an article on Rosenzweig, briefly discusses his
       debate with Buber on Jewish law. While Rosenzweig saw
       the law as God's living command, Buber saw it as man's
       own creation in response to an encounter with God.

B426   Kegley, Charles W. "Martin Buber's Ethics and the
       Problems of Norms." *Religious Studies*, 5 (December
       1969), 181-94.

       Buber was generally skeptical of philosophical ethics
       which he believed lacked religious insights and moti-
       vational power. Ethics must be God-related. The onto-
       logical ground of the good is the will of God. The
       author attacks Buber's position on two main points:
       (1) that to do good is to do the will of God, and
       (2) the lack of criteria to judge ethical decisions.
       Buber claims that in a dialogue each situation provides
       its own interpretation, but he fails to provide cri-
       teria to judge the correctness of that interpretation.
       This has the sound of dangerous subjectivism. Buber's
       thought makes clear the need for action-guiding norms
       in ethics.

B427   Kiner, Edward D. "Martin Buber's Concept of 'Living
       Truth' and Jewish Education." *CCAR Journal*, 16
       (April 1969), 73-6.

       The concept of "living truth," of truth found
       through authentic living, is applied to the roles of
       the teacher and the student.

B428   Kiner, Edward D. "Some Problems in a Buber Model for
       Teaching." *Educational Theory*, 19 (Fall 1969),
       396-403.

       A response to Scudder's proposal (item B407) to use
       Buber's philosophy as a paradigm for the teaching pro-
       cess. Treats two problems in Scudder's article, that
       of norms and models in Buber's thought, and Scudder's

"dialogue with the academic world." The author feels
that Buber's concept of the "great character" implies
norms and models which Scudder overlooked when he rejected the existence of generally accepted principles
of thought and action. Furthermore, Scudder states
that the teacher's authority is derived from an I-Thou
"dialogue with the academic world." The author has
difficulty defining this phrase. Does it mean a dialogue with texts, facts, and ideas? This seems to be
counter to Buber's definition of dialogue. But grant-
ing this dialogue is possible, how does one distinguish
between a valid and invalid dialogue with the academic
world? The author attempts to formulate this concept
in terms of Scudder's goals.

B429 Lewis, H.D. "The Elusive Self and the I-Thou Relation."
        Talk of God. Royal Institute of Philosophy Lectures
        1967-1968. London: Macmillan, 1969, pp. 168-84.

        Discusses the following problems in Buber's thought:
        (1) the self exists only in certain relations; (2) the
        distinction between inner and outer things is passed
        over too lightly; (3) the religious aspect of the I-Thou
        relation tends to eclipse its other aspects; (4) empha-
        sis on the encounter with God without knowledge about
        God turns religion into a mere sense of the being of
        God; (5) any information on how this relationship takes
        place is thus precluded; (6) we never treat another
        person strictly as a thing, as an It; (7) the moment of
        standing in relation is, to man and to God, too detached
        from the content of previous experiences.

B430 May, Harry S. "Martin Buber and Mohammed Iqbal: Two
        Poets of East and West." *Judaism*, 18 (Spring 1969),
        177-87.

        Believes that Iqbal, an Indian Muslim thinker and
        poet, was indebted to Buber for many of his religious
        ideas. Both tried to bring their people back to their
        heritage utilizing the Bible and the Koran. Iqbal's
        description of the "I" and its relationship with God is
        similar to Buber's I-Thou relationship.

B431 Moore, Stanley R. "Religion as the True Humanism:
        Reflections on Kierkegaard's Social Philosophy."
        Journal of the American Academy of Religion, 37
        (March 1969), 15-25.

        Argues against Buber's thesis that anti-humanism lies
        at the heart of Kierkegaard's thinking.

B432 Morgan, George W. "Martin Buber and Some of His
      Critics." *Judaism*, 18 (Spring 1969), 232-41.

      A review essay of *The Philosophy of Martin Buber*
      (item B377). The author feels that much of the criti-
      cism of Buber contained in this book is the result of
      the critics' inclination to philosophize. They mani-
      fest presuppositions characteristic of Western philo-
      sophy and react against the lack of these presupposi-
      tions in Buber's thought. They are concerned with
      systematizations, universal propositions, and criteria
      for testing the validity of beliefs and actions. They
      overlook the unique form of philosophizing which char-
      acterizes Buber's work.

B433 Morrison, Harriet B. "The Successful Teacher." *Pea-
      body Journal of Education*, 47 (November 1969), 156-9.

      Uses Buber's I-Thou relation as a paradigm for the
      successful teacher. Emphasizes the need for the teacher
      to encourage the formation of a community in the class-
      room. Education is seen ultimately as the development
      of character.

B434 Mulligan, Joseph E. "Teilhard and Buber." *Religion
      in Life*, 38 (Autumn 1969), 362-82.

      A comparison of the two thinkers on seven shared
      positions. Both viewed the world sacramentally, believ-
      ing that God presents himself to us in the everyday
      world. Related to this is their belief that the reli-
      gious man is responsible for this everyday world. Both
      define the person as an individual-in-relation. On the
      question of freedom, they see freedom *from* as a prelimi-
      nary to freedom *to*. Both feel that the true community
      requires a center: for Teilhard, Christ; and for Buber,
      God. On the question of mysticism, they take pains to
      separate themselves from the pantheistic concept of the
      absorption in the All. On the last point of comparison,
      evolution, the author finds evidence that Buber might
      have been receptive to Teilhard's insights.

B435 Nissenson, Hugh. "An Event of the Night." *Jewish
      Heritage*, 11 (Summer 1969), 37-41.

      Report of an interview in which Buber discussed the
      holocaust and the problem of evil in the context of
      monotheism.

B436 Oliver, Roy. "Martin Buber's Vision." *Jewish
      Quarterly*, 17 (Winter 1969), 46-7.

      A review of *A Believing Humanism* (item A261), *On
      Judaism* (item A327), and *The Philosophy of Martin Buber*
      (item B377). While the more orthodox Jews rejected
      Buber's views on Jewish law, the author feels that his
      influence on Judaism as a whole is still an open
      question.

B437 Rudavsky, David. "Martin Buber's Existentialism:
      Sources, Influences and Interpretation." *Journal of
      Hebraic Studies*, 1 (1969), 41-59.

      An overview of Buber's philosophical and religious
      thought which the author sees as an attempt to formu-
      late a religious faith midway between conventional
      religion and the godlessness of the modern age.

B438 Sadler, William A., Jr. "Witnesses to Love: Some Con-
      tributions of Martin Buber and Gabriel Marcel."
      Existence and Love. New York: Charles Scribner's
      Sons, 1969, pp. 96-105.

      Contrasts Heidegger's affirmation of being in the
      face of death with Buber's I-Thou relationship, as an
      approach to the wholeness of the individual. Wonders
      if Buber's emphasis upon relationship does justice to
      what individualists such as Heidegger and Kirkegaard
      mean when they speak of authentic individual existence.
      Buber's ambivalence toward freedom, lodging it in rela-
      tionship, overlooks the individual who is burdened with
      relationships that curtail his freedom. The problem of
      verifying Buber's anthropological statements is also
      discussed.

B439 Schreiber, Mordecai. "Rav Kuk and Martin Buber on
      Teshuvah." *CCAR Journal*, 16 (June 1969), 31-5.

      Compares their use of the concept of teshuvah (repen-
      tance or returning to God) and finds them very similar.
      While Kuk spoke in the traditional kabbalistic language,
      Buber spoke in terms of turning, of entering into an
      I-Thou relation. Both saw teshuvah as existing on
      three levels: that of the individual, that of Israel,
      and that of the world. For both, all three levels were
      inter-related and interdependent.

B440   Scott, Nathan A., Jr. "Martin Buber--Guide to the
       World of Thou." *The Unique Vision: Mirrors of Man in
       Existentialism.* New York: World Publishing Company,
       1969, pp. 150-79.

       An overview of Buber's philosophy of dialogue as an
       example of religious existentialism.

B441   Shaffer, Carolyn R. "A Jewish View of Redemption."
       Commonweal, 22 August 1969, pp. 512-5.

       The Hasidic basis of Buber's "hallowing of the every-
       day" gives religious overtones to an essentially secular
       message. While the goal of one's life is an intimate
       relationship with God, this is accomplished not through
       seeking God directly, but through concentrating on
       everyday life and one's relationships with his fellows.
       He thus relegates the notion of God to a peripheral
       position. "Hallowing of the everyday" is, in fact, a
       secular concept with the trappings of religious language

B442   Silberman, Lou H. "Concerning Jewish Theology in North
       America: Some Notes on a Decade." *American Jewish
       Year Book*, 70 (1969), 37-58.

       In a general article on current Jewish theology, sug-
       gests that Buber's influence is more pervasive than
       depicted by some writers. He and Franz Rosenzweig have
       made it possible for non-traditionalists to understand
       the thought and the deeds of Judaism. Briefly discusses
       Eliezer Berkovits' and Mordecai Kaplan's expositions of
       Buber's views on Judaism.

B443   Simon, Charlie M. *Martin Buber: Wisdom in Our Time.*
       New York: Dutton, 1969. 191 pp.

       A biography covering the whole of Buber's life and a
       superficial presentation of his thought. Appears to
       have been written for younger readers. There is a sub-
       ject index.

B444   Streiker, Lowell D. *The Promise of Buber.* Philadel-
       phia: J.B. Lippincott, 1969. 92 pp.

       An introduction to Buber's thought and its applica-
       tion to modern life. Sees Buber's greatest accomplish-
       ment as his attempt to demonstrate the relevance of
       the ancient faith of Judaism to contemporary life. His
       central teachings, the life of dialogue and the in-
       separability of the God-man dialogue from the man-man

dialogue, relate his understanding of this Jewish way
of life. Buber's primary struggle was that of a religious man with an unredeemed world. Particular emphasis
is placed upon Buber's concept of good and evil. There
is no index.

B445 Vogel, Manfred. "Buber's Ethics and Contemporary
      Ethical Options." *Philosophy Today*, 13 (Spring
      1969), 3-18.

Most current approaches to ethics fall within two
radically different approaches, one whose guidelines
are the ideal requirements of the ethical, and the
other whose guidelines are the authentic capacity of
the human. Buber's ethical formulation attempts to
satisfy the basic considerations of each and is an alternative to both. It avoids having to take either an
objective or subjective stance, and has the advantage
of maintaining an absolutist formulation while at the
same time remaining situational.

B446 Weiner, Herbert. *9½ Mystics: The Kabbala Today*. New
      York: Holt, Rinehart and Winston, 1969, pp. 109-39.

While agreeing that Buber presented the message of
Hasidism in terms acceptable to the modern Western mind,
the author criticizes his interpretation from two points
of view. First, he reiterates Gersham Scholem's argu-
ments (see index). Second, he compares Buber's concept
of Hasidism with an existing Hasidic community, the
Belz Hasidim, and finds a strong element of the absurd
ignored by Buber.

B447 Wood, Robert E. *Martin Buber's Ontology: An Analysis
      of I and Thou*. Evanston, Ill.: Northwestern Univer-
      sity Press, 1969. 139 pp.

A systematic analysis of *I and Thou* (item A17), beginning with an overview of Buber's life and thought,
followed by sections on the plan of the book, the
philosophy of dialogue, the person and the social environment, God and the God-man relationship, and the
ontological foundation of the work. There is an index.

B448   Berkovits, Eliezer. "God's Silence in the Dialogue
        According to Martin Buber." *Tradition*, 11 (Summer
        1970), 17-24.

        Buber's attempt to establish a dialogical basis for
        ethical absoluteness is seen as a failure. Man's dia-
        logue with God, as conceived by Buber, cannot form
        this basis because (1) it is contentless and therefore
        gives man no objective way to judge his subsequent
        behavior, and (2) man has no obligation to enter into
        the dialogue in the first place.

B449   Buchanan, Scott. "Second Edition/Civil Disobedience:
        Martin Buber." *Center Magazine*, May-June 1970,
        pp. 65-8.

        To illuminate the problem of civil disobedience, uses
        Buber's concept of Jewish law as a teacher or questions
        to be pursued, rather than dogma to be accepted.

B450   Cohen, Aharon. *Israel and the Arab World*. Translated
        by Aubrey Hodes, Naomi Handelman, and Miriam Shimeoni.
        New York: Funk and Wagnalls, 1970, pp. 239-42.

        Brief discussion of Buber's early concern about
        Jewish-Arab relations in Palestine and the effect of
        this concern on the Zionist movement.

B451   Curtis, Charles J. "Christianity and Judaism: Buber."
        Contemporary Protestant Thought. New York: Bruce
        Publishing Co., 1970, pp. 117-33.

        An overview stressing the philosophy of dialogue,
        Hasidism, and Zionism.

B452   Dale, John. "Martin Buber's Semantic Puzzle."
        Religious Studies, 6 (September 1970), 253-61.

        An analysis of Buber's use of language, particularly
        as seen in *I and Thou* (item A17). Discusses his pre-
        ference for nominal rather than verbal expressions,
        the rhetorical richness of his language, and its
        anthropological and dialogic status. For Buber language
        is a basic capacity of the human community, existing
        between men rather than within the various individuals.
        His nominal syntax is the result of this focus on the
        interhuman. His nouns are not names but human events
        that cannot be analyzed in conceptual terms. He must

depend upon metaphor to express much of his thought.
The author likens Buber's literary form not to poetry
or an account of mysticism, but to literary criticism.

B453 DeVitis, Joseph L. "Ethical and Educational Autonomy
in Buber's 'Great Character.'" *Journal of Critical
Analysis*, 2 (July 1970), 13-9.

Buber defines his "great character" as a person who
transcends and yet penetrates man's habitual context.
Before man can enter into mutual relationships, he must
achieve autonomy. He uses the technique of distancing,
or learning to see what he experiences as independent
existents. With distancing comes the development of
genuine communication and "dialectical inner line," the
ethical line of demarcation between oneself and the
other. The person is thus freed from his dependence
upon the world's values. Buber's paradox is that only
an autonomous person can build genuine relationships.
But is the great character beyond norms? According to
Buber he responds to commands of the spirit and dialogical existence before earthly norms. The purpose of
education is to bring each member of the community up
to this level of personhood.

B454 Edwards, Paul. *Buber and Buberism: A Critical Evaluation*. Lawrence, Kan.: University of Kansas, Department of Philosophy, 1970. 49 pp.

Buber's theology "cannot withstand critical scrutiny
and ... is a melange of dogmatisms, non-sequiturs, inconsistencies, and evasions." Evaluates Buber's I-Thou
and I-It relationships, his concept of God, and his
description of the hiddenness of God. Buber's concept
of the I-Thou relation incorrectly implies: (1) a break-
down of determinism, (2) the possibility of an I-Thou
relationship with an inanimate object, (3) an unneces-
sary redefinition of 'presentness,' and (4) the impos-
sibility of a conceptual representation of this
relationship. Buber's concept of God is derived from
religious experience, but he offers no criteria to distinguish authentic from illusory experience. The author
questions the very existence of these experiences.
Also, while Buber affirms God's ineffability, he appears
to have a good deal of knowledge about his nature and
his intentions. Lastly, Buber's concept of the hiddenness of God does not avoid the specter of a God of
perfect goodness allowing great evil.

B455   Friedman, Maurice. "Martin Buber's Encounter with
       Mysticism." *Human Inquiry: Review of Existential
       Psychology and Psychiatry*, 10 (1970), 43-81.

       An historical treatment of the effect of various
       mystical writers on Buber's thought. Particular atten-
       tion is paid to the influence of Jacob Boehme, Meister
       Eckhart, Nicholas of Cusa, Buddhism, Hinduism, Taoism,
       and Gustav Landauer. Mysticism gave Buber a new approac
       to reality, enabling him to break through the sense of
       aloneness and the superficiality fostered by mass cul-
       ture to the immediacy of the spiritual life. But it
       also served to cut him off from the claim of the im-
       mediate moment. This dividing of the inner and outer
       life, with a higher value placed on the inner, is what
       Buber later rejected. His conversion of 1916 did not
       mean, however, that he rejected mysticism completely.
       It continued to influence his thought.

B456   Friedman, Maurice. "Revelation and Reason in Buber's
       Philosophy of Religion." *Bucknell Review*, 18 (Fall
       1970), 69-77.

       Reason can function as a means of communicating the
       experience of faith and the reality of relationship.
       But if reason demands that all other faculties become
       subordinate to it, it becomes dubious. Revelation for
       Buber is neither fixed objective truth nor subjective
       inspiration, but address and response. The content of
       revelation is the reality one meets and responds to
       each moment.

B457   Hawton, Hector. *The Feast of Unreason*. Westport,
       Conn.: Greenwood Press, 1970, pp. 141-3.

       Discusses the I-Thou relation as solipsism and an
       attack on objective knowledge necessary for science.

B458   Hopper, Stanley Romaine. "The 'Eclipse of God' and
       Existential Mistrust." *Eastern Buddhist*, n.s. 3
       (October 1970), pp. 46-70.

       Uses Buber's concepts of the eclipse of God and mis-
       trust to introduce a discussion of these topics. Finds
       neither concept radical enough to embrace the predica-
       ment of modern man. Believes we also lack the grammar
       for grasping Buber's existential relations.

B459   Kaplan, Edward K. "Bachelard and Buber: From Aesthetics
       to Religion." *Judaism*, 19 (Fall 1970), 456-7.

       Contends that the philosophy of Gaston Bachelard is
       helpful in understanding the first two sections of *I
       and Thou* (item A17).

B460   Kaufmann, Walter. "I and You: A Prologue." *I and
       Thou*, by Martin Buber. Translated by Walter Kaufmann.
       New York: Charles Scribner's Sons, 1970, pp. 9-48.

       A long and curious introduction to his translation.
       Although Kaufmann acknowledges the significant ideas
       contained in the book, including the sacredness of the
       here and now, God as subject rather than object, and
       the endowment of the social sphere with a religious
       dimension, he implies that Buber has deceived his
       readers by simplifying the world as his readers wish to
       have it simplified. He rejects Buber's twofold world
       for a manifold world. He also implies that Buber is
       deliberately obscure. Kaufmann's writing style often
       appears to mimic Buber's own style.

B461   Martin, Bernard. "Martin Buber." *Great Twentieth
       Century Jewish Philosophers*. New York: Macmillan
       Company, 1970, pp. 238-65.

       Overview emphasizing Buber's I-Thou, I-It relation-
       ships, his interpretation of the Bible, and his teach-
       ing about God. Criticizes Buber's refusal to recognize
       the centrality of the Sinai event which leads him to a
       weak and unsatisfactory view of the Torah and the
       Halakhah.

B462   Moore, Donald J. "Martin Buber on Jesus: A Jewish
       Reading." *America*, 13 June 1970, pp. 630-3.

       Buber confronted Christians with a knowledge of Jesus
       inaccessible to the non-Jew, a knowledge of his Jewish-
       ness. For Buber Jesus was a Jew to the core, one of a
       series of suffering servants. The mystery of these
       messianic servants is rooted in their hiddenness. But
       Jesus stepped out of this hiddenness. He became the
       first of the auto-Messiahs, a mishap in the relations
       between man and God. Jesus lived in openness to God
       and wished to bring others to this openness. He warded
       off belief in himself. Thus the deification of Jesus
       is in opposition to what he taught. It destroys the
       immediacy between man and God.

B463   Mosse, George L.   "The Influence of the Volkish Idea on
       German Jewry." *Germans and Jews*. New York: Howard
       Fertig, 1970, pp. 85-94.

       Buber was much influenced in his early attempts to
       revitalize Judaism by a revival of interest in the
       German mystics and by the Volkish movement. His Hasi-
       dism served a purpose similar to that of mystical thought
       in the Volkish idea, and his use of myth closely paral-
       leled important German writers of the time. The author
       argues that this relationship between Buber's interpre-
       tation of Judaism and the then-current German ideas, as
       well as his substitution of mysticism and intuition for
       the traditional context of Jewish religion, introduced
       a vagueness into the quest for a Jewish identity and
       made it difficult to disentangle the Jewish from the
       German.

B464   Sachs, Mendel.   "Positivism, Realism, and Existentialism
       in Mach's Influence on Contemporary Physics."
       Philosophy and Phenomenological Research, 30 (March
       1970), 403-20.

       Briefly notes that Buber's I-Thou and I-It relation-
       ships are consistent with the Mach principle in rela-
       tivity theory.

B465   Sevilla, Pedro C.   *God as Person in the Writings of
       Martin Buber*. Manila: Atenco de Manila University,
       Loyola House of Studies, 1970.   170 pp.

       While Buber rejects any tendency to reduce God to the
       realm of the finite, he also insists on the necessity
       of describing God as a person, believing that while we
       cannot know God's essential being, whatever God is, he
       is also a person. Buber's view is derived from the
       biblical description of God as entering into direct
       relationships with men. The author analyzes Buber's
       concepts of relationship and personhood and applies
       them to the biblical description of God and his inter-
       actions with the people of ancient Israel. For Buber
       these interactions were historical events, experienced
       by a faithful people as the actions of God. The author
       takes issue with Buber's ambivalent attitude toward
       using philosophy to understand these events. He ques-
       tions whether the dialogical principle is sufficient
       to explain the development of human thought and under-
       standing. Insights and images gained in previous
       encounters can be used to enrich future encounters.

Reflection is as indispensable as dialogue. The author then attempts to develop a theory of cognition which will harmonize with Buber's writings. There is an index.

B466 Vogel, Manfred. "The Concept of Responsibility in the Thought of Martin Buber." *Harvard Theological Review*, 63 (April 1970), 159-82.

Buber's thought is based upon one fundamental insight consisting of two parts: (1) primary reality lies in relation, and (2) there are two kinds of relation, I-Thou, and I-It. Buber's ethics are based upon this ontological principle. His fundamental ethical concept is that of responsibility, responsibility for responding and responsibility to a Thou. This Thou has been given two formulations, the true self and the Absolute Thou. But the true self is an It and therefore cannot be grounded in the I-Thou relation. Only the Absolute Thou provides a source of responsibility which is not only absolute but a Thou. Thus Buber's ethics are not an independent system but are grounded in his ontological formulation and culminate in his religious formulation.

B467 Wijnhoven, Jochanan H.A. "Gersham G. Scholem: The Study of Jewish Mysticism." *Judaism*, 19 (Fall 1970), 468-81.

In an article on Scholem, Wijnhoven briefly contrasts his approach to the study of Hasidism with that of Buber. Buber stressed the subjective element of scholarship, the intuitive grasp of the essence, and the creative reformulation of the object of one's research. Scholem, a more academic scholar, accused Buber of distorting historical fact for the sake of a message. Buber's picture of Hasidism, for all its appeal, was not based on a study of Hasidic writings, but on anecdotal material.

B468 Wormann, Curt D. "German Jews in Israel: Their Cultural Situation Since 1933." *Leo Baeck Institute Year Book*, 15 (1970), 73-103.

In a general article, briefly discusses Buber's influence or lack of influence on Israeli Jews.

1971

B469   Allentuck, Marcia. "Martin Buber's Aesthetic Theories:
       Some Reflections." *Journal of Aesthetics and Art
       Criticism*, 30 (Fall 1971), 35-8.

       Buber's ideas on aesthetics provide insights into the
       work of the artist and into the creative process. His
       conception of the human psyche as a battleground, in
       which the formative and the formless struggle for mas-
       tery, appears early in his work. The source of art is
       man meeting the world and being addressed by form. The
       artist is the great bringer out of form through the
       psyche's intention and the will to form. The work of
       art produced is the medium through which the artist com-
       municates this form in a dialogue with his audience.

B470   Altizer, Thomas J.J. "A Response to Stanley Romaine
       Hopper." *Eastern Buddhist*, 4 (May 1971), 158-61.

       Discussion of Hopper's article on the eclipse of God
       (item B458).

B471   Borowitz, Eugene B. "Education Is Not I-Thou."
       Religious Education, 66 (September-October 1971),
       326-31.

       Buber stated that education is essentially the educa-
       tion of character. This is achieved through a genuine
       human encounter between teacher and student. For many
       this relationship has taken the place of learning. But
       here Buber broke with his own system. Education, al-
       though centered on the person, is not I-Thou. The
       teacher must select and present that part of the world
       which will bring his students into the world. This
       presentation is not accomplished in a fully reciprocal
       relationship. The teacher addresses the student as
       Thou but does not present himself as a Thou. This is
       as close as Buber came to the concept of role.

B472   Ferrell, Donald. "Anxiety and the Death of God."
       National Catholic Guidance Conference Journal, 15
       (Spring 1971), 200-5.

       (Not available for annotating.)

B473   Forth, David S. "Berkeley and Buber: An Epistemological
       Comparison." *Dialogue: Canadian Philosophical Review*,
       10 (December 1971), 690-707.

The ground for the similarity between these two
philosophers is their religious orientation. Their
theories of knowledge are theories of revelation. While
Berkeley claims that our knowledge of others is mediated
by signs, he recognizes that we have intuitive knowledge
of our own mind. Buber extends this intuitive direct
knowledge outward to others. Buber's meeting God in
the hallowing of the everyday is remarkably like Berkeley's concept of the divine visual language and the
nearness of God it implies. That God meets us and deals
with us in the minute-by-minute everyday world is the
basis of their epistemological agreement. For both the
causal interpretation of man's world is an error of
judgment on the part of the experiencing subject. They
reach similar positions on metaphysical questions because of their similar epistemologies.

B474   Fox, Everett.   "We Mean Voice: The Buber-Rosenzweig
          Translation of the Bible." *Response*, 5 (Winter 1971-
          72), 29-42.

Buber and Franz Rosenzweig, when translating the
Bible into German, tried to: (1) return to the spoken-
ness of the original Hebrew, (2) reproduce the primal
meanings revealed in the word roots, and (3) bring out
the leading-word repetitions which were used in the
Hebrew to signal the underlying theme. Their translation stressed the unity of the text rather than, as is
common in Western scholarship, breaking it down into
sources.

B475   Friedman, Maurice.   "Dialectical Faith Versus Dialogi-
          cal Trust." *Eastern Buddhist*, n.s. 4 (May 1971),
          162-70.

Criticism of Hopper's interpretation of Buber
(item B458).

B476   Friedman, Maurice.   "Martin Buber." *Encyclopaedia
          Judaica*, vol. 4.   New York: Macmillan Co., 1971,
          pp. 1430-3.

Overview of Buber's life and philosophy.

B477   Hodes, Aubrey.   *Martin Buber: An Intimate Portrait*.
          New York: Viking Press, 1971.   242 pp.

A blending of the author's personal reminiscences of
his meetings with Buber from 1953 to 1965, biographical
material on Buber, and discussion of his thought.
There is an index.

B478   Idinopulos, Thomas A. *The Erosion of Faith: An Inquiry
       into the Origins of the Contemporary Crisis in
       Religious Thought.* Chicago: Quadrangle Books, 1971,
       pp. 178-208.

       An overview concluding with a comparison of Buber's
       thought with that of Nicolas Berdyaev and, to a lesser
       extent, Paul Tillich and Jacques Maritain.

B479   Johannesen, Richard L. "The Emerging Concept of Com-
       munication as Dialogue." *Quarterly Journal of Speech,*
       57 (December 1971), 373-82.

       An investigation of communication as dialogue using
       Buber, among others, as a theoretical base.

B480   Lyon, James K. "Paul Celan and Martin Buber: Poetry as
       Dialogue." *PMLA,* 86 (January 1971), 110-20.

       For both Buber and Celan, the meeting of man with
       what is over against him leads to the realization of
       self. They see the human imagination as the impulse
       to transform everything into a Thou. Both are God-
       seekers in an age which considers this unfashionable.

B481   Moore, Donald J. "Martin Buber: 'Friend of the Court.'"
       America, 6 March 1971, pp. 231-4.

       Buber, a lifelong Zionist, called for a commonwealth
       of Jewish and Arab communities in the Near East as early
       as 1921. Prior to the establishment of the state of
       Israel, he worked on behalf of a binational state. He
       later accepted Israel as a fact of history but saw it
       as a vehicle by which to realize the truth and justice
       embodied in Judaism. He continued to work for Jewish-
       Arab rapprochement throughout his life.

B482   Rosenblatt, Howard S. "Martin Buber's Concepts Applied
       to Education." *Educational Forum,* 35 (January 1971),
       215-8.

       Sees the assessment approach to students as the I-It
       relationship in education, useful but secondary to the
       teacher-student dialogue.

B483   Scholem, Gersham. "At the Completion of Buber's Trans-
       lation of the Bible." *The Messianic Idea in Judaism.*
       New York: Schocken Books, 1971, pp. 314-9.

       A brief talk given at Buber's home on the completion
       of his translation of the Hebrew Bible into German.

Discusses Buber's emphasis on scripture as spoken word,
the urbanity of language used, the substitution of I,
Thou, and He for the name of God, and Buber's use of
secondary sources.

B484   Scholem, Gersham. "Martin Buber's Interpretation of
        Hasidism." *The Messianic Idea in Judaism*. New York:
        Schocken Books, 1971, pp. 228-50.

Slight revision of two *Commentary* articles (items
B191 and B250).

B485   Siegel, Seymour. "Contemporary Jewish Theology: Four
        Major Voices." *Journal of Church and State*, 13
        (Spring 1971), 257-70.

Although Buber is the best known writer on Judaism
in our time, his rejection of any religious form not in
the category of I-Thou separated him from the organized
ongoing life of the Jewish believing community. His
exposition of Hasidism overlooked their faithful adher-
ence to Jewish practice and observance. Further, his
early advocacy of a binational state alienated him from
the Jewish masses. His positive influence on contemporary Judaism is found in his emphasis on the encounter
with God as a real relationship in the midst of the
everyday world.

B486   Simon, Howard A. "Martin Buber and the Law." *CCAR
        Journal*, 18 (April 1971), 40-4.

When speaking of the halakah, Buber was primarily
concerned with the individual and his response. The
law is a vehicle for an I-Thou relation between man and
God. But Buber places the burden on man. The law must
be believed in as God's address to the individual.
Each individual must turn toward the law and relate it
to his own authentic life. The entire law may not
reach out to him. This does not diminish the law, but
merely indicates the individual's authentic response
to this address from God.

B487   Spear, Otto. "Martin Buber on Nations and World Peace."
        Universitas, 13 (1971), 269-76.

Buber thought that the best way to contribute to world
peace was to bring peace to the specific situation in
which one found oneself. Although his Zionism contained
the concept of nationhood, he rejected the nationalism
of power. Any nationalism must include the concept of
supra-nationalism, of being a part of humanity.

B488   Vermes, Pamela. "Martin Buber: A New Appraisal."
        Journal of Jewish Studies, 22 (1971), 78-96.

        In a three-part article, first discusses seven major
        interpreters of Buber. Then focuses on Buber's concepts
        of God, as rooted in the Bible, and the perfect man, as
        exemplified by the Hasidic zaddic. The third section
        criticizes Walter Kaufmann's introduction to his trans-
        lation of *I and Thou* (item B460).

                                1972

B489   Friedman, Maurice. "The Ontology of the Between."
        Review of Existential Psychology and Psychiatry, 11
        (1972), 183-90.

        A review of Robert Woods' *Martin Buber's Ontology*
        (item B447) in which the reviewer criticizes Wood for
        subsuming Buber under a metaphysic, and thus obscuring
        Buber's central message.

B489a   Glanz, David. "Buber's Concept of Holocaust and His-
            tory." *Elul*, February 1972, pp. 29-31.

        (Not available for annotating.)

B490   Herberg, Will. *Martin Buber: Personalist Philosopher
            in an Age of Depersonalization*. McAuley Lecture XV.
            West Hartford, Conn.: St. Joseph College, McAuley
            Institute of Religious Studies, 1972. 15 pp.

        Buber's writings on the philosophy of dialogue were
        part of the upsurge of personalism that followed the
        First World War. *I and Thou* (item A17), based upon the
        phenomenological description of the primordial words,
        opened this new personalistic period. Buber applied
        this personalism to the religion of ancient Israel,
        Christianity, ethics, and to the problems of modern man.

B491   Hodes, Aubrey. *Encounter with Martin Buber*. London:
            Penguin Press, 1972, 243 pp.

        A slightly revised edition of *Martin Buber: An Inti-
        mate Portrait* (item B477).

B492   Johnston, William M. *The Austrian Mind: An Intellec-
            tual and Social History, 1848-1938*. Berkeley: Uni-
            versity of California Press, 1972, pp. 214-20.

A brief discussion of Buber and his relationship to
the Austrian intellectual scene of the time. Compares
Buber and Ferdinand Ebner, who independently discovered
the I-Thou relation.

B493   Kauf, Robert. "Verantwortung: The Theme of Kafka's
       Landarzt Cycle." *Modern Language Quarterly*, 33
       (December 1972), 420-32.

In an article about Franz Kafka, briefly discusses
two letters exchanged with Buber, then the editor of
Der Jude, who had invited Kafka to submit some stories.

B494   Kohanski, Alexander S. "Martin Buber's Restructuring
       of Society into a State of Anocracy." *Jewish Social
       Studies*, 34 (January 1972), 42-57.

Buber holds that modern technological society has
created instruments that threaten man's inter-human
relations. He distinguishes between the social principle and the political principle which differ in their
methods of forming the human community. In the former
I-Thou relation is predominant while in the latter
individuals are subordinated to a common purpose. While
Buber recognizes the necessity of the political principle, he feels that because of the excess of power
available to the modern state, it has overwhelmed the
social principle. His solution is the formation of a
religious socialism with an anocratic or nondominant
government whose function would be administrative
rather than governmental. This is to be accomplished
through the education of men who value the social principle. The author points out that Buber fails to indicate what instrumentality these men will use to create
their new society.

B495   Kraut, Benny. "The Approach to Jewish Law of Martin
       Buber and Franz Rosenzweig." *Tradition*, 12 (Spring-
       Winter 1972), 49-71.

Three factors influenced Buber's interpretation of
Jewish law. First, he was more concerned with the religious problems of man in general and thus viewed
Jewish law from a general human rather than an exclusively Jewish point of view. He also held that the
free expression of the inner self was more important
than obedience to dogma. Finally, he viewed the biblical description of the Sinai event as a human interpretation of this revelation. The content of revelation

is the presence of God. The laws derived from revelation are man's interpretation of this encounter. Buber's
views are irreconcilable with both Rosenzweig's and
traditional interpretations.

B496   Moran, James A. "Martin Buber and Taoism." *Judaism*,
       21 (Winter 1972), 98-103.

In 1909 Buber wrote an essay on Taoism and the Taoist
philosopher Chuang Tzu (item A155). Taoist ideas later
influenced his own writings. Their emphasis on humility,
silence, and inner freedom appears throughout *I and Thou*
(item A17), and the concept of nonaction was incorporated
into Buber's account of the I-Thou relation. Parallels
can also be found between the message of Chuang Tzu and
Buber's interpretation of Hasidism. Both philosophers
show a respect for the uniqueness of individual things
and an abhorrence of excessive organization, categoriz-
ing, measurement, and evaluation.

B497   Morse, Benjamin J. "Rainer Maria Rilke and Martin
       Buber." *Alles Lebendige meinet den Menschen:*
       Gedenkbush für Max Niehans. Bern: Francke, 1972,
       pp. 102-28.

The author finds parallels between Rilke's "Ninth
Duino Elegy" and Buber's *Legend of the Baal-Shem*
(item A133). Suggests that these parallels are the
result of Buber's influence on Rilke.

B498   Oliver, Roy. "The Baal Shem's New Year's Sermon."
       Jewish Quarterly, 20 (Summer 1972), 9-13.

Suggests that interpreters of Buber have often
emphasized non-Jewish elements in his work to make him
more acceptable to the academic world. As an example,
discusses Friedman's exclusion of the Hasidic story
"The Baal Shem's New Year's Sermon" from his translation of *The Legend of the Baal Shem* (item A133). This
story, which is included in item A6, is the source of
Buber's expression "the narrow ridge."

B499   Rothschild, Fritz, and Seymour Siegel. "Modern Jewish
       Thought." *The Study of Judaism: Bibliographic Essays*.
       New York: Anti-Defamation League of B'nai B'rith,
       1972, pp. 146-52.

An overview of Buber's thought through brief summa-
ries of his major works.

B500   Schulweis, Harold S. "Buber's Broken Dialogue."
       Reconstructionist, December 1972, pp. 7-12.

       Criticizes Buber's concept of God as absolute per-
sonality. Buber misconstrues the individual's intense
personal experience of God as proof of the personality
of God. In addition, God as absolute personality is
supramoral, his moral qualities being incomprehensible
to man. This separates the I of man from the Thou of
God and morality from faith.

B501   Simpson, Douglas T. "Some Implications of the I-I
       Concept for Education." *Negro Educational Review*, 23
       (October 1972), 126-31.

       Posits an I-I relation, the individual's relation to
his own selfhood. This I-I relation can be based either
on an I-It or I-Thou attitude toward the self, depend-
ing to a great extent upon how others are relating to
him. Relating to a person as a Thou will help him relate to himself as a Thou and later help him enter into
I-Thou relations with others. The author briefly discusses how schools can contribute to this process.

B502   Steinkraus, Warren E. "Berkeley and Inferred Friends."
       Dialogue: Canadian Philosophical Review, 11 (December
       1972), 592-5.

       Criticism of Forth's article (item B473). Argues
that Buber's I-Thou and I-It relationships do not involve an epistemological theory.

                                 1973

B503   Clark, Allen. "Martin Buber, Dialogue, and the Philo-
       sophy of Rhetoric." *Philosophers on Rhetoric*. Edited
       by Donald G. Douglas. Skokie, Ill.: National Text-
       book Company, 1973, pp. 225-42.

       Attempts to construct a theory of communication based
on Buber's thought.

B504   Freed, L.F. "Who Is Martin Buber?" *South African
       Medical Journal*, 47 (1973), 163+.

       (Not available for annotating.)

B505   Glatzer, Nathum. Foreword to *On Zion: A History of an
       Idea*, by Martin Buber. New York: Schocken Books,
       1973, pp. vii-xiv.

Explores Buber's relationship to the Zionist movement.
Buber saw Zion as a sacred mission to found a just
society. This meant keeping Palestine free of Western
power politics and economics. A crucial test for this
mission was the creation of a community in which Jews
and Arabs could share all areas of public life.

B506   "God as the Absolute Thou." *Times Literary Supplement*,
        28 December 1973, pp. 1577-8.

In an unsympathetic article, the author analyzes the
rise of Buber's influence on theology in the 1920s,
and what he sees as the demise of this influence in the
mid-1950s. Argues that the early influence was the
result of the postwar positivists' destruction of spec-
ulative theology, leaving a vacuum which was filled by
Buber's thought. The demise of Buber's influence was
the result of a resurgence of traditional theology on
the one hand, and an application of logical empiricism
to encounter theology on the other. The author believes
that if a renaissance of Buber's influence were to occur,
it would be reflected in man's social and political relationships, rather than in theology.

B507   Gordon, Haim. "Would Martin Buber Endorse the Buber
        Model?" *Educational Theory*, 23 (Summer 1973), 215-23.

A criticism of Scudder's "Buber model" for teaching
(item B407). Scudder interprets the I-Thou relation as
something the teacher must consciously develop with his
students in order to impart knowledge while avoiding
authoritarianism. But in the I-Thou realm of existence,
this type of goal-directed decision does not exist.
Establishing this relationship is in part a matter of
grace and not a procedure to be planned, while the
knowledge imparted is not academic knowledge but the
ontological knowledge of reality as relationship.
Scudder's model confines education to the I-It world
of skill and intellect.

B508   Gutsch, Kenneth U., and Howard S. Rosenblatt. "Coun-
        selor Education: A Touch of Martin Buber's Philosophy."
        Counselor Education and Supervision, 13 (September
        1973), 8-13.

The I-Thou, I-It philosophy provides a theoretical
framework for many aspects of counseling including the
self understanding achieved by the client through dialogue with the counselor, the inner struggle within the

client, and the existence of many non-reciprocal relationships in the client's life.

B509 Hill, Brian V. *Education and the Endangered Individual:*
      A Critique of Ten Modern Thinkers. New York: Teachers
      College Press, 1973, pp. 183-201, 241-54.

      Presents an overview of Buber's philosophical anthro-
      pology as an alternative to the picture of man derived
      from modern philosophy and science, and as a defense of
      the sanctity of the individual. Also briefly explores
      Buber's philosophy of education, comparing it to that
      of Jacques Maritain.

B510 Hill, Brian V. "Martin Buber, Jacques Maritain, Rein-
      hold Niebuhr: Modern Religious and Educational
      Thinkers." *Intellect*, 102 (December 1973), 191-5.

      Although recognizing the contributions of science to
      the study of man, these thinkers suggest the use of
      additional vocabularies which partly shift the burden
      of proof from the objective to the subjective sphere.
      Compares them on their approaches to the study of man
      and on educational theory. All three would focus edu-
      cation on the development of the individual, but the
      individual within a community.

B511 Hilliard, F.H. "A Re-examination of Buber's Address on
      Education." *British Journal of Educational Studies*,
      21 (February 1973), 40-9.

      A discussion of Buber's criticism of education.
      Buber criticized both traditional authoritarian educa-
      tion and the "new" education which stresses freedom,
      spontaneity, and creativity. The former gave too much
      prominence to the role of the teacher, while the latter
      over-emphasized the centrality of the pupil. The
      teacher and the child together are at the center of
      the educational process.

B512 Jung, C.G. "Religion and Psychology: A Reply to
      Martin Buber." *Spring* (1973), 196-203.

      (Not available for annotating.)

B513 Largo, Gerald A. "Two Prophetic Voices: Macmurray and
      Buber." *America*, 31 March 1973, pp. 283-6.

      There has been a shift away from the traditional
      approaches in theology toward a non-scholastic,

personalistic, phenomenological emphasis. This new
approach focuses on man as the center of reflection.
John Macmurray and Buber are seen as leaders in this
shift. Macmurray's belief that significance in life is
to be found in the mutual relationship of persons is
parallel to Buber's concept of the I-Thou relationship.
Both require a fundamental change in attitude on the
part of human beings toward their fellows, a change
that must be rooted in religion.

B514   Lunn, Eugene. *Prophet of Community: The Romantic
       Socialism of Gustav Landauer.* Berkeley: University
       of California Press, 1973, pp. 246-7.

       Brief discussion of Buber's conflict with Landauer
over the First World War.

B515   Marra, Gianfranco. "Man According to Buber."
       L'Osservatore Romano: Weekly Edition in English,
       7 June 1973, p. 9.

       A brief overview of Buber's thought. Buber points to
a solution of society's problems through a middle way
between individualism and collectivism. However, he
fails to describe a way of achieving this middle way.

B516   Schaeder, Grete. *The Hebrew Humanism of Martin Buber.*
       Translated by Noah J. Jacobs. Detroit: Wayne State
       University Press, 1973. 503 pp.

       A scholarly overview of Buber's life and thought.
The author is particularly interested in the intellectual background of each stage of Buber's thought. Primary subjects discussed are: (1) Buber's early development, (2) his studies of German, Jewish, and Oriental
mysticism and myth, (3) the philosophy of realization,
(4) Buber's part in the renewal of German Judaism and
in the Zionist movement, (5) the philosophy of dialogue,
(6) the message of Hasidism, (7) the translation of the
Hebrew Bible and its influence on Buber's thought,
(8) his interpretation of Christianity, its relationship
to Judaism, and the roles of Jesus and Paul, and (9) his
contribution to philosophical anthropology. While there
is a name index, the unfortunate omission of a general
subject index from a book of this size and complexity
limits its role as a reference work.

B517 Schroeder, Janet E. *Dialogue with the Other: Martin Buber and the Quaker Experience.* Pendle Hill Pamphlet 192. Wallingford, Pa.: Pendle Hill Publications, 1973. 30 pp.

Author cites several aspects of the Quaker experience which correspond to Buber's thought, namely the dialogical nature of Quaker worship, the use of stories to teach truths of religion, the stress on the everyday, and the concept of God found in relationship.

B518 Schwarcz, Moshe. "Ontology of Mystery and Ontology of Covenant: Phenomenology as Directing the Mind to a Divine." *Traces of God in a Secular Culture.* Edited by George F. McLean. Staten Island, N.Y.: Abba House, 1973, pp. 211-35.

A comparison of the thought of Buber and Gabriel Marcel. While the author finds basic structural similarities, he emphasizes differences resulting from their philosophical and religious backgrounds. For Buber the decisive factors are the Hebrew Bible, Jewish mysticism, and Hasidism. For Marcel they are phenomonology and the Thomistic-scholastic tradition. He compares the two on the relationship of religion to philosophy, nominalism versus realism, the content of revelation, Thou as the ultimate principle of Being, the God-man relationship, and transcendence versus immanence.

B519 Seckinger, Donald S. "Martin Buber and the One-Sided Dialogical Relation." *Journal of Thought*, 8 (November 1973), 295-301.

Buber's philosophy of dialogue is seen as an alternative to one-sided action and material achievement. It goes beyond the "originator instinct." Human freedom must be characterized not merely by minimal external restraints or maximum external opportunities, but as a path toward communion with others. Freedom in education is the possibility of this communion. However, the dialogical relation in education is, by necessity, one-sided and often fails, despite the teacher's efforts.

B520 Shute, Clarence. "Aristotle's Interactionism and Its Transformations by Some 20th Century Writers." *Psychological Record*, 23 (Summer 1973), 382-93.

Briefly describes Buber's betweenness as the highest
expression of "contextual interactionism." His thought
is seen as similar to Plato's in that both were absorbed
in the subjective universe.

B521   Tallon, Andrew. "Person and Community: Buber's Category
        of the Between." *Philcsophy Today*, 17 (Spring 1973),
        62-83.

How does one become a person? According to Buber, in
the enactment of community. Buber gives this answer
more implicitly than explicitly. He avoids discussing
the effect of the I-Thou relation on the self and pays
almost exclusive attention to its effect on the other.
In doing so he is resisting psychologism and ego-centered
individualism. Communion is the act but community is
the habit, the will to make the act last. An occasional
I-Thou relation is not enough for personalization or
for constituting community. Underlying all consciousness, all relation, and all the ontological reality of
the between is the will to community. To work toward
community is to work for conditions that promote
personalization.

B522   Vermes, Pamela. "Buber's Understanding of the Divine
        Name Related to Bible, Targum, and Midrash." *Journal
        of Jewish Studies*, 24 (Autumn 1973), 147-66.

Buber and Rosenzweig translated ehyeh, God's name in
his own mouth, as "I am there/I will be there" and, in
the light of this, translated YHWH, God's name as spoken
by man, as "He is there/He will be there." Buber tried
to find biblical support of this, and Vermes extends
this search to the Targums and the Midrash. She finds
that the notion of God present with the world is a per-
sistent theme. This supports Buber's concept of the
"everlasting you" and his whole teaching of dialogue
as part of the living body of Jewish belief.

B523   Weiss-Rosmarin, Trude. "Jewish Books--Then and Now."
        Jewish Spectator, 38 (December 1973), 5-6, 32.

A brief note about the difficulty of finding a United
States publisher for Buber's works during the 1930s and
1940s.

B524   Wingerter, J. Richard. "Pseudo-Existential Writings in
        Education." *Educational Theory*, 23 (Summer 1973),
        240-59.

A review of existential thought as applied to education with particular reference to Scudder's and Etscovitz's articles on Buber (items B407 and B416). The author's primary criticism is that these writers degrade Buber's ontological thinking to a level where the original thought is lost. Neither Scudder nor Etscovitz realizes that Buber is speaking ontologically when he describes dialogue and the I-Thou relation. Both try to systematize and objectivize Buber's thought so that it can be utilized in the business of education. Scudder takes Buber's distinction between the I-Thou and the I-It and insists on a choice between the two, ignoring Buber's claim that both are necessary modes of existence.

1974

B525   Bender, Hilary E. *The Philosophy of Martin Buber: Monarch Notes.* New York: Monarch Press, 1974. 111 pp.

An overview in outline form covering all of Buber's major concepts. Intended for the college student.

B526   Berkovits, Eliezer. *Major Themes in Modern Philosophies of Judaism.* New York: Ktav Publishing House, 1974, pp. 68-137.

A brief overview of Buber's thought followed by a highly critical evaluation. The author concludes that: (1) the I-Thou relation need not be considered the ultimate form of reality, (2) meaning brought from the dialogical relationship lacks objective validity, (3) the concept of obligation cannot be derived from Buber's relational philosophy, and (4) while the I-Thou relation may serve as a basis for a personal religion of the individual soul, it cannot account for Judaism. Buber's revelation without content places him in the Pauline tradition and reduces religion to individual piety.

B527   Borowitz, Eugene B. "Comments." *Leo Baeck Memorial Conference on Jewish Social Thought: 1973-1974.* Edited by Herbert A. Strauss. New York: American Federation of Jews from Central Europe, 1974, pp. 16-25.

A response to Simon's article (item B554). Believes that Buber has much to offer the Jewish people, as well

as the world at large. The problem for the Jews is
Buber's approach to the law. Nevertheless he, rather
than Leo Baeck, is seen as an appropriate guide to the
reconstruction of Jewish social life.

B528   Brusin, David. "Rosenzweig's Approach to Jewish Law."
       Reconstructionist, June 1974, pp. 7-12.

       Outlines Buber's objections to Jewish law and Rosen-
       zweig's response to these objections.

B529   Buss, Janet L. "The 'I' and 'Thou' in Theater Games."
       Paper presented at the 65th Annual Convention.
       Washington, D.C.: Eastern Communication Association,
       1974, 12 pp. (ERIC Document Reproduction Service
       ED 013 371)

       The application of Buber's I-Thou relation to acting.

B530   Cain, Seymour. "Berrigan, Buber, and the 'Settler
       State.'" *Christian Century*, 26 June 1974, pp. 664-8.

       A brief discussion of why the binational Palestinian
       state, which Buber hoped for, was never achieved.

B531   Cohn, Ellen. "'I and Thou'--As a Personal Experience."
       Sh'ma, 11 January 1974, pp. 35-6.

       The effect of *I and Thou* (item A17) on the author.

B532   Diamond, Malcolm L. "Martin Buber: On Meeting God."
       Contemporary Philosophy and Religious Thought. New
       York: McGraw-Hill, 1974, pp. 101-29.

       A discussion of I-Thou and I-It relationships empha-
       sizing the man-God encounter and the epistemological
       aspects of this encounter. For Buber, verifiable knowl-
       edge is a part of the I-It mode. The I-Thou relation-
       ship is on a higher level of truth. Objective knowledge
       about God is impossible because the I-Thou nature of
       the man-God encounter places God beyond the reach of
       checkability. God's existence and his qualities cannot
       be verified during the encounter or after encounter
       because in both cases it would force the individual
       into an I-It attitude. One of Buber's weakest points
       is his vagueness about the interaction between the It
       and the Thou. The author argues that this interaction
       is greater than Buber acknowledges. I-It checking is
       crucial to the discrimination between genuine and mis-
       taken perceptions of the Thou.

B533 Fackenheim, Emil L. "Martin Buber: Universal and
Jewish Aspects of the I-Thou Philosophy." *Midstream*,
20 (May 1974), 46-56.

Attempts to show that the universal philosophy contained within Buber's thought cannot be separated from
its particularistic or Jewish elements. The first is
derived from and depends upon the second. The author
sees the divine-human relation as the animating principle of *I and Thou* (item A17). In describing this
relation Buber rejects both the subjectivist's reduction of God to a projection of man's unconscious, and
the mystic's flight from earthly necessity. This rejection appears arbitrary but the basis for it can be
found in Buber's encounter with the Bible. The covenant
between God and Israel is a mutual relationship between
the particularity of the Jewish people and a universal
God. This mutual relationship is the basis for Buber's
philosophy.

B534 Friedman, Maurice. "'I and Thou'--How a Book Came Into
Being." *Sh'ma*, 11 January 1974, pp. 33-5.

Brief discussion of the writing of *I and Thou* (item
A17), including Buber's intellectual outlook at the
time of its writing, the book's relationship to the
ideas of other thinkers, particularly Ferdinand Ebner,
and its central position in Buber's thought.

B535 Gordon, Haim. "Existentialist Education as Expressed
in the Hasidic Stories of Martin Buber." *Religious
Education*, 69 (September-October 1974), 579-92.

Buber's Hasidic stories are used to illuminate his
educational thought.

B536 Gordon, Murrary. "Indian-Israeli Relations: Perspective and Promise." *Midstream*, 20 (November 1974),
13-36.

Briefly discusses Buber's response to Gandhi's 1938
statements on the Jewish problems in Germany and
Palestine.

B537 Jackson, G. "Interpreters of Our Faith: Martin Buber."
A.D., June 1974, pp. 17-9.

Overview with excerpts from Buber's works.

B538   Jacob, Walter. *Christianity Through Jewish Eyes*. New
       York: Hebrew Union College Press, 1974, pp. 172-86.

       A review of Buber's interpretation of Christianity.
       While Buber recognized Christianity as a path to God,
       he rejected its claim to be the sole path. Jesus was
       seen as a Jew whose basic teachings fell within the
       faith of Judaism. Jesus did not reject Israel or wish
       to separate himself from the Covenant. Paul made this
       break. Buber rejected Paul's basic thought and those
       periods of history dominated by this thought. He wished
       to reclaim Jesus for Judaism.

B539   Johnston, William M. "Martin Buber's Literary Debut:
       'On Viennese Literature.'" *German Quarterly*, 47
       (November 1974), 556-8.

       Brief introduction to a translation of Buber's "On
       Viennese Literature" (item A376).

B540   Klink, William H. "Environmental Concerns and the Need
       for a New Image of Man." *Zygon*, 9 (December 1974),
       300-10.

       The answer to the anthropological question concerning
       the essence of man must take into account his relation-
       ship with the environment as a whole. This relationship
       has been changed by post-World War II technology and is
       defined here by an extension of Buber's concept of the
       I-Thou relationship.

B541   Kovacs, George. "Atheism and the Ultimate Thou."
       International Journal for Philosophy of Religion, 5
       (Spring 1974), 1-15.

       An analysis of the place of atheism in the philosophy
       of dialogue. Atheism is a sign of alienation, an ob-
       struction of man's ability to enter into dialogue. As
       this ability is the essence of man, there is an implica-
       tion that the atheist is less human than the believer.
       But Buber also states that if the atheist addresses
       another Thou with his whole being, he is addressing
       God. This implies that even an atheist, if he is truly
       human, is a believer. Thus the philosophy of dialogue
       can both dehumanize or baptize an atheist, but it cannot
       meet him on his own ground.

B542   Lescoe, Francis J. *Existentialism: With and Without
       God*. New York: Alba House, 1974, pp. 135-70.

       A lengthy overview.

B543 Manheim, Werner. *Martin Buber*. New York: Twayne
      Publishers, 1974. 106 pp.

An overview concentrating on the development of the
philosophy of dialogue and Buber's interpretation of
Hasidism. The author has excluded discussion of Buber's
biblical studies and his social philosophy. There is a
very meager subject index.

B544 Moore, Donald J. "Buber's Secular Spirituality."
      Religion in Life, 43 (Summer 1974), 183-91.

Buber calls religion the great temptation of man.
Institutional religion tends to withdraw man from the
world where real communion with God takes place and becomes a substitute for this communion. Furthermore, in
the institution's need to manipulate God, it turns God
into an It. The author believes, however, that organized
religion can provide a basis for the community desired
by Buber. The forms of organized religion also allow
the great religious encounters of mankind to be passed
from one generation to the next. Moore proposes prayer
as a link between the secular spirituality of Buber and
institutional religion.

B545 Moore, Donald J. *Martin Buber: Prophet of Religious
      Secularism*. Philadelphia: Jewish Publication Society
      of America, 1974, 264 pp.

An overview of Buber's thought with an emphasis upon
his criticism of religion. The author finds the source
of this criticism first in his writings on the Bible,
Hasidism, and Judaism, and second in his personalism
and philosophy of dialogue. Buber criticizes religion
as a system exemplified by organized churches, theology,
gnosticism, and magic. At the same time he recognizes
man's need, often supplied by religion, for law, structure, tradition, and community. The choice between the
system and the spirit is left up to each person. In
the final chapter the author discusses Buber's critique
of religion as it applies to the Catholic Church. There
is no index.

B546 Moran, James A. "Buber and Dewey: The Redemption of
      Personal Experience." *Philosophy Today*, 18 (Spring
      1974), 32-40.

Argues for the relevance of John Dewey's theory of
experience in interpreting Buber's I-Thou relation.
Dewey widens the meaning of experience to include the
moral and the aesthetic as well as scientific cognition.

He objects to the image of man, presented by the em-
piricists and rationalists, as a spectator who detachedly
observes the mechanisms of nature. To clarify the role
of cognition in experience, Dewey distinguishes between
having an experience and reflecting on that experience.
An I-Thou encounter can be seen as something that is
had rather than thought about. Buber's claim that the
objective stance of the I-It cannot capture the reality
of the I-Thou can also be understood in these terms.
The concrete experience is much richer than the later
reflective accounts. The convergence of these two
thinkers is based upon their shared goal of widening
man's view of experience by challenging our narrow
scientific rationalism.

B547   Pincus, Lily. *Death and the Family*. New York: Pan-
        theon Books, 1974, pp. 14-22.

        Relates a discussion with Buber concerning marital
        interactions and family therapy.

B548   Plaut, W. Gunther. "Long-hand with Buber." *Judaism*,
        23 (Winter 1974), 61-9.

        A review of the first volume of Buber's letters
        published in German. These letters focus on the rise
        of Zionism and the German-Jewish relationship.

B549   Popel, Stephen. "Martin Buber: The Art of the Unpoliti-
        cal." *Midstream*, 20 (May 1974), 56-61.

        A re-examination of Buber's Zionism and his place in
        the Zionist movement. Buber's difficulties at the
        fifth and twelfth Zionist Congresses are attributed to
        his cultural Zionism and his opposition to Jewish
        nationalism. His Zionist writings are criticized for
        their mystification, their justification of Palestine
        for the Jews on the basis of Israel's subjective per-
        ception of history, and their unrealistic insistence
        on binationalism.

B550   Rachlis, Arnold. "Martin Buber's Dialogical Principle
        in Religious Education." *Reconstructionist*, June
        1974, pp. 18-25.

        An overview of Buber's philosophy of education and
        its application to religious education.

B551 Rinott, Chanoch. "Major Trends in Jewish Youth Move-
    ments in Germany." *Leo Baeck Institute Year Book*, 19
    (1974), 77-95.

    Discusses Buber's involvement in this movement.

B552 Rose, Neal. "Factor Analysis of Martin Buber's 'The
    Legend of the Baal Shem.'" *Hebrew Abstract*, 15
    (1974), 128-30.

    A comparison of Buber's Hasidic stories contained in
    item A133 with the original legends. The author finds
    that Buber selected stories that projected the Baal
    Shem as a zaddik or perfected man. Buber's stories
    are also longer than the originals. The added material
    includes: (1) descriptions of natural beauty, psycho-
    logical states, and mystical consciousness, (2) re-
    interpretation of the ideological struggle between the
    Hasidim and their opponents, and (3) vocabulary and
    conceptualizations from the German mystical tradition.

B553 Seligman, Paul. "A New Look at Buber's Philosophy of
    Man and God." *Studies in Religion*, 4 (1974-75),
    129-36.

    The I-Thou, I-It philosophy shows that we can realize
    our humanity over and above the realization of our par-
    ticular aims and pursuits. It offers an alternative to
    doctrines that make realization an inner human rather
    than an inter-human concern. It also opposes the gener-
    al tendency to psychologize and reduce God to our image
    of God. However, Buber brought the human and the divine
    spheres too close to one another. He did not allow any
    qualitative distinction between our relations to the
    human Thou and the eternal Thou. The author also dis-
    agrees with Buber's belief that the psychotherapeutic
    relationship is not a fully mutual I-Thou relation.
    Suggests solutions to the latter two problems.

B554 Simon, Ernst A. "Baeck's and Buber's Social and
    Political Thought--Paradigms for Today?" *Leo Baeck
    Memorial Conference on Jewish Social Thought: 1973-
    1974.* Edited by Herbert A. Strauss. New York:
    American Federation of Jews from Central Europe,
    1974, pp. 7-15.

    The differences between Leo Baeck and Buber discussed
    in terms of the synagogue, their relationship to Franz
    Rosenzweig, Jewish apologetics, their approach to
    Christianity, their relationship to Zionism, and their

influence upon the Jewish community. As to the social
values held by each, the author states that neither
will serve as a paradigm for today.

B555   Steffney, John. "Heidegger and Buber: Ontology and
           Philosophical Anthropology." *Religion and Life*, 43
           (Spring 1974), 33-41.

       Heidegger believed that philosophical anthropology is
       superficial and one must pass beyond it to more pro-
       found territory. He saw the question--What is man?--as
       indefinite. This is based, according to Buber, on his
       misreading of Kant. Man *is* finite but in such a way
       that he can know and act with a certain amount of
       assurance. Meaning, while very fragile, does come into
       being when we act fully human. Buber believed that
       neither philosophical anthropology nor ontology can
       serve as a foundation for philosophy. Any system is
       the substitution of an It for a Thou.

B556   Stone, Charles. "Two Types of Knowledge in Bergson and
           Buber." *Dialogue* (Phi Sigma Tau), 17 (October 1974),
           10-2.

       Compares the epistemologies of Henri Bergson and
       Buber and finds that while differing in terminology,
       they come to roughly the same conclusions about man's
       knowing faculty. Both propose a fundamental dualism
       inherent not in the world, but in man's way of knowing
       it.

B557   Thomas, Joseph. "Martin Buber's Doctrine of God."
           Encounter (Christian Theology Seminary), 35 (Summer
           1974), 184-203.

       A description of Buber's concept of God in terms of
       his philosophy of dialogue, the influence of Jewish
       religious tradition, and his philosophical theology.
       Author concludes that Buber's description of revelation
       rests upon personal experience and faith.

B558   Ticho, Ernst A. "Donald W. Winnicott, Martin Buber,
           and the Theory of Personal Relationships." *Psychiatry*,
           37 (August 1974), 240-53.

       A comparison of Buber and Winnicott reveals similar
       views about the nature of personal relationships and
       life goals. While Buber describes these phenomenologi-
       cally, Winnicott takes a genetic developmental approach.
       The author believes that in psychotherapy the I-Thou,

I-it polarity breaks down because there are many situations that are partly I-Thou and partly I-It. He also believes that Buber does not deal with the universality of aggression and lacked the psychological tools to explain what happened in Nazi Germany. Buber was handicapped because he did not understand man's dynamic unconscious, and dealt only with the mature aspects of the psyche. Nevertheless, his thought is useful to psychotherapists and complements Winnicott's work.

B559 Vermes, Pamela. "Martin Buber's Correspondence." *Journal of Jewish Studies*, 25 (Winter 1974), 444-50.

A review of the first two volumes of *Briefwechsel aus sieben Jahrzehnten*, a selection of Buber's correspondence. Takes issue with the number and importance of the letters included.

B560 Wieseltier, Leon Sol. "'I and Thou'--An Intellectual Experience." *Sh'ma*, 11 January 1974, pp. 36-7.

Buber's greatest legacy is his uncompromising dedication to the actuality of the world. Human existence in this world is not an obstacle but the condition for the spiritual life.

1975

B561 Berry, Donald L. "Mutuality in Jerusalem." *Religion in Life*, 44 (Autumn 1975), 281-90.

Argues that Israel has gone too far in the direction of the 'political' Zionism of Ben-Gurion as opposed to the 'cultural' Zionism of Buber. Buber felt that the Jewish population had, by forming a Jewish state, cut themselves off from significant relations with their Arab neighbors. The philosophy of dialogue could form the framework through which these relationships could be established.

B562 Branson, Roy. "The Individual and the Commune: A Critique of Martin Buber's Social Philosophy." *Judaism*, 24 (Winter 1975), 82-96.

Buber rejects the extremes of individualism and collectivism and argues for a third alternative, the small community held together through close personal contacts. The state, political parties, and large commercial

organizations thwart these personal contacts. The
ideal community is exemplified by the Israeli commune.
The author argues that Buber does not provide for the
protection of the individual against domination by the
group, or for the defense of the group against the
tyranny of individual members. In Buber's framework,
the individual may not go outside the community, even
to the External Thou, for universal truths by which to
judge community actions. One reason Buber underestimate:
the value of norms and the structures of justice in a
community is his concept of evil. Evil is human vitalit·
in search of focus. This focus is found through relationships, not through the restraints of institutions
or laws.

B563   Davies, Alan T. "Paul Tillich on Judaism and Martin
       Buber on Christianity." *Studies in Religion*, 5
       (1975-76), 66-74.

       Outlines similarities in these two religious thinkers
and compares their views on each other's religion.
Buber broke with centuries of Jewish mistrust of Christianity and the old anathema surrounding Jesus. He was
willing to speculate about the messianic consciousness
of Jesus and the gentile acceptance of Jesus as messiah.
Buber saw the two religions as based upon two polar concepts of faith, Jewish trust and Christian belief, a
questionable typology according to the author. Also
discussed is the possibility that Buber was rephrasing
the old Jewish polemic that Christianity is a debased
Judaism, dominated by pagan (Hellenistic) elements.

B564   Ehrlich, Leonard H. *Karl Jaspers: Philosophy as Faith.*
       Amherst: University of Massachusetts Press, 1975,
       pp. 77-97.

       Contrasts Buber's philosophy of dialogue with Jaspers'
ideal of communication. Cites similarities but concen-
trates on the differences. Jaspers sees communication
as essentially a struggle for truth in time. Dialogue
is the recognition of God through communion with his
creatures. Buber criticizes both Jaspers and Karl Barth
for appropriating the principle of dialogue. The author
finds inconsistencies in this criticism. Buber also
objects to Barth's repudiation of the validity of the
Jewish faith but then rejects the validity of Jaspers'
faith. The author questions whether Buber's conception
of testimony allows for dialogue with someone of another
faith.

B565 Flohr, Paul R. "The Road to 'I and Thou': An Inquiry
      into Buber's Transition from Mysticism to Dialogue."
      Texts and Responses. Edited by Michael A. Fishbane
      and Paul R. Flohr. Leiden: E.J. Brill, 1975, pp.
      201-25.

      Buber's early mysticism attributed a crucial role to
      Erlebnis, the affective experience that could overcome
      the isolation of the individual. He greeted the onset
      of World War I with enthusiasm because the Erlebnis
      produced by the war would usher in an era of realiza-
      tion, a consciousness of Gemeinschaft. Men were re-
      leased from petty instrumental aims to devote themselves
      to absolute value. Jewish participation in the various
      armies would result in the birth of the heroic Jew.
      These views brought Buber into conflict with Frederick
      van Eeden, a Dutch pacifist, and Buber's friend Gustav
      Landauer. After an exchange of letters with Landauer
      in 1916, Buber changed his views. His subsequent writ-
      ings contained explicit opposition to the war, a re-
      evaluation of the meaning of Erlebnis, and a shift in
      the axis of Gemeinschaft from consciousness to the
      relations between men.

B566 Forrester, David. "Martin Buber." *Tablet* (London),
      14 June 1975, pp. 549-50.

      A brief memorial on the tenth anniversary of Buber's
      death.

B567 Gillin, Charles Talbot. "Freedom and the Limits of
      Social Behaviorism: A Comparison of Selected Themes
      from the Works of G.H. Mead and Martin Buber."
      Sociology, 9 (January 1975), 29-47.

      Mead and Buber have fundamentally different perspec-
      tives on man. Mead sees society as the dominant factor
      in the development of the social self, while for Buber
      neither the self nor society but relationship is the
      basic reality. Those who suggest Mead's generalized
      other is basically the same as Buber's Eternal Thou
      are mistaken. In addition, Mead presents a theory of
      inner dialogue while Buber rejects this concept. The
      author argues that Buber's philosophical anthropology
      encompasses the basic insights of Mead plus the concept
      of reification, and more adequately accounts for human
      freedom.

B568   Hynson, Leon O. "Theological Encounter: Brunner and
        Buber." *Journal of Ecumenical Studies*, 12 (Summer
        1975), 349-66.

        An analysis of the ways in which the I-Thou personal-
        ism of Buber had a major influence on Emil Brunner's
        interpretation of the Christian faith.

B569   Jones, David A. "The Third Unrealized Wonder: The
        Reality of Relation in D.H. Lawrence and Martin
        Buber." *Religion in Life*, 44 (Spring 1975), 178-87.

        A discussion of the similarities between Lawrence's
        and Buber's diagnoses of the ills of modern society.
        Both dislike the overly rationalized, technological
        society where the worth of the individual is minimized
        or lost. For both the individual is of supreme impor-
        tance, but the individual in a relationship. For
        Lawrence this relationship is sexual, but not sex as
        an end in itself. Through this relationship a man and
        a woman enter a new dimension of reality not possible
        for either alone, the 'third unrealized wonder.' This
        is compared with Buber's I-Thou relationship.

B570   Katz, Robert L. "Martin Buber and Psychotherapy."
        Hebrew Union College Annual, 46 (1975), 413-31.

        Buber's primary criticism of psychotherapy was that
        it lacked an overview of what man is and what he is
        called to be. Buber tried to fill this need. Accord-
        ing to his formulation, psychological sickness is a
        sickness in relationships. What emerges in the between
        cannot be reduced to the sum of psychological or intra-
        psychic responses of the two individuals involved.
        This, however, is the focus of psychotherapists. They
        also do not distinguish between neurotic guilt and real
        or existential guilt resulting from failure to respond
        to the call from beyond man. The task is to become
        aware of this guilt and, by responding to the call,
        become reconciled. Buber did not recommend the I-Thou
        relationship as a model for therapy. He saw this
        relationship as inherently unequal and suggested inclu-
        sion as a method of communication. The author likens
        this to empathy.

B571   Katz, Steven T. *Jewish Philosophers*. New York: Bloch
        Publishing Co., 1975, pp. 190-6.

        An overview of Buber's life, his philosophy of dia-
        logue, and his interpretation of Hasidism and

Christianity. Criticizes Buber's view of revelation
and Hasidism.

B572 Kohanski, Alexander S. *An Analytical Interpretation of
      Martin Buber's I and Thou*. Woodbury, N.Y.: Barron's
      Educational Series, 1975. 176 pp.

      A guide for the student and general reader intended
      to be read in conjunction with *I and Thou*. Page refer-
      ences to both the Kaufmann and Smith translations
      (items A370 and A17) are given for each section. An
      overview of Buber's thought introduces the volume.
      There is no index.

B573 Kohanski, Alexander S. "Martin Buber's Approach to
      Jesus." *Princeton Seminary Bulletin*, 67 (Winter
      1975), 103-15.

      A Christian analysis of Buber's approach to Jesus.
      Buber does not contend against historical Christianity
      or its dogmas. His work focuses on the person of
      Jesus as he appears in the synoptic Gospels. In dis-
      tinguishing between two types of faith, the Jewish
      "trust in" and the Christian "belief that," Buber tries
      to demonstrate that Jesus was a man of the first type
      and therefore not an originator of a new religion. He
      likens Jesus' message to that of the Pharisees and
      claims that his denunciation of that group was directed
      at the pseudo-Pharisees, the same men that the true
      Pharisees denounced. Jesus' most radical deviation
      from the Pharisees was his demand for human perfection.
      Finally, Buber sees Jesus as the first of a series of
      Jewish messianic forerunners. The author finds insuf-
      ficient evidence to support this view of Jesus.

B574 Kohanski, Alexander S. "Martin Buber's Philosophy of
      Judaism." *Judaism*, 24 (Winter 1975), 69-81.

      Discussion of the early phase of Buber's philosophy
      of Judaism. Judaism was substance in the act of reali-
      zation. Buber's purpose was to bring the individual
      Jew to the awareness of the Jewishness which lay dormant
      in his blood, awaiting a conscious act of realization.
      Self-realization was achieved through identification
      with the Jewish people and a complete return to the
      fundamental spiritual process called Jewishness. This
      Jewishness manifests itself in three strivings; for
      unity of soul and community, for action, and for a
      future of absolute justice and love. A decision to

return will lead to religiosity rather than religion,
a distinction which brought Buber into conflict with
rabbinic Judaism.

B575   Matott, Glenn. *The Funnel and the Pump: Variations on
       a Theme by Martin Buber.* Paper presented at the
       26th Annual Meet⸝   . St. Louis: Conference on Col-
       lege Compositior   ⸝d Communication, 1975. 9 pp.
       (ERIC Document Reproduction Service ED 103 884)

       Brief overview of Buber's views on education and the
       teacher-pupil relationship.

B576   Mersch, Arnold. "Whitman and Buber: In the Presence of
       Greatness." *Walt Whitman Review*, 21 (September 1975),
       120-5.

       Similarities found in their definitions of life as
       meeting in the everyday world. For both God exists in
       all earthly things and is thus to be found through this
       meeting.

B577   Moonan, Willard. "Writings About Martin Buber in
       English." *Bulletin of Bibliography*, 32 (January-
       March 1975), 28-32.

       A preliminary secondary bibliography of 224 items.
       Not annotated.

B578   Moran, James A. "Martin Buber: Mystic of the Everyday."
       Studies in Religion, 5 (1975-76), 162-70.

       Discusses the early influence of mystical writers on
       Buber. Then enumerates the similarities between his
       description of the I-Thou relation and descriptions
       of the mystical experience. Both relationships are
       ineffable, involve direct contact with the real, cannot
       be sustained for long periods of time, are received as
       a gift of grace, and help the individual to realize the
       full dimensions of the self. The confusion over the
       mystical nature of the I-Thou relation can be reduced
       if we realize that many mystics were interested in
       deepening and expanding human experience. The I-Thou
       relation embodies a mysticism of the everyday.

B579   Park, O'Hyun. "Chinese Religions and the Religion of
       China." *Perspectives in Religious Studies*, 2 (Fall
       1975), 160-90.

A highly critical view of Buber's interpretation of
Asian religions. Buber saw Confucianism as excessively
supernatural, ignoring its central existential spirit.
Similarly he understood Taoism as a mysticism of unity
that overlooked human individuality, and wu-wei as nonaction, a retreat from man's ethical activity. This
rejection of Taoism as an escape from the world is
described as a result of a Western prejudice. Finally,
Buber's concept of Zen was confused by his dualism and
his view of Zen enlightenment as a psychological experience indifferent to the man-man relationship. His
evaluation of Zen was dictated by the need to see Hasidism as mankind's supreme religious achievement.

B580   Scudder, John R., Jr. "Why Buber Would Not Endorse a
       Pseudo-Existentialist." *Educational Theory*, 25
       (Spring 1975), 197-201.

A continuing discussion of the application of Buber's
thought to education begun by this author (item B407)
and involving Haim Gordon (item B507), J. Richard Wingerter (item B524), and Edward David Kiner (item B428).
The author is primarily concerned here with his own
reasoning and that of his critics, rather than Buber's
thought per se. He does admit that in his previous
work he had missed the ontic dimension of Buber's
thought.

B581   Weinstein, Joshua. *Buber and Humanistic Education.*
       New York: Philosophical Library, 1975. 102 pp.

A general introduction to Buber's educational theory.
The author begins with an overview of Buber's life and
thought. He focuses on those ideas which bear upon the
process of education, particularly the education of
character, the education of adults and youths, the
qualifications and role of the teacher, moral education,
and the goals of national education. There is no index.

B582   Worob, Avaham. *Duties of the Mind: Essays on Jewish
       Philosophy.* Spring Valley, N.Y.: Shaare Emet, 1975,
       pp. 3-39.

Argues Buber's concept of the self needs to be expanded beyond his basic relationships. Reviews other
attempts to do this. Then states seven criteria Buber
uses to establish separate kinds of relationships.
Four new combinations, I-You, I-We, I-Me, and I-Some-
thing are described and found to fit these criteria.
But even these six relations are not seen as exhaustive.

1976

B583   Alperson, Burton L. "On Shibboleths, Incantations, and
       the Confusion of the I-Thou and the Oh-Wow."
       Humanist, 36 (January-February 1976), 12-4.

       Includes Buber among thinkers who have suffered at
       the hands of "second-generation humanistic psychologists'
       who stress the adjustment concept of personality. In
       defining the I-Thou relationship as a peak experience,
       a be-all and end-all of human behavior, they ignore
       Buber's view that it is necessary to live in both the
       world of Thou and the world of It. He summarizes this
       pop psychology interpretation of Buber as: "Oh wow to
       I-Thou, Aw shit to I-It."

B584   Amey, L.J. *Visual Literacy: Implications for the Pro-
       duction of Children's Television Programs*. Halifax:
       Dalhousie University, School of Library Service, 1976.
       55 pp.

       Uses several theories, including Buber's philosophy
       of dialogue, to explain the relationship between the
       perceiver and the perceived.

B585   Artz, Johannes. "Newman as Philosopher." *International
       Philosophical Quarterly*, 16 (September 1976), 263-87.

       In an article on John Henry Newman, the author briefly
       draws parallels between the religious philosophies of
       Newman and Buber. Both understood religion as essen-
       tially personal and historical, a meeting with God, and
       not a product of rational deduction.

B586   Berenbaum, Michael G. "Franz Rosenzweig and Martin
       Buber Reconsidered." *Response*, 10 (Winter 1976-77),
       25-40.

       Compares the two on their conceptions of Jewish law
       and contends that Buber's non-nomistic position is more
       in line with the needs of modern Jews. Buber challenged
       the normative structure of Judaism in search of an en-
       counter with God.

B587   Berry, Wanda W. "The Binocular Vision: The Philosophi-
       cal and Religious Imagination in W.H. Auden's Critical
       Essays." *Soundings*, 59 (Summer 1976), 164-85.

       Briefly argues that while Auden never explicitly
       refers to Buber, the influence of Buber's philosophy of

dialogue can be seen in *Secondary Words*. In this work
Auden shifts toward the language of personal being and
occasionally uses Thou to delineate the personal.
Existence as a person is achieved through hearing Thou
spoken to us by other persons. His analysis of language
is also close to Buber's.

B588   Breslauer, S. Daniel. "The Three Strands in Martin
       Buber's Understanding of Jewish Ritual." *Hebrew
       Studies*, 17 (1976), 167-70.

       Buber's opposition to institutional ritualism is well-
       known. He did, however, recognize its usefulness. It
       can act as a channel for religiosity, a precondition
       for encounters, a help in constituting a community, and
       a method to transform a natural entity into a real other.

B589   Cheshire, Ardner R., Jr. "Invisible Man and the Life
       of Dialogue." *CLA Journal*, 20 (September 1976), 19-34.

       A discussion of Ralph Ellison's novel *Invisible Man*
       in terms of Buber's philosophy of dialogue.

B590   Eakin, Frank E., Jr. *A Buberian Approach to Faculty
       Development*. Washington, D.C.: American Council on
       Education, 1976. 28 pp. (ERIC Document Reproduction
       Service ED 156 045)

       Uses Buber's philosophy of dialogue to establish
       guidelines for a college faculty development program.

B591   Eakin, Frank E., Jr. "Martin Buber--A Christian View."
       Jewish Spectator, Spring 1976, pp. 41-3.

       An appreciation of Buber's impact on Christian
       thought. His relational anthropology is important for
       its ethical implication as well as its emphasis on the
       everyday world. His writings also point the way toward
       a de-Hellenized Christology.

B592   Edelman, Sam. *Martin Buber's Essays on Theatre: A
       Philosophical Look at Theatre of the Mind*. 1976.
       13 pp. (ERIC Document Reproduction Service ED 130 364)

       Buber's concepts of polarity, dialogue, and inclusion
       are used to understand the interrelationships between
       the actors, the play, and the audience in the readers
       theatre.

B593 Friedman, Maurice. "Martin Buber and Asia." *Philosophy East and West*, 26 (October 1976), 411-26.

Although Asia was not a primary field of scholarship for Buber, he did have an active interest in Asian re-ligions. Hinduism and Buddhism were early influences but they did not form a central part of his thought as did Taoism and Zen. The author discusses two Taoist concepts, man as involved in a reciprocal relationship with nature, and wu wei or nonaction, both of which are useful in understanding Buber's philosophy of dialogue. There are also many similarities with Hasidism as inter-preted by Buber. Taoism and Zen are, like Hasidism, mysticisms of the particular and not based upon the bond between the general and the Absolute. It is the present moment that is important and no dualism is re-cognized between the sacred and the secular. Both Zen and Hasidism stress the one-to-one relationship between teacher and pupil as essential to the transmission of knowledge from one generation to the next. The Hasidic concept of kavna or intention is similar to the philo-sophies of action implicit in Hinduism, Taoism, and Zen, in that fulfillment comes through the intention one brings to one's acts. Additional similarities are discussed.

B594 Friedman, Maurice. "The Self and the World: Psycholo-gism and Psychotherapy in Martin Buber's 'I and Thou.'" *Review of Existential Psychology and Psychiatry*, 15 (1976), 163-72.

Although Buber retained an interest in psychology and psychotherapy throughout his life, he opposed psycholo-gism's attempt to subsume all reality under psychologi-cal categories. Psychologism regards the world as idea, while cosmologism regards the soul as a product of the world. For Buber both pervert the relationship between the I and the world. By emphasizing the basic reality of the between, he offered a third perspective in which the soul is contained in the world and the world in the soul, while both retain their independence. In opposi-tion to the reflective attitude toward the self implied by psychologism, Buber described the spontaneous aware-ness of self within the I-Thou relationship. In oppo-sition to Freud's psychoanalysis, he suggested the process of psychosynthesis, based upon his understanding of the healing practiced by the zaddik among the Hasidim.

B595 Gordon, Haim. "A Method of Clarifying Buber's I-Thou
      Relationship." *Journal of Jewish Studies*, 27 (Spring
      1976), 71-83.

      Analyzes three attempts to clarify the I-Thou relation-
      ship, labeled the simplifying approach, the philosophical
      approach, and the detached correcting approach, and finds
      all three inadequate. States that the I-Thou relation-
      ship resists definition because: (1) to define something
      one must be external to it, and the I-Thou relationship
      requires participation, (2) it is difficult to find one
      thing in common for all I-Thou relationships, and (3)
      even if one could define it, the essence of the rela-
      tionship is to live it, not to verbally express it.
      Buber suggests that each reader search his own personal
      experiences for moments that will clarify the relation-
      ship. *I and Thou* (item A17) must be lived, not just
      read.

B596 Hart, Richard. "The Uses of Dialogue in Education:
      Martin Buber." *Aitia*, 4 (Winter-Spring 1976-77), 30-8.

      (Not available for annotating.)

B597 Jay, Martin. "Politics of Translation: Siegfried
      Kracauer and Walter Benjamin on the Buber-Rosenzweig
      Bible." *Leo Baeck Institute Year Book*, 21 (1976),
      3-24.

      The Buber-Rosenzweig translation of the Hebrew Bible
      into German is not only a model for other translations,
      but serves to articulate the translators' religious
      philosophies. In addition, the controversy that greeted
      its publication throws light on the Weimar Jewish in-
      telligentsia. An analysis is made of this controversy,
      particularly the criticism of Kracauer and Benjamin.

B598 Kaufman, William E. *Contemporary Jewish Philosophers*.
      New York: Reconstructionist Press, 1976, pp. 55-77,
      257-9.

      After a discussion of Buber's development emphasizing
      the influence of Kant, Nietzsche, and Feuerbach, the
      author concentrates on Buber's concept of the man-God
      relationship. Feels that the heart of Buber's religious
      message is that God can be encountered but not inferred.
      But, the author asks, what of those who have never had
      this encounter, or have experienced evil such that the
      encounter is put into question? Buber's answer to both
      the situation of the atheist and the Holocaust are seen

as inadequate. The author argues that our historical
hour demands a different concept of God. God must be
defined in such a way that he can be expressed as well
as addressed.

B599 Kegan, Robert. *The Sweeter Welcome: Voices for a
      Vision of Affirmation, Bellow, Malamud, and Martin
      Buber*. Needham Heights, Mass.: Humanities Press,
      1976. 169 pp.

      Analysis of the novels of Saul Bellow and Bernard
      Malamud in terms of Buber's writings on Hasidism and
      the philosophy of dialogue. Following a brief overview
      of Buber's thought, the author focuses on the affirma-
      tion expressed by these novelists, and their portrayal
      of the holy in everyday life. There is a subject index.

B600 Lawton, Philip N., Jr. "Love and Justice: Levinas'
      Reading of Buber." *Philosophy Today*, 20 (Spring
      1976), 77-83.

      Discusses three criticisms of Buber made by Emmanuel
      Levinas: (1) the original reciprocity of the I-Thou
      relation implies a pre-original obligation to enter
      into dialogue, (2) the formulation of the I-Thou rela-
      tion conserves a formal character, and (3) in the
      exclusiveness of the I-Thou relation, the participants
      forget the universe. It is a rapport of love, not jus-
      tice. Levinas sees Buber's alleged insensitivity to
      questions of social justice as a betrayal of the Jewish
      spirit.

B601 Lilker, Shalom. "The Kibbutz and Martin Buber."
      Reconstructionist, May 1976, pp. 12-9.

      For Buber, community was an essential aspect of
      Judaism. He felt that although it was based upon a
      humanistic faith, the Kibbutz movement, as true com-
      munity, would lead inevitably to God. This goal was
      never realized. The movement rejected Buber's religious
      socialism and the unrealistic demands he placed upon
      the lives of its members. They were disappointed in
      his idealized teachings on the communal life.

B602 Matott, Glenn. "In Search of a Philosophical Context
      for Teaching Composition." *College Composition and
      Communication*, 27 (February 1976), 25-31.

      The modern trend in teaching composition stresses
      the development of self-awareness and self-expression.

It does not require that the product of this self-
expression be measured against any norm. The author
agrees with Buber that this can lead to a new human
isolation through lack of communication, a process that
fits with Sartre's view of the human condition. Suggests adopting Buber's view of education where the
teacher not only helps the student discover his uniqueness but helps bring this uniqueness into dialogue.

B603 Mendes-Flohr, Paul R. "Martin Buber's Concept of Centre
      and Social Renewal." *Jewish Journal of Sociology*, 18
      (June 1976), 17-26.

While Buber was influenced by Ferdinand Tonnies'
Gemeinschaft und Gesellschaft, he redefined Gemeinschaft
in terms of I-Thou relationships. True community arises
when men have a common relationship to the centre. This
relationship is realized when they encounter a common
revelation, an unconditionality. Sensitivity to this
centre is the "essential We" and must be renewed by
subsequent generations. Buber's concept of social
renewal was influenced by Gustav Landauer, who taught
that it was not a function of institutional change so
much as the result of a fundamental transformation of
interpersonal relationships.

B604 Panko, Stephen M. *Martin Buber*. Waco, Tex.: World
      Books, 1976. 135 pp.

Overview of Buber's life and thought including dis-
cussions of his philosophy of dialogue and philosophy
of religion, his interpretations of Hasidism, the Hebrew
Bible, Judaism, and Zionism, and finally his interpretation of and influence upon Christianity. There is no
index.

B605 Scholem, Gersham. "Martin Buber's Conception of
      Judaism." *On Jews and Judaism in Crisis*. Edited by
      Werner J. Dannhauser. New York: Schocken Books,
      1976, pp. 126-71.

Buber sought and failed throughout his life to influence his fellow Jews. In attempting to reformulate
Judaism, he rejected its historical formulation, the
halakah, equating it with the unproductive aspect of
the Diaspora. His early mystical philosophy evolved
into the philosophy of dialogue which he saw as the
great discovery of Israel. His principal works on
the interpretation of Judaism concerned the Bible and

Hasidism, both of which proclaimed this message of
authentic Judaism. In the Bible, true dialogue became
true revelation. Thus Buber attains an extraordinary
loosening of the texts which are the basis of historical
Judaism, equating them with those revelations which may
be encountered at any time by the individual. The central concept of Hasidism became the realization of the
I-Thou relation in the concrete world, reflecting more
of Buber's outlook than that of the Hasidim.

B606   Seckinger, Donald S. "Buber-Rogers Dialogue: Theory
       Confirmed in Experience." *Journal of Thought*, 11
       (April 1976), 143-9.

       Discusses the similarities and differences in Buber's
       concept of teaching and Carl Rogers' concept of psycho-
       therapy. While they share the belief in helping
       through relationships, Buber does not hesitate to in-
       clude the guidance function in the teacher's role,
       something rejected by Rogers for the psychotherapist.

B607   Spear, Otto. "Martin Buber's Dialogue--Topics and
       Partners." *Universitas*, 18 (1976), 75-83.

       A brief review of some of the correspondence contained
       in *Martin Buber: Briefwechsel aus sieben Jahrzehnten*.

B608   Stitskin, Leon D. *Jewish Philosophy: A Study in
       Personalism*. New York: Yeshiva University Press,
       1976, pp. 275-80.

       A brief comparison of the concept of revelation in
       the thought of Buber and Franz Rosenzweig, the former
       positing a revelation of presence, and the latter a
       revelation of content.

B609   Talmon, Shemaryahu. "Martin Buber's Ways of Interpre-
       ting the Bible." *Journal of Jewish Studies*, 27
       (Autumn 1976), 195-209.

       Buber should not be seen as a professional biblical
       exegete who approaches his material with scholarly de-
       tachment, but as a Jewish thinker who used the methods
       and results of contemporary biblical scholarship to
       arrive at an existential appreciation of the Bible.
       Buber used these methods only so long as they further
       his overall purpose. He was concerned not with the
       history of biblical faith but with a presentation of
       the fundamentals of this faith. While he wished to
       transmit the text as it stood, he did not hesitate to

emend it, without, however, dealing with the methodology
of emendation. His emphasis on the unity of the Bible
led him to overlook internal diversity. He also did not
fully grasp the centrality of the law for historical
Judaism, and undervalued it as against ethical monotheism based on revelation.

1977

B610   Berry, Donald L. "Buber's View of Jesus as Brother."
       Journal of Ecumenical Studies, 14 (Spring 1977),
       203-18.

Buber's view of Jesus as brother helps him to find a
genuinely Jewish way of interpreting Jesus. This interpretation is discussed in relation to three topics:
God, faith, and messianism. (1) Jesus is perceived as
a prophet, not an incarnation of God. Jesus speaks the
I of unconditional relation with the external Thou and
is thus a paradigm of the "fulfilled person in relation
to God." (2) This unconditional relation of trust in
God ranks Jesus as a man of faith, but not an object of
faith. He is a mediator of faith, a brother who points
the way. (3) Buber views Jesus as a messianic person,
a suffering servant of God, but not the messiah.
Messianism is an ongoing process, and the messianic
person is a recurring figure. The author, in evaluating
these views, argues that several must be abandoned or
modified as the result of New Testament scholarship.

B611   Birnbaum, Ruth. "The Man of Dialogue and the Man of
       Halakhah." *Judaism*, 26 (Winter 1977), 52-62.

A study of Buber and Joseph B. Soloveitchik on the
meaning of revelation and its relation to Jewish law.
Buber saw revelation as unfinished teaching, to be
accepted or rejected on the basis of whether it is
addressed to the individual. Soloveitchik saw revelation as law, to be accepted with submission. Where
Buber looks for subjectivity and openness to continuing
revelation, Soloveitchik finds objectivity in an historical revelation complete and binding for all time.

B612   Charmé, Stuart. "The Two I-Thou Relations in Martin
       Buber's Philosophy." *Harvard Theological Review*, 70
       (January-April 1977), 161-73.

The author identifies two modes of I-Thou relations,
that between man and God and that between man and man.
The first is seen as an epistemological issue dealing
with the way God is known. This relation is contentless
and involves a special direct knowing of reality. The
second mode of I-Thou relation is the ethical mode between persons. This relationship is immersed in the
concrete world and based upon responsibility to, and
objective knowledge of, the Thou. Each of these modes
of I-Thou relations should be evaluated in its own
right. When Buber equates the first mode with the I-
Thou relation between persons, he reduces our knowledge
of other persons to a mysticism, devoid of ethical
dimensions, upon which no concrete way of life may be
built.

B613   Cunningham, Lawrence S.   "Spiritual Classics Revisited--
       Martin Buber: 'I and Thou.'"   *Christian Century*,
       16 March 1977, pp. 246-7.

       Brief overview of *I and Thou* at the time of Kaufmann's
       translation (item A370).

B614   Fisch, Harold.   "Buber's Interpretation of Zionism: A
       New Analysis."   *Forum* (Jerusalem), 1977.

       (Not available for annotating.)

B615   Gordon, Haim.   "Martin Buber's Impact on Religious
       Education."   *Religious Education*, 72 (November-
       December 1977), 580-94.

       Discussion of what the author sees as the limited
       effect Buber has had on his readers. To understand
       any one of Buber's works requires: (1) an acquaintance
       with his overall thought, (2) an involved, non-detached
       approach to the work, (3) a period of self examination,
       and (4) a change in one's mode of existence. This re-
       quires an arduous effort on the part of the reader.
       Religious educators who have been influenced by Buber's
       thought see education in terms of a meeting of persons,
       a quest for simplicity, and a rejection of the super-
       ficial.

B616   Gordon, Haim.   "Religious Education as Expressed in
       the Hasidic Stories of Martin Buber."   *Religious
       Education*, 72 (January-February 1977), 61-73.

Using Buber's Hasidic stories, Gordon tries to solve
three problems that face religious educators: (1) how
to convey the spirit of a religious heritage, (2) how
to help the pupil become aware of the nearness of God,
and (3) how to prepare the pupil for future battles
with evil.

B617   Katz, Steven T. "Buber's Concept of Revelation: Some
       Critical Reflections." *Proceedings of the Seventh
       World Congress of Jewish Studies*, 1977.

       (Not available for annotating.)

B618   Kayser, Rudolf. *The Saints of Quran*. Edited by Harry
       Zohn. Cranbury, N.J.: Associated University Press,
       1977, pp. 114-9.

       A brief overview of Buber's thought on his eightieth
       birthday.

B619   Mendes-Flohr, Paul R. "Martin Buber and the Moral
       Dilemma of Zionism: A Believing Realism." *Jerusalem
       Quarterly*, No. 3 (Spring 1977), 74-84.

       The moral ambiguity of the Zionist goal of Jewish
       settlement in Palestine resulted from the possible dis-
       lodgement of the native Arab population. As early as
       1921 Buber urged a rejection of chauvinistic national-
       ism in favor of a commonwealth of Arabs and Jews. He
       saw the Jewish problem as one of spiritual and cultural
       confusion that would be compounded by a policy of
       nationalistic politics. In the face of the political
       realities of Palestine, Buber developed a philosophy of
       ethical action which responded to the unique demands of
       each situation. His prophetic politics were aimed at
       preserving the community without succumbing to the will
       to power.

B620   Susser, Bernard. "Ideological Multivalence: Martin
       Buber and the German Volkish Tradition." *Political
       Theory*, 5 (February 1977), 76-96.

       Discusses the parallels between Buber's thought and
       various romantic, irrationalist, volkish tenets then
       current in Weimar Germany, and which later contributed
       to National Socialism. Buber's early writings inter-
       preted Judaism in terms of the volkish concepts of
       blood and national consciousness. He attempted to
       establish a spiritual kinship between the German and
       the Jewish soul, thereby enabling Jews to partake of

the spiritual life of the German Volk. Buber's interpretation of Hasidism and Zionism also reflects this
volkish preoccupation. He rejected bourgeois society
for a social order arising from the principle of Gemeinschaft, a third way between the traditional left and
right. Parallels are also drawn between the I-Thou
relation and the charismatic relation between the
people and the führer.

B621   Taylor, Katharine W., and Harry B. Scholefield.
       Martin Buber and the Life of Dialogue. Cassette
       Tapes. Berkeley: University of California Extension
       Media Center, 1977, 8 hours.

       Cassette tapes on which the authors give an overview
       of Buber's thought in discussion form.

B622   Ternent, William A., and Janet A. Ternent. *Toward a
       Communication Theory Focused on Humankind's Future.*
       Paper presented at the 63rd Annual Meeting.
       Washington, D.C.: Speech Communication Association,
       1977. 22 pp. (ERIC Document Reproduction Service
       ED 147 901)

       Uses Buber's philosophy of dialogue as a model for a
       human communication system to fit Jonas Salk's theory
       of mankind's future.

B623   Vermes, Pamela. "Man's Prime Peril: Buber on Religion."
       Journal of Jewish Studies, 28 (Spring 1977), 72-8.

       Author feels that Buber's aversion to religion has
       been largely overlooked. He preached the abandonment
       of institutional religion. His primary objection was
       that religion tends to separate the sacred from every-
       day life. It breaks down the immediacy necessary for
       true relation between God and man. God becomes an
       object of knowledge, an It.

1978

B624   Agus, Jacob B. *Jewish Identity in an Age of Ideologies.*
       New York: Frederick Ungar Publishing Co., 1978.,
       pp. 182-6, 327-33.

       Explores Buber's views on socialism and ancient
       Israel. Buber saw the ideal society as one that fosters
       the I-Thou relationship among its members. This would

require small socialist communities linked in nationhood. The Kibbutz movement expressed many of his ideas.
Buber's writings on the Bible were an attempt to prove
that the I-Thou relation was central to biblical faith
and exemplified in the folk feeling of direct relation
to God as king. The experience of God's thou was the
event of revelation. The author finds Buber's interpretation of Judaism one-sided, emphasizing the role of
the prophets at the expense of the rites of the priests
and the wisdom of the sages.

B625 Baker, Leonard. *Days of Sorrow and Pain: Leo Baeck and*
        the Berlin Jews. New York: Macmillan Publishing Co.,
        1978, pp. 175-80.

      Describes the work of Buber and Baeck to improve
Jewish education in Germany at the time of the Nazi
takeover.

B626 Bender, Hilary E. "The Contemporary Human Service
        Professional: A Buberian Analysis." *Thought*, 53
        (September 1978), 272-82.

      Buber wrote about the role of the social services
professional in terms of the teacher, the psychotherapist, and the religious leader. He distinguished
between the authority figure and the helper, identify-
ing the helper as what is needed for our age. In
describing the work of the helper, he emphasized the
social context in which he must work, that of radical
alienation. The helper must overcome this alienation
by working through the modern institutions which foster
it.

B627 Ben-Horin, Meir. "On Mordecai M. Kaplan's Critique of
        Buber." *Judaism*, 27 (Spring 1978), 161-74.

      While there are many points of similarity between
Kaplan and Buber, major fundamental differences exist.
Kaplan's thought is grounded in Western philosophical
and scientific precepts which Buber seems to reject in
favor of Jewish religious traditions. Buber wishes to
avoid imposing modern critical insights upon the Bible,
while Kaplan uses these insights to re-interpret fundamental Biblical concepts. Kaplan, in supporting his
position, shows that Buber overstates his reliance on
Jewish religious tradition. Buber's modifications of
this tradition clearly indicate the influence of Western
philosophy. Buber's concept of God as absolute

personality is also discussed as a point of conflict
between the two philosophers.

B628   Borowitz, Eugene B.   "Humanism and Religious Belief in
         Martin Buber."   *Thought*, 53 (September 1978), 320-8.

       Addresses the problem of Buber's lack of influence
upon both orthodox and non-orthodox Jews. Buber took a
stance between humanism and religiosity. He deviated
from secular humanism in his insistence that to be truly
human one must form a relationship with God. His belief
that Jewish life must have God as its focus made him too
religious for the non-orthodox. On the other hand, his
views on revelation and history, making traditional
Jewish law just one possibility of the I-Thou relationship with God, separated him from Jewish orthodoxy.
Buber was, suggests the author, an embarrassment to
Jews.

B629   Breslauer, S. Daniel.   "Baruch Spinoza and Martin
         Buber on the Bible."   *Journal of the Central Con-
         ference of American Rabbis*, 25 (Winter 1978), 27-36.

       Argues that Spinoza's approach to the Bible has
dominated Western thought. But for the modern Jew to
return to the Bible as a text of faith, he must move
beyond Spinoza's critique. The author recommends
Buber's interpretation of the Bible as a record of
the personal human-divine dialogue. Compares Spinoza
and Buber on biblical miracles, prophecy, and the law,
and finds that Buber's sensitivity to the personal
element reveals hidden dimensions overlooked by
Spinoza.

B630   Briggs, Kenneth A.   "Buber Emerges Anew As Figure of
         Debate."   *New York Times*, 19 February 1978, p. 51.

       Report on a U.S. conference on Buber in which positive
views were opposed by Walter Kaufmann. In his opening
address, Kaufmann stated that Buber failed in most of
his undertakings and, in *I and Thou* (item A17), approxi-
mated the "oracular tone of false prophets."

B631   Fisch, Harold.   *The Zionist Revolution: A New Perspec-
         tive*.   New York: St. Martin's Press, 1978, pp. 66-78.

       Buber saw the history of the Jewish people as a dia-
logue between man and God involving the creation of a
sacred community. He saw this community as an answer
to the alienation of modern man. However, he remained

largely aloof from the actual struggle to create a
Jewish state. Reasons for this are found in his adher-
ence to Abad Ha'am's spiritual interpretation of Zionism, and in his selection of Hasidism as the model for
the sacred community. Buber did not recognize the day-
to-day mode of dialogue found in the halakah, or the
dialogue inherent in the challenge and response of the
Jewish nation.

B632   Fishbane, Michael. "Martin Buber as an Interpreter of
       the Bible." *Judaism*, 27 (Spring 1978), 184-95.

    Buber's translation of the Bible was greatly influ-
enced by his understanding of the purpose of the Bible.
For Buber the Bible was not a text, but the voice of
God addressing man and the responding voice of man.
He often put this in terms of his philosophy of dialogue. The purpose of a translation was to put the
Bible in language which would lead the individual reader
to respond in his own life to the Thou which called him
through the scriptures. A translation should be judged
not by its authenticity as a historical record but by
the authenticity of the faith expressed.

B633   Friedman, Maurice. "The Intellectual Challenge Buber
       Has Left Us." *Thought*, 53 (September 1978), 329-42.

    The author touches on many aspects of Buber's thought
and discusses each briefly. Included are sections on
philosophical anthropology, the possibility of error in
I-Thou knowing, the dialogical faith as relationship
without content, biblical creation, psychologism, the
contemporary emphasis on feeling, the concept of con-
firmation, the basis of community, existential trust,
and the eclipse of God in modern life. The author views
Buber's thought as an active personal response to the
human condition.

B634   Goldstein, Jeffrey. "Buber's Misunderstanding of
       Heidegger." *Philosophy Today*, 22 (Summer 1978),
       156-67.

    Buber's criticisms of Heidegger resulted from his
confusing fundamental ontology with philosophical
anthropology. He saw the latter as the only worthwhile
philosophical task and judged Heidegger's thought in
these terms. He interpreted the a priori investigation
of Dasein's structure as an arbitrary abstraction from
man's lived life, overlooking Heidegger's distinction

between ontic and ontological inquiry. The investigation of what man is is an ontical inquiry. Heidegger's
ontological investigation is an inquiry into what this
"is" means. When Heidegger discussed Dasein as having
a certain relation to its own Being, it was interpreted
by Buber as man having a relationship with himself.
Buber saw man as man only in relation to other men or
to God and felt that Heidegger ignored this necessity.
However, Heidegger did stress that a basic aspect of
Dasein is being with other Daseins. The author feels
that much of this disagreement is based upon Buber's
misunderstanding of Heidegger's revolutionary use of
language.

B635   Goodman, Ruth. "Dialogue and Hasidism: Elements in
       Buber's Philosophy of Education." *Religious Educa-
       tion*, 73 (January-February 1978), 69-79.

       Summary of Buber's views on education as derived
from his philosophy of dialogue and his studies of
Hasidism. The teacher's role in the educational process is to form a dialogical relationship with the
student in which the teacher not only imparts subject
matter, but exemplifies society and ethics in personal
conduct.

B636   Gordis, Robert. "Martin Buber at His Centennial."
       Judaism, 27 (Spring 1978), 131-2.

       A brief introduction to an issue of *Judaism* commemora-
ting the centennial of Buber's birth. Author notes
that while Buber has had an extraordinary influence on
twentieth-century religious thought, his influence on
Jewish thought has been limited. Suggests two reasons:
(1) the highly individualistic nature of Buber's
thought, and (2) his stress on the experience of revelation rather than its content.

B637   Gordon, Haim. "An Approach to Martin Buber's Educa-
       tional Writings." *Journal of Jewish Studies*, 29
       (Spring 1978), 85-97.

       Feels that many have misinterpreted Buber's writings
on education, ignoring the existential dimension of his
thought in a desire for philosophical or scientific
objectivity. Buber rejects the detached outlook as a
basis for participating in the educational process.
The educator must become personally involved with his
pupils, relating his entire being to them, and helping
each student in his quest for self-fulfillment.

B638   Gordon, Haim.   "Can Literature Clarify Existential
          Encounters?"   *Educational Forum*, 42 (January 1978),
          189–202.

          Uses literary examples to clarify Buber's concept of
          the I-Thou encounter.

B639   Gordon, Haim.   "Martin Buber's Life and Thought:
          Bibliographical Retrospect."   *Religious Studies
          Review*, 4 (July 1978), 193–201.

          A brief discussion of some writings about Buber.
          Finds few works dealing with the philosophy underlying
          Buber's ideas or how these ideas may be realized in
          everyday life.

B640   Grady, L. Augustine.   "Martin Buber and the Gospel of
          St. John."   *Thought*, 53 (September 1978), 283–91.

          Uses Buber's framework to analyze the person of Jesus
          as presented in the Gospel of John.   Jesus, as the Word
          of God, is God's offer of dialogue.   The body of the
          gospel is a "Book of Signs" through which we are
          addressed by God.   Jesus replaces the institutions and
          feasts of the Old Testament which belong to the world
          of It.   He establishes the world of Thou with his own
          presence.

B641   Hatt, Harold E.   "Dialogue: Interpersonal and Inter-
          .faith."   *Encounter* (Christian Theological Seminary),
          39 (Summer 1978), 215–31.

          (Not available for annotating.)

B642   Hellwig, Monika K.   "Gifts and Insights from the
          Hasidim."   *Listening*, 13 (Fall 1978), 268–78.

          Uses Buber's interpretation of the central themes of
          Hasidism in a discussion of the movement's meaning for
          Christians.

B643   Hendley, Brian.   "Martin Buber on the Teacher/Student
          Relationship: A Critical Appraisal."   *Journal of
          Philosophy of Education*, 12 (1978), 141–8.

          Argues against Buber's rigid characterization of the
          teacher-student relationship as one-sided.   The author
          grants that there cannot be a fully mutual relationship
          but feels that mild friendships and even mutual affec-
          tion are possible if both parties are committed to the
          educational task.

B644   Horwitz, Rivka. *Buber's Way to I and Thou: An His-*
       torical Analysis and the First Publication of Martin
       Buber's Lectures "Religion als Gegenwart." Heidel-
       berg: Verlag Lambert Schneider, 1978, 301 pp.

       An analysis of the development of the philosophy of
       dialogue and the writing of *I and Thou* (item A17), based
       upon material found in the Martin Buber Archives. The
       1922 lectures "Religion as Presence," reproduced here
       in German, appear to be an early version of *I and Thou*
       and are used to trace the development of these ideas.
       The lectures and correspondence also testify to the
       early influence of Ferdinand Ebner. The author con-
       tends that an encounter with Ebner's writings may have
       been the turning point in Buber's development. A cor-
       responding influence by Hermann Cohen is ruled out.
       Later Buber's relationship with Franz Rosenzweig became
       crucial, particularly in the development of Buber's
       concept of dialogue and in the elimination of the terms
       "realization" and "orientation" from Buber's philosophy.
       There is a name index and a subject index.

B645   Jordan, Pat. "Martin Buber: What Is to Be Done?"
       Catholic Worker, February 1978, pp. 4-5.

       A brief overview of Buber's life and the development
       of his thought.

B646   Jospe, Eva. "Encounter: The Thought of Martin Buber."
       Judaism, 27 (Spring 1978), 135-47.

       An overview. Sees Buber's primary purpose as the
       creation of a philosophical anthropology, a view of man
       in his totality and a way of life, rather than a syste-
       matic philosophical outlook. Major themes discussed
       are the religious inwardness and sanctification of
       everyday life of the Hasidic world-view, and the prin-
       ciple of duality underlying I-Thou, I-It relations.

B647   Kaplan, Edward. "Martin Buber and the Drama of Other-
       ness: The Dynamics of Love, Art, and Faith."
       Judaism, 27 (Spring 1978), 196-206.

       While Buber is known as the philosopher of human
       relationship, he postulates the inescapable reality of
       alienation. While his philosophy of dialogue represents
       a protest against this alienation, the I-Thou relation-
       ship requires acknowledgment of this separateness, of
       a fundamental otherness. Separateness is overcome, if
       only for a moment, through dialogue. Art and poetry

are methods of actualizing otherness within dialogue
to create dialogue. Buber interprets modern man's
estrangement from God as a recognition of otherness
without the ability to bring this otherness into dialogue. His solution is twofold: to prepare ourselves
for dialogue by striving for individual wholeness, and
to trust otherness, be it human or divine.

B648   Katz, Steven T. "Dialogue and Revelation in the
       Thought of Martin Buber." *Religious Studies*, 14
       (March 1978), 57-68.

Argues that Buber's dialogical account of revelation
is logically and philosophically deficient because it
is based upon a set of misleading analogies between
inter-human and divine-human relations. All interpersonal relations require objective concepts if the
reality of the other is not to evaporate. The same is
true of the man-God relationship. Buber's separation
of 'belief in' and 'belief that' is erroneous and leads
to disastrous consequences. How does one meet God if
one knows nothing about him? One cannot believe in
something that is unintelligible. Actually, Buber's
statements about the unknowable Thou contain four
examples of 'belief that.'

B649   Katz, Steven T. "Reflections on Martin Buber's Cen-
       tennial." *Expository Times*, 90 (December 1978), 71-6.

Brief evaluation of Buber's work among German Jews,
as well as his scholarly achievements in the areas of
biblical studies, the philosophy of dialogue, and Hasidic studies. Attributes much of Buber's influence to
his role as a rediscoverer of transcendence. While the
author praises Buber's emphasis upon the social nature
of man and the pre-eminence of relation over substance,
he criticizes the concepts of the between and God as
Eternal Thou. He also suggests the need for scholarly
correction of Buber's interpretation of Hasidism.

B650   Kaufman, William E. "The Mysticism of Martin Buber:
       An Essay on Methodology." *Judaism*, 27 (Spring 1978),
       175-83.

There are wide differences of opinion as to the role
of mysticism in Buber's thought. Some feel that he
overcame early mystical tendencies, while for others
mysticism is a constant throughout his work. The problem is seen as one of the definition of mysticism.

188 Writings about BuberWritings about Buber

Several are given to illustrate the differences in emphasis in each, and the difficulty of using any one of
them to judge Buber's thought. Buber's own definition
is discussed as a dualistic, theistic mysticism in which
man directly encounters the personhood of God. Thus if
the definition of mysticism contains the concept of
union or total absorption of the self with God, Buber
is not a mystic. If, however, mysticism is defined
theistically, as a direct encounter with God in which
contact with the world is intensified rather than
negated, Buber's mature thought remains mystical.

B651   Kaufmann, Walter. "Buber's Failures and Triumph."
       Revue Internationale de Philosophie, 32 (1978),
       441-59.

A recounting of Buber's failures; very little about
his triumph. His method of translating the Hebrew
Bible, striving for the original voice, is ignored by
current publishers who want easily read idiomatic ver-
sions. His writings about the Bible are also ignored.
His interpretation of Judaism has few adherents today.
I and Thou (item A17) is seen as a flawed work, inau-
thentic and simplistic. The author interprets Buber's
I-Thou, I-It dichotomy as an expression of a deep
existential malaise, perhaps the result of his mother's
abandonment of him when he was a child. While Buber's
translations of Hasidic tales are seen as classics of
religious literature, his portrait of Hasidic life does
not stand up to scholarly criticism. Thus his effort
to create a humanistic religion was a failure.

B652   Ketcham, Charles B. *A Theology of Encounter: The
       Ontological Ground for a New Christology*. University
       Park: Pennsylvania State University Press, 1978,
       pp. 26-43.

Includes an overview of Buber's I-Thou and I-It relations and their importance in understanding personal
identity and the God-man relationship. Argues that
Buber's thought has revolutionized theological anthropology and prepared the way for a new theology. The
major part of the book deals with the application of
these insights to Christian theology and the Christ
event.

B653   Lai, Whalen W-L. "Inner Worldly Mysticism: East and
       West." *Zen and Hasidism*. Compiled by Harold Heifetz.
       Wheaton, Ill.: Theosophical Publishing House, 1978,
       pp. 186-207.

A comparison of Hasidism and Zen using the interpretations of Buber and D.T. Suzuki.

B654   Link-Salinger, Ruth. "Buber, the Man of Letters."
       Judaism, 27 (Spring 1978), 207-13.

A review of the three-volume German publication of
Buber's correspondence.

B655   Link-Salinger (Hyman), Ruth. "Friends in Utopia:
       Martin Buber and Gustav Landauer." *Midstream*, 24
       (January 1978), 67-72.

Historical study of the relationship between Buber
and Landauer, characterizing them as men devoted to
cultural revolution, spiritual renaissance, and the
recasting of society.

B656   *Martin Buber 1878-1978; Exhibition.* Jerusalem: Jewish
       National and University Library, 1978, 75 pp.

A catalog of an exhibition of material from the Buber
Archives held in April 1978.

B657   Moore, Donald J. "Martin Buber and Religion." *Thought*,
       53 (September 1978), 258-71.

Buber saw himself as a man of faith, a witness to the
biblical faith in a God who called his people to a dialogical relationship. This is the heart of religion,
the dialogical confrontation between God and the human
person. Buber distinguishes between religiosness and
religion. Religiousness implies an active relationship
with God. Religion as a system may obscure this relationship. The author believes that the two should com-
plement each other. Religiousness needs the structure
of religion which in turn needs the continual openness
of dialogue.

B658   Rotenstreich, Nathan. "Immediacy and Dialogue."
       Revue Internationale de Philosophie, 32 (1978), 460-72.

An exploration of Buber's concept of immediacy as
seen in the I-Thou relation. The author finds three
underlying philosophical motifs; a search for certainty,
the possibility of perceiving a thou as opposed to an
object, and the distinction between illusion or dreams
and reality. The acceptance of the world revealed
through immediacy leads to an attitude of care and to
responsiveness. The author questions Buber's dichotomy
between immediacy and discursive thought. Argues that

the content of immediate contact is not only the presence of the other, but an awareness of features and an
act of recognition. These aspects are missing from
Buber's concept.

B659   Schatzker, Chaim. "Martin Buber's Influence on the
       Jewish Youth Movement in Germany." *Leo Baeck Insti-
       tute Year Book*, 23 (1978), 151-71.

       Explores the atmosphere in which these youth organi-
       zations existed, to explain their acceptance of some of
       Buber's ideas. Pictures these youths as torn between
       their Jewishness and their German heritage. They took
       the thought patterns and educational methods of the
       German youth movement and adapted it to the Jewish
       situation. Some of Buber's ideas, such as his emphasis
       on striving for community, and his view of religion
       as an emotional experience, helped in this transition.
       When they later rejected the German youth movement,
       they also rejected Buber's thought.

B660   Shapira, Avraham. "Meetings with Buber." *Midstream*,
       24 (November 1978), 48-54.

       Reminiscences of conversations between Buber and
       kibbutz members held during the last five years of
       Buber's life. In these conversations Buber repeatedly
       emphasized that he did not wish to teach a doctrine,
       nor to see himself as a rabbi. His thought was a method
       of approach. He insisted on discussing problems in
       terms of the existential moment and the personal element
       of that moment. The author feels that this stemmed not
       from a conscious philosophical stand, but from profounder
       levels of Buber's personality.

B661   Shestov, Lev. "Martin Buber." *Midstream*, 24 (November
       1978), 41-8.

       Author sees *I and Thou* (item A17) as an attempt to
       construct a modern theophany. To find God in the every-
       day as presented to modern man is the dominant goal of
       Buber's thought. Modern philosophies of God have tended
       to parallel Spinoza's attempt to purify God, removing
       him from historically-bound world views. Buber leads
       in the opposite direction. He accepts the theophanies
       of the Hasidism and of the Bible, placing them alongside
       his modern theophany. We must live through all of these
       theophanies to understand the fate of God in our world.

B662 Simon, Ernst. "The Builder of Bridges." *Judaism*, 27
(Spring 1978), 148-60.

The author identifies three primary stages of development in Buber's thought. At each stage Buber won
disciples among groups with divergent outlooks. As his
thought developed, earlier adherents did not move on
with him, but became fixed upon earlier stages. In the
first stage he was seen as a mystic who emphasized the
realm of aesthetics. Later he turned to the question
of the individual Jew in contemporary Western civilization and had great influence upon European Jews seeking
a practical Jewish identification. Finally his interpretations of Judaism and Christianity had great influence among Christians who mistakenly saw him as a
spokesman for traditional Judaism. At each stage Buber
influenced groups that ignored other areas of his thought
and tended to identify him with their particular stage.

B663 Stewart, John. "Foundations of Dialogic Communication."
Quarterly Journal of Speech, 64 (April 1978), 183-201.

Uses Buber's thought to express the relationship
between dialogic communication and the holistic approach
to man.

B664 Tallon, Andrew. "Intentionality, Intersubjectivity,
and the Between: Buber and Levinas on Affectivity and
the Dialogical Principle." *Thought*, 53 (September
1978), 292-309.

By relocating the locus of the event of meaning from
inside one's head to the realm of the between, Buber
pointed to a way out of psychologism, rationalism, and
intellectualism. Thus he started a major revolution in
philosophy, but he failed to complete it. His central
concept, the between, must be studied to establish its
meaning, how it is constituted, and how it can be used
in the building of community. The author outlines a
phenomenological approach to this task.

B665 Walters, James W. "Martin Buber's Philosophy of
Relationality and Mysticism." *Encounter: Creative
Theological Scholarship*, 39 (Spring 1978), 189-201.

Defends Buber's mysticism of communion against the
criticism of Walter T. Stace (item B178). Argues that
Stace's insistence that Buber's dualism is inferior
to the unitive mystical vision is based upon an arbitrary philosophical assumption.

B666   Woocher, Jonathan S.   "Martin Buber's Politics of
       Dialogue." *Thought*, 53 (September 1978), 241-57.

   Buber's concerns with political and social justice
antedated his philosophy of dialogue but were later
framed in terms of this philosophy. The dialogical community, his social-political ideal, would be achieved
through a turning from instrumental relationships to
those of I and Thou by slowly bringing social and political institutions under the influence of this spirit.
Buber applied this to Zionism through his commitment to
the cooperative socialist movement and to Arab-Jewish
reconciliation. Is his teaching appropriate today?
The politics of dialogue have been subjected to two
criticisms: that the hard realities of political life
are not given adequate consideration, and that one cannot extrapolate from the personal sphere of I and Thou
to the social process. The author discusses these
criticisms.

B667   Wood, Robert E.   "Buber's Conception of Philosophy."
       Thought, 53 (September 1978), 310-19.

   Countering criticism of his philosophical approach to
Buber's thought, the author discusses Buber's concept
of philosophy. The task of philosophy is to develop a
universally valid conceptual account of Being. For
Buber, philosophical works are creations of the spirit,
begun in an I-Thou relationship, within which mankind
may dwell. To produce them demands a special type of
unity within the philosopher. Working within the world
of It, he must remain open to the world of Thou.
Philosophy may contribute to religion by a critique of
idols and by pointing toward the fulfillment only possible in the religious life.

Indexes

TITLE INDEX:
WRITINGS BY BUBER

(Translated titles. For other translations
with variant titles, see numbered entries.)

Abraham the Seer A139, A346
Abstract and Concrete A176
Addresses on Judaism A237
Adult Education in Israel A108
Advice to Frequenters of Libraries A21
After Death A324
The Altar A152
'And If Not Now, When?' A90
Arab-Jewish Unity: Testimony before the Anglo-American
    Inquiry Commission for the Ihud (Union) Association A47
At the Turning: Three Addresses on Judaism A109
Authentic Bilingualism A280
Autobiographical Fragments A240

The Baal-Shem-Tov's Instruction in Intercourse with God A183
The Beginnings A194
Beginnings A258
The Beginnings of Chassidism A44
The Beginnings of Hasidism A61
The Beginnings of the National Ideal A31
Believing Humanism A211, A292
A Believing Humanism: My Testament, 1902-1965 A261
Bergson's Concept of Intuition A160
Beside Me A321
Between Man and Man A48, A227
Between Man and Man: Education A140
Biblical Humanism A361
Biblical Humanism: Eighteen Studies A342
Biblical Leadership A38, A80, A354
The Bi-National Approach to Zionism A58
Books and Men A149, A260
Books and People A204
Brother Body A153

TRANSLATOR INDEX: WRITINGS BY BUBER

Gordon, Haim   B507, B535,
  B595, B615, B616, B637,
  B638, B639
Gordon, Murrary   B536
Gordon, Rosemary   B398
Gotshalk, Richard   B267
Grady, L. Augustine   B640
Granatstein, Melvin   B424
Gregory, T.S.   B316
Griffiths, B.   B74
Gruenthaner, Michael J.
  B29
Gumbiner, Joseph H.   B30
Gutsch, Kenneth U.   B508

Haberman, Joshua O.   B425
Halevi, Jacob L.   B98, B160
Halio, Jay L.   B226
Hammer, Louis Z.   B227,
  B358
Harper, Ralph   B317
Hart, Richard   B596
Hartshorne, Charles   B359
Hatt, Harold E.   B641
Hawton, Hector   B457
Heiman, Leo   B228
Helen James John, Sr.
  B187, B205
Heller, Arthur D.   B134
Hellwig, Monika K.   B642
Hendley, Brian   B643
Herberg, Will   B58, B75,
  B110, B135, B270, B490
Hill, Brian V.   B509, B510
Hilliard, F.H.   B511
Himmelfarb, Milton   B318
Hodes, Aubrey   B399, B477,
  B491
Holmer, Paul L.   B188
Hopper, Stanley Romaine
  B458
Horowitz, David   B206
Hort, Greta   B17
Horwitz, Rivka   B644
Howe, Reuel L.   B111
Hynson, Leon O.   B568

Idinopulos, Thomas A.   B478
Infield, Henrick   B99

J.G.W.   B272
Jackson, G.   B537
Jacob, Walter   B229, B538
Jarrett-Kerr, Martin   B18
Jay, Martin   B597
Johannesen, Richard L.   B479
Johnston, William M.   B492,
  B539
Jones, David A.   B569
Jones, Edgar   B136
Jordan, Pat   B654
Jospe, Eva   B646
Jude Michael, Bro.   B231
Judges, A.V.   B161
Jung, C.G.   B512

Kaplan, Edward K.   B459,
  B647
Kaplan, Mordecai   B60, B246,
  B360
Kappler, Frank   B275
Katz, Robert L.   B570
Katz, Steven T.   B571, B617,
  B648, B649
Kauf, Robert   B493
Kaufman, William E.   B598,
  B650
Kaufmann, Fritz   B361
Kaufmann, Walter   B137,
  B362, B460, B651
Kayser, Rudolf   B618
Kegan, Robert   B599
Kegley, Charles W.   B426
Kehoe, R.   B61
Kerenyi, Carl   B363
Ketcham, Charles B.   B652
Kiner, Edward D.   B427, B428
Kingsley, Ralph P.   B247
Klink, William H.   B540
Kloman, William   B276
Kohanski, Alexander S.
  B494, B572, B573, B574
Kohn, Hans   B4, B10

SUBJECT INDEX:
WRITINGS BY AND ABOUT BUBER

(Item numbers preceded by A refer to writings
by Buber. Those preceded by B refer to writings
about Buber.)

Arab-Jewish relations (see also Israel, modern; Palestine)
    A19, A46, A54, A58, A187, A371, B76, B185, B190, B194,
    B202, B203, B309, B313, B325, B330, B331, B336, B399,
    B403, B450, B477, B481, B505, B530, B549, B561, B619,
    B666
Aristotle (see also Greek philosophy)   A53, A106, B91, B520
Ark of the Covenant   A95, A353
Art (see also Aesthetics)   A218, B263, B358, B370, B379,
    B447, B469, B647
Art education   B379
Asian religions (see also Buddhism; Confucionism; Hinduism;
    Taoism; Zen)   A14, A119, A191, A332, B579, B593
Assagioli, Roberto   B594
Atheism   A118, B447, B532, B541, B598
Auden, W.H.   B587
Audio-visual material   B310, B621
Augustine, Saint   A53, B361
Auschwitz, see Holocaust
Austria, see Vienna
Authenticity (see also Self, the; Self realization; Unique-
    ness; Wholeness)   B179, B184, B204, B351, B355, B427,
    B490
Authority (see also Leadership; Political philosophy; Power,
    political)   B27, B407, B562, B631
Autonomy (see also Self, the)   B95, B453, B558
Avesta   A124, B72
Awards, see Tributes

Baal   A45, A95, A326
Baal Shem Tov (see also Hasidic stories; Hasidism)   A7, A42,
    A44, A62, B169, B516, B543, B552
Bachelard, Gaston   B459
Baeck, Leo   B116, B200, B527, B554, B625
Bahr, Hermann   A376, B539
Baillie, John   B88, B95
Bakanurskii, G.L.   B412
Balthasar, Hans Urs Von   A341
Barth, Karl   A228, B42, B95, B500, B564
Baumgartner, Walter   A326
Beauty, see Aesthetics
Becoming   A17, B95, B359, B447, B521
Beer-Hafmann, Richard   A278
Behaviorism   B567
Being   A17, A113, A145, B95, B118, B365, B447, B518
Belief (see also Trust in versus belief that)   A73, A163,
    B188, B648
Belief in versus belief that, see Trust in versus belief that
Bellow, Saul   B599

Book reviews:
    At the Turning B58
    A Believing Humanism B402, B436
    Between Man and Man B26, B30, B39
    Briefwechsel aus sieben Jahrzehnten B548, B559, B607,
       B654
    Daniel B240, B245, B289, B292, B297
    Eclipse of God B58, B62, B68, B70, B74, B75, B77, B91,
       B156
    For the Sake of Heaven B15, B82
    Good and Evil B69
    Hasidism B23
    Hasidism and Modern Man B137, B156
    I and Thou B66, B506, B613
    Images of Good and Evil B61
    Israel and Palestine B58, B78, B81
    Israel and the World B41
    Kingship of God B371, B391, B401
    Knowledge of Man B405
    The Legend of the Baal-Shem B123
    Martin Buber by Arthur Cohen B156
    Martin Buber by Maurice Friedman B115, B156
    Martin Buber's Ontology by Robert E. Wood B489
    Moses B31, B137
    A New German Translation of the Bible B3
    On Judaism B392, B402, B436
    Origin and Meaning of Hasidism B177, B314, B405
    Paths in Utopia B49, B50, B53
    Philosophy of Martin Buber edited by Paul Arthur Schilpp
       and Maurice Friedman B432, B436
    Pointing the Way B133, B137, B142, B156
    Prophetic Faith B45, B47, B48
    Tales of Rabbi Nahman B156
    Tales of the Hasidim: The Early Masters B29, B34
    Tales of the Hasidim: The Later Masters B23
    To Hallow this Life B137
    Two Types of Faith B93
    Way of Man B156
Books A21, A149, A150
Borowitz, Eugene B454
Boszormenyi-Nagy, Ivan B633
Bovillus, Carolus A53
Brunner, Emil B568
Buber, Paula Winkler A274, B422, B423, B443
Buber, personal contact with A209, B54, B63, B119, B125,
    B134, B194, B225, B228, B237, B422, B435, B660
Buber, pictures of A209, A213, A218, B4, B10, B14, B112,
    B115, B119, B126, B133, B169, B190, B201, B203, B210,

B307, B312, B327, B338, B375, B384, B389, B390, B408,
B437, B442, B444, B447, B461, B465, B486, B516, B522,
B526, B527, B533, B545, B554, B557, B574, B586, B598,
B604, B605, B620, B628, B640, B651
Judaism, ancient, see Israel, ancient
Judaism, liberal (see also Judaism; Judaism, reform) B155,
B157
Judaism, modern, essence of (see also Judaism) A10, A302,
A329, A330, A335, A362, B4, B20, B52, B80, B95, B113,
B118, B200, B301, B307, B309, B339, B365, B574
Judaism, reform (see also Judaism; Judaism, liberal) A206,
B157
Der Jude B493, B662
Judges (Hebrew Bible) A38, A326, B444
Jung, Carl G. A118, A122, A146, B74, B94, B150, B156, B174,
B378, B395, B458, B475, B516, B621
Justice B20, B600

Kabbalah A35, A41, A42, A43, A66, A333, A341, B163, B169,
B191, B484
Kafka, Franz A107, A146, B123, B343, B493
Kant, Immanuel A53, A73, A78, A105, A172, A238, A248, B92,
B117, B124, B361, B385, B410, B447, B516, B555, B598
Kaplan, Mordecai A142, B219, B442, B627
Kaufmann, Fritz A341
Kaufmann, Walter B488, B532, B582, B595, B630
Kavanah, see Intention
Keyserling, Hermann A85
Kibbutz movement (see also Community) B224, B379, B477,
B601, B624
Kierkegaard, Søren A50, A53, A120, A228, B11, B25, B26, B30,
B33, B88, B97, B118, B120, B124, B139, B160, B169, B179,
B326, B338, B351, B364, B382, B385, B408, B431, B437,
B438, B516, B543
Kiner, Edward David B580
King, William A94
Kingdom of God B20
Kings, biblical A38, A326, B356
Kingship of God A95, A147, A326, B86, B95, B148, B157, B158,
B343, B356, B368, B397, B624
Kittel, Gerhard B116
Knowing (see also Cognition; I-It knowledge; I-Thou knowledge)
A160, A223, A297, B85, B95, B128, B156, B188, B242, B254,
B263, B365, B394, B465, B473, B490, B502, B525, B532,
B556, B612, B658
Knowledge (see also I-It knowledge; I-Thou knowledge; Knowing;
Objective knowledge; Truth) A124, A155, B95, B465, B661
Kohn, Hans B488, B619